INEQUALITY

INEQUALITY

SOCIAL CLASS AND ITS CONSEQUENCES

edited by
D. Stanley Eitzen and Janis E. Johnston

Paradigm Publishers
Boulder • London

Paradigm Publishers is committed to preserving our environment. This book was printed on recycled paper with 30% post-consumer waste content, saving approximately 8 trees and avoiding the creation of more than 3 thousand gallons of wastewater, nearly 4 hundred pounds of solid waste, more than 7 hundred pounds of greenhouse gases, and using approximately 1400 kilowatt hours less of electricity than if it had been printed on paper manufactured from all virgin fibers.

Due to space limitations on this page, source notes and permission credits for all of the readings in this volume appear in the Credits section beginning on page 217.

All rights reserved. No part of the publication may be transmitted or reproduced in any media or form, including electronic, mechanical, photocopy, recording, or informational storage and retrieval systems, without the express written consent of the publisher.

Copyright © 2007 Paradigm Publishers

Published in the United States by Paradigm Publishers, 3360 Mitchell Lane, Suite E, Boulder, CO 80301 USA.

Paradigm Publishers is the trade name of Birkenkamp & Company, LLC, Dean Birkenkamp, President and Publisher.

Library of Congress Cataloging-in-Publication Data

Inequality : social class and its consequences / edited by D. Stanley Eitzen and Janis E. Johnston.
   p. cm.
  Includes bibliographical references and index.
  ISBN 978-1-59451-357-2 (hardcover : alk. paper)
  1. Social classes—United States. 2. Equality—United States. 3. United States—Social conditions—1980–   I. Eitzen, D. Stanley. II. Johnston, Janis E., 1957–
  HN90.S6I54 2007
  305.50973—dc22
                                                  2007002224

Printed and bound in the United States of America on acid free paper that meets the standards of the American National Standard for Permanence of Paper for Printed Library Materials.

Designed and Typeset by Straight Creek Bookmakers.

11 10 09 08 07   1 2 3 4 5

Contents

Preface	ix
Introduction	1

Part I: Dimensions of Social Stratification

Chapter 1: Social Class in America	9
1. Shadowy Lines That Still Divide *Janny Scott and David Leonhardt*	11
2. A Statistical Portrait of the U.S. Working Class *Michael D. Yates*	19
3. The Other America: An Enduring Shame *Jonathan Alter*	35
Chapter 2: The Inequality Gap	43
4. Tilting the Tax System in Favor of the Rich *The New York Times*	45
5. Income and Inequality: Millions Left Behind *Woodrow Ginsberg*	52
6. The Perks of Privilege *Clara Jeffery*	61
Chapter 3: The Disappearing Middle	67
7. Our Society's Middle Is Shrinking from View *Louise Auerhahn*	69

8. The Vanishing Middle-Class Job:
    As Income Gap Widens, Uncertainty Spreads
    Griff Witte
	71

Chapter 4: Social Mobility	81

9. The Death of Horatio Alger: Our Political Leaders Are Doing
    Everything They Can to Fortify Class Inequality
    Paul Krugman
	83

10. Rags to Riches? The American Dream Is Less Common in the
     United States Than Elsewhere
     Bernard Wasow
	85

Part II: The Consequences of Class

Chapter 5: Work — 93

    11. Still Not Getting By in Bush's America — 95
        Joel Wendland
    12. America's Low-Wage Workers: The Demography of a Caste — 97
        Beth Shulman

Chapter 6: Health Care — 103

    13. As the Rich Get Richer, Do People Get Sicker? Researchers Debate Whether Income Inequality Impairs Public Health — 105
        Lila Guterman
    14. Sick of Poverty — 110
        Robert Sapolsky

Chapter 7: Education — 117

    15. A Wider Lens on the Black-White Achievement Gap — 120
        Richard Rothstein
    16. Does Meritocracy Work? — 129
        Ross Douthat

Chapter 8: Justice and Injustice — 139

    17. The Rich Get Richer and the Poor Get Prison — 141
        Jeffrey Reiman
    18. Poverty and Violent Crime — 145
        Elliott Currie
    19. The Civil Rights Act of 1964: The Social Class Exclusion — 150
        Janis E. Johnston

Chapter 9: Natural Disasters — 157

    20. Dying Alone: An Interview with Eric Klinenberg — 159
        University of Chicago Press
    21. The Nation: Cast Away: Broken Levees, Unbroken Barriers — 163
        Jason DeParle
    22. New Orleans by the Numbers — 165
        Peter Wagner and Susan Edwards

Chapter 10: Unequal Sacrifice in War — 171

    23. Sacrifices of War Remain Unshared — 173
        Chuck Raasch

24. Their Last Resort 174
    Ann Scott Tyson

Chapter 11: Environmental Classism 179

25. Bioethics, Social Class, and the Sociological Imagination 181
    Leigh Turner
26. Poverty and Pollution in the United States 186
    Robert D. Bullard

Part III: Reducing Inequality

Chapter 12: Progressive Solutions for Reducing Inequality 197

27. Narrowing the Income Gap Between Rich and Poor 199
    Michael Hout and Samuel R. Lucas
28. Millennium Development Goals for Children in the
    United States to Be Achieved by 2015 203
    Children's Defense Fund
29. Taxing Concentrated Wealth to Broaden the American Dream:
    Good Policy, Good Politics, Good for America 204
    Dedrick Muhammad and Chuck Collins

Websites *213*
Credits *217*
Index *219*
About the Editors *235*

PREFACE

Inequality is a fact of social life. All known societies have some system of ranking individuals and families along a superiority-inferiority scale. The bases for ranking are, typically, family of origin, race/ethnicity, gender, and economic position. While each of these is important and the intersections among them crucial to understanding the complexities of social inequality, the focus of this book is on economic position. Wealth and income separate people into social classes. Access to money determines the chance to obtain those things that are highly valued in society. The term *life chances* refers to the chances throughout one's life cycle to live and experience the good things in life. Thus, the social class that one occupies has consequences for health, longevity, prestige, treatment in the criminal justice system, marital stability, whether one gives orders or takes orders at work, success in school, and the like. These are the topics of this book.

The goal underlying this collection of articles is to provide an understanding of social class and its consequences in the United States. Our decision to include each selection has been purposed by three questions: Will the reader find it interesting? Insightful? Sociologically meaningful?

Social class is at the heart of sociology. It affects nearly every dimension of people's lives. It is a crucial variable for explaining human behavior. It is a key structural component of social organizations. We feel strongly that social class should be central to many sociology courses. Thus, this anthology is intended to be a useful companion to the textbook or other sources chosen for courses such as Introduction to Sociology, Social Problems, and Social Stratification as well as for any course with an emphasis on diversity. Although social class may be more tangential in other academic contexts, this book will also be of value in such courses as Political Sociology, Social Policy, Sociology of Families, and Social Welfare.

We are grateful to Dean Birkenkamp and his colleagues at Paradigm Publishers for their help with and support of this project. We also acknowledge the contribution of our colleagues at Colorado State University, the University of Wyoming, and elsewhere.

—*D. Stanley Eitzen and Janis E. Johnston*

INTRODUCTION

Is the United States an egalitarian society? Are its inhabitants participating on a level playing field where any of them can move up if they work hard enough? Consider the following facts concerning the inequities in contemporary U.S. society:

- At a time (2004) when there were 374 billionaires in the United States (*Forbes,* 2005), 37 million people were living below the official poverty line (U.S. Census Bureau, 2005).
- In a society with the best medical technology, hospitals, and physicians, 46.6 million had no health insurance in 2005.
- In Pitkin County, Colorado (where Aspen is located), there are seventeen houses larger than 15,000 square feet (the largest is 55,000 square feet) (Kenworthy, 2006), yet about 2 million Americans are homeless at some time during any given year.
- In 2005, more than 25 million Americans turned to food banks, soup kitchens, and shelters for meals (Ohlemacher, 2006).
- The five Wal-Mart heirs have a combined fortune of $84 billion. In 2005 they received $884.3 million in dividends from their inherited Wal-Mart stock. Since dividends are taxed at a lower rate than wages, the annual tax savings on these dividends to the Waltons are $51 million (Hopkins, 2005).
- From 1980 to 2000, the top 0.1 percent of income earners increased their average annual incomes by $1.8 million while the income of the bottom 90 percent of taxpayers actually fell over those 20 years (Zweifel, 2005).
- A 2005 study by the Institute for Policy Studies and United for a Fair Economy found that the ratio between chief executive officer and worker pay was 431 to 1. This amounts to $11.8 million in annual earnings for the average CEO compared to $27,460 for the average worker (reported in Talvi, 2005).

These data reveal striking disparities in economic resources, as uncovered in greater depth in the following pages. As we shall see, the maldistribution of wealth and income in the United States deeply affects people's lives.

THE CLASS STRUCTURE IN THE UNITD STATES

This book is about the U.S. stratification system. The distribution of economic resources sorts individuals and families into social classes. In effect, when a number of individuals occupy the same relative economic rank in the stratification system, they form a social class (much of this discussion comes from Eitzen and Baca Zinn, 2007: chs. 9 and 10). The lines identifying a class are fuzzy, except perhaps those delineating the highest and lowest classes. While a social class is not a completely homogeneous group, there is some degree of identification with other people in similar economic situations, and people have a sense of who is superior, equal, and inferior to them. Similarly, among people in a similar economic position there tend to be commonalities in lifestyles, behaviors, tastes, and worldviews. As noted, however, the lines separating the classes are inexact.

While we lack clarity about the exact boundaries of the social classes, sociologists are clear on the following points:

- Economic resources—wealth and income—are the central criteria for classification.
- Economic resources determine the degree to which people will experience the good things in life (the concept of "life chances" refers to this probability).
- Social class implies having or not having status, power (giving orders or taking orders), self-determination, access to services, good medical care, safety, satisfying work, and educational opportunities.
- In particular, economic resources are directly related to educational attainment. And the amount of formal education an individual achieves is a major determinant of her or his occupation, income, and prestige.
- Our social class position affects our health and shapes our values, politics, and family life.

While social class is fundamentally based on wealth, we define a social class as composed of people who rank close to one another in wealth, power, and prestige. Based on these elements, the class structure of the United States can be conceptualized as a ladder. At the top rung of this stratification ladder is the *upper class* (sometimes referred to as the *ruling class* or the *capitalist class*). Totaling less than 1 percent of the population, these folks constitute a small but wealthy and powerful elite. Included are those who have had great wealth for generations (e.g., the DuPonts and the Rockefellers) as well as those who have recently become rich (e.g., Larry Page and Sergey Brin, the co-founders of Google, who, though only in their early 30s, were worth an estimated $10 billion each in early 2006). The net worth of these top 1 percent is greater than that of the bottom 90 percent of Americans. They control the stock in corporations, and their money is a potent influence in politics. Their children are privileged, attending the most exclusive private schools and inheriting their parents' assets and social networks.

Right below is the *upper-middle class,* which comprises those with relatively high incomes and high social prestige. Specifically, this class is composed of well-educated professionals (doctors, lawyers, engineers) and business executives with key decisionmaking roles in large organizations. Their jobs require considerable formal education and have a high degree of autonomy and responsibility.

At the next rung is the *lower-middle class,* made up of families clustered around the median income level. Included in this class are white-collar workers (accountants, teachers), small-business owners, the self-employed, and skilled craftspeople.

The *working class,* which comes next, includes relatively unskilled blue-collar (manual labor) and service workers such as secretaries, clerks, and hairdressers. They hold jobs that are routine and closely supervised, they follow orders rather than giving them, and they have less education and lower incomes compared with those in the lower-middle class.

Those in the *lower class,* one rung down, are unemployed or, if employed, work at menial jobs. They are poor or near-poor. In 2004 some 2.8 percent of all workers, working full-time and year-round, lived below the official poverty line. They do society's dirty work for low pay (the minimum wage is $5.15, and a mere $2.13 for wait staff) and no benefits. The poor, who are disproportionately women and people of color, live in substandard housing and their children go to underfinanced schools.

The *underclass* constitutes the lowest rung in the stratification ladder. These are the chronically poor. Among poor people in 2004, the average deficit (the dollar amount below the poverty line) was $7,775. During the same year, some 42 percent of the poor population (15.6 million Americans) were living at or below the official poverty line (U.S. Census Bureau, 2005: 14). These severely poor people typically use 50 percent or more of their meager income for housing.

In Part I of this book we explore four dimensions of the social class system in the United States. We begin with descriptions of the class divisions, the working class, and the poor. Next we examine the very real inequality gap, which continues to widen. The inequality gap refers to the divide between the "haves" and the "have-nots." One measure of this economic inequality is the Gini coefficient (Boushey and Weller, 2005). This coefficient ranges from 0 (whereby everyone's income is exactly the same) to 1 (whereby all income goes to a single person). The Gini coefficient was 0.388 in 1968 and 0.470 in 2004, reflecting a substantial rise in inequality. While the inequality gap expands, the middle class shrinks. This slowly disappearing middle is our third topic. As Holly Sklar states: "Middle-class households are a medical crisis, outsourced job or busted pension away from bankruptcy.... We are living the American Dream in reverse" (Sklar, 2006: 16). A related issue is the final one discussed in this first section: How much social mobility (i.e., the movement from one class to another) is present in U.S. society? A commonly held belief among Americans is that the United States is a land of opportunity where hard work and perseverance will lead to upward mobility. To which we ask: To what degree is this true?

In Part II we consider the consequences of social class. Social class matters. Indeed, it matters in two key ways. First, people in the same social class tend to behave in similar ways and to interpret the world similarly. Second, and this is our focus, social class has consequences for how enjoyable our lives will be. Bill Moyers in his foreword to *Inequality Matters* demonstrates this vividly:

> Under a six-column headline across the top, the [*New York*] *Times* of March 10, 2004, tells us that the annual tuition at Manhattan's most elite private schools has reached $26,000—for kindergarten as well as high school. Lower down the page, in a story with a two-column headline, we learn about a school in Mount Vernon, New York, just across the city line from the Bronx. Its student body is 97 percent black. Nine out of ten kids qualify for free lunches. One out of ten lives in a homeless shelter." (Moyers, 2005: 1)

The consequences of social class are at the heart of this book.

The first consequence of social class that we consider is work. Jobs vary according to social class in terms of how satisfying they are, whether they involve physical risks, the monetary rewards they bring, and their requirements for creativity and decisionmaking.

Second, we examine how social class is related to the uneven distribution of health care. Social class literally affects our chances of living and dying. Economic disadvantage is closely associated with health disadvantages. Put another way: "How people live, get sick, and die depends not only on their race and gender, but primarily on the class to which they belong" (Navarro, 1991: 2).

Third, the amount and quality of education one receives depend on economic background, not just on cognitive ability. Inequality of educational opportunity occurs at all educational levels and takes many forms—some subtle, others not so subtle. The quality of education varies by school district, because schools are funded based on their tax base. Within each school, regardless of the district, children are given standardized tests that have a middle-class bias. The results of these tests place children in tracks according to ability. These tracks coincide with social class position inasmuch as economically advantaged students have educational advantages (e.g., preschool, access to tutors, specialized training, a variety of experiences), in contrast to disadvantaged students, many of whom speak English as a second language, missed out on preschool, suffered exposure to lead and other toxic chemicals in their formative years, or have parents who are uneducated. Especially harmful is the tendency of teachers to have low expectations of students placed in a lower track.

Fourth, the higher one's social class, the more likely one is to escape the harsh penalties of the criminal justice system. Indeed, the lower classes are disproportionately found in prison and on probation and parole. The administration of justice is unequal in the United States precisely because the affluent can afford to hire the best lawyers for their defense and to appeal an adverse decision to a series of appellate courts, whereas the poor must rely on court-appointed lawyers, who are usually among the least experienced and often have heavy caseloads.

Fifth, the higher one's social class, the more likely one is to survive a natural disaster such as Hurricane Katrina or even a heat wave. Consider, for example, the official casualty lists of the transatlantic luxury liner *Titanic,* which rammed an iceberg in 1912: Three percent of the first-class female passengers died as compared to 16 percent of the second-class female passengers and 45 percent of the third-class female passengers (Lord, 1955: 107).

Sixth, the higher one's social class, the less likely one is to serve in the military—or, if in the military, to die or be injured in battle. During periods when the draft is not in force (as is the case at present), the personnel in the lower ranks of the military come disproportionately from the disadvantaged segments of society.

The final consequence of social class discussed here involves environmental classism. This refers to the environmental dangers confronting the lower classes because they live where housing is cheapest, which tends to be near polluting factories, hazardous waste facilities, and excessive noise. Racial minorities, who are disproportionately found in the lower classes, are especially vulnerable to these environmental hazards—an issue known as environmental racism.

Part III of this book provides some examples of progressive solutions for reducing the inequities in U.S. society. These examples include universal health care; redistribution of resources, especially as a way of alleviating the problems of economically disadvantaged children; and alteration of the tax code, which currently favors the already advantaged.

References

Boushey, Heather, and Christian E. Weller. 2005. "What the Numbers Tell Us." Pp. 27–40 in *Inequality Matters: The Growing Economic Divide in America and Its Poisonous Consequences,* edited by James Lardner and David A. Smith. New York: The New Press.

Eitzen, D. Stanley, and Maxine Baca Zinn. 2007. *In Conflict and Order,* 11th ed. Boston: Allyn and Bacon.

Forbes. 2005. "The Forbes 400" (October 10):89–320.

Hopkins, Jim. 2005. "Wal-Mart Family Funds Causes, Candidates Backing Tax Cuts," *USA Today* (April 6): 1B–2B.

Kenworthy, Tom. 2006. "Oversize Homes Wear Out Welcome," *USA Today* (February 21): 1A.

Lord, Waler, 1955. *A Night to Remember.* New York: Henry Holt.

Moyers, Bill. 2005. "The Fight of Our Lives." Pp. 1–13 in *Inequality Matters: The Growing Economic Divide in America and Its Poisonous Consequences,* edited by James Lardner and David A. Smith. New York: The New Press.

Navarro, Vicente. 1991. "Class and Race: Life and Death Situations," *Monthly Review* 43 (September): 1–13.

Ohlemacher, Stephen. 2006. "Nation's Largest Food Bank Served More Than 25 Million," Associated Press (February 23).

Sklar, Holly. 2006. "Happy New Year, American Dream," *The Progressive Populist* (February 1): 16.
Talvi, Silja J. A. 2005. "Alls or Nothings," *In These Times* (October 24): 10.
U.S. Census Bureau. 2005. "Income, Poverty, and Health Insurance Coverage in the United States: 2004, *Current Population Reports,* P60–229.
Zweifel, Dave. 2005. "Super-Rich Leaving Even the Rich Behind," *The Progressive Populist* (July 15): 14.

Part I
Dimensions of Social Stratification

Chapter 1
Social Class in America

One's position in the American class system defines the opportunities that she or he has within that system. People live in neighborhoods with others of their social class, they go to schools with people who share their social class, and they marry within their social class. The lines between the social classes act as barriers that most people never cross. In general, if you begin life in the lower class, you end life in the lower class. If you begin life in the upper class, you end life in the upper class. As Scott and Leonhardt point out in the first reading, however, the line that divides the social classes is no longer as apparent as the line that existed when our grandparents, or their grandparents, were young.

The blurring of the lines between the classes has led some to believe that the United States is moving toward a society in which class is no longer the factor that it once was. The evidence, however, points to the contrary. Membership in the upper class really does provide people with opportunities that are not available to the lower classes. Students from the upper class have access to the best schools, the best teachers, and the best technology. The affluent have access to the highest-quality health care, and can afford to follow doctors' recommendations and pay for prescription medications. People in the upper class have access to better legal advice, are better equipped to survive a natural disaster, and live in safer neighborhoods than people in the lower classes.

Social class even affects how people travel; for example, the well-to-do can better afford to fly. A more pressing difference between the social classes, however, concerns automobile travel—specifically, access to safe vehicles and highways. Members of the upper class are not only likelier to drive automobiles that are equipped with the latest in safety technology (anti-lock braking systems, computer adjustment to the wheels in bad weather, air bags, and access to immediate help through satellite systems), but they also enjoy greater access to safe roads. Toll roads are the latest in safe roads, but they require travelers to pay a fee. The number of toll roads is increasing, as is the cost. Consider E-470, for example. This is a toll road that skirts the east side of Denver, Colorado. A driver who traverses the entire 46.10 miles of E-470 in a standard passenger car now pays $9.75 one-way. Moreover, the building of toll roads often means that public roads in adjacent areas receive only minor attention and may not be improved as conditions warrant, so as to encourage drivers to take the toll road instead. This problem has recently come to public attention in the form of a debate over toll roads. Consider the proposed improvements to C-470, another toll road in Colorado. As noted in the *Denver Post* (Leib, 2006, p. 1A), the proposed improvements are "an expensive approach to congestion that favors a minority of motorists who can afford high tolls, leaving most drivers mired in clogged, adjacent, free lanes at peak travel times." Additionally, Denver has just opened its "high-occupancy vehicle" lanes to solo drivers who agree to pay a toll. Yes, social classes still exist, and one's membership in a social class does matter.

Children born in the baby-boom generation grew up with the idea that they would have a better life than their parents—that they would be upwardly mobile. They also believed that their own children would be better off than they themselves, a dream that is rapidly becoming more difficult to obtain. Upward mobility is elusive, whereas its counterpart, downward mobility, is a reality for many Americans. With company downsizing, the movement of technical jobs out of the United States, bankruptcies and scandals resulting in the elimination of jobs and retirement accounts, and the crash of the "dot-commer" industry, many people in this country have learned, firsthand, what downward mobility really means.

Social class is not a choice, it is not an option, and it is not disappearing. Social class colors every aspect of a person's life. Part I of this book introduces the issues related to social class with three readings that discuss class in U.S. society. The first of these describes the class system in the United States; the second one describes the working class; and the final selection portrays the lower class.

REFERENCES

Leib, Jeffrey. 2006. "A Fork in C-470 May Sway How State Adds Lanes," *Denver Post,* May 30, pp. 1A, 12A.

1. Shadowy Lines That Still Divide
Janny Scott and David Leonhardt

There was a time when Americans thought they understood class. The upper crust vacationed in Europe and worshiped an Episcopal God. The middle class drove Ford Fairlanes, settled the San Fernando Valley and enlisted as company men. The working class belonged to the A.F.L.-C.I.O., voted Democratic and did not take cruises to the Caribbean.

Today, the country has gone a long way toward an appearance of classlessness. Americans of all sorts are awash in luxuries that would have dazzled their grandparents. Social diversity has erased many of the old markers. It has become harder to read people's status in the clothes they wear, the cars they drive, the votes they cast, the god they worship, the color of their skin. The contours of class have blurred; some say they have disappeared.

But class is still a powerful force in American life. Over the past three decades, it has come to play a greater, not lesser, role in important ways. At a time when education matters more than ever, success in school remains linked tightly to class. At a time when the country is increasingly integrated racially, the rich are isolating themselves more and more. At a time of extraordinary advances in medicine, class differences in health and lifespan are wide and appear to be widening.

And new research on mobility, the movement of families up and down the economic ladder, shows there is far less of it than economists once thought and less than most people believe. In fact, mobility, which once buoyed the working lives of Americans as it rose in the decades after World War II, has lately flattened out or possibly even declined, many researchers say.

Mobility is the promise that lies at the heart of the American dream. It is supposed to take the sting out of the widening gulf between the have-mores and the have-nots. There are poor and rich in the United States, of course, the argument goes; but as long as one can become the other, as long as there is something close to equality of opportunity, the differences between them do not add up to class barriers.

Over the next three weeks [May and June 2005], *The [New York] Times* will publish a series of articles on class in America, a dimension of the national experience that tends to go unexamined, if acknowledged at all. With class now seeming more elusive than ever, the articles take stock of its influence in the lives of individuals: a lawyer who rose out of an impoverished Kentucky hollow; an unemployed metal worker in Spokane, Wash., regretting his decision to skip college; a multimillionaire in Nantucket, Mass., musing over the cachet of his 200-foot yacht.

The series does not purport to be all-inclusive or the last word on class. It offers no nifty formulas for pigeonholing people or decoding folkways and manners. Instead, it represents an inquiry into class as Americans encounter it: indistinct, ambiguous, the half-seen hand that upon closer examination holds some Americans down while giving others a boost.

The trends are broad and seemingly contradictory: the blurring of the landscape of class and the simultaneous hardening of certain class lines; the rise in standards of living while most people remain moored in their relative places.

Even as mobility seems to have stagnated, the ranks of the elite are opening. Today, anyone may have a shot at becoming a United States Supreme Court justice or a C.E.O., and there are more and more self-made billionaires. Only 37 members of last year's Forbes 400, a list of the richest Americans, inherited their wealth, down from almost 200 in the mid-1980's.

So it appears that while it is easier for a few high achievers to scale the summits of wealth, for many others it has become harder to move up from one economic class to another. Americans are arguably more likely than they were 30 years ago to end up in the class into which they were born.

A paradox lies at the heart of this new American meritocracy. Merit has replaced the old system of inherited privilege, in which parents to the manner born handed down the manor to their children. But merit, it turns out, is at least partly class-based. Parents with money, education and connections cultivate in their children the habits that the meritocracy rewards. When their children then succeed, their success is seen as earned.

The scramble to scoop up a house in the best school district, channel a child into the right preschool program or land the best medical specialist are all part of a quiet contest among social groups that the affluent and educated are winning in a rout.

"The old system of hereditary barriers and clubby barriers has pretty much vanished," said Eric Wanner, president of the Russell Sage Foundation, a social science research group in New York City that recently published a series of studies on the social effects of economic inequality.

In place of the old system, Dr. Wanner said, have arisen "new ways of transmitting advantage that are beginning to assert themselves."

FAITH IN THE SYSTEM

Most Americans remain upbeat about their prospects for getting ahead. A recent *New York Times* poll on class found that 40 percent of Americans believed that the chance of moving up from one class to another had risen over the last 30 years, a period in which the new research shows that it has not. Thirty-five percent said it had not changed, and only 23 percent said it had dropped.

More Americans than 20 years ago believe it possible to start out poor, work hard and become rich. They say hard work and a good education are more important to getting ahead than connections or a wealthy background.

"I think the system is as fair as you can make it," Ernie Frazier, a 65-year-old real estate investor in Houston, said in an interview after participating in the poll. "I don't think life is necessarily fair. But if you persevere, you can overcome adversity. It has to do with a person's willingness to work hard, and I think it's always been that way."

Most say their standard of living is better than their parents' and imagine that their children will do better still. Even families making less than $30,000 a year subscribe to the American dream; more than half say they have achieved it or will do so.

But most do not see a level playing field. They say the very rich have too much power, and they favor the idea of class-based affirmative action to help those at the bottom. Even so, most say they oppose the government's taxing the assets a person leaves at death.

"They call it the land of opportunity, and I don't think that's changed much," said Diana Lackey, a 60-year-old homemaker and wife of a retired contractor in Fulton, N.Y., near Syracuse. "Times are much, much harder with all the downsizing, but we're still a wonderful country."

The Attributes of Class

One difficulty in talking about class is that the word means different things to different people. Class is rank, it is tribe, it is culture and taste. It is attitudes and assumptions, a source of identity, a system of exclusion. To some, it is just money. It is an accident of birth that can influence the outcome of a life. Some Americans barely notice it; others feel its weight in powerful ways.

At its most basic, class is one way societies sort themselves out. Even societies built on the idea of eliminating class have had stark differences in rank. Classes are groups of people of similar economic and social position; people who, for that reason, may share political attitudes, lifestyles, consumption patterns, cultural interests and opportunities to get ahead. Put 10 people in a room and a pecking order soon emerges.

When societies were simpler, the class landscape was easier to read. Marx divided 19th-century societies into just two classes; Max Weber added a few more. As societies grew increasingly complex, the old classes became more heterogeneous. As some sociologists and marketing consultants see it, the commonly accepted big three—the upper, middle and working classes—have broken down into dozens of microclasses, defined by occupations or lifestyles.

A few sociologists go so far as to say that social complexity has made the concept of class meaningless. Conventional big classes have become so diverse—in income, lifestyle, political views—that they have ceased to be classes at all, said Paul W. Kingston, a professor of sociology at the University of Virginia. To him, American society is a "ladder with lots and lots of rungs."

"There is not one decisive break saying that the people below this all have this common experience," Professor Kingston said. "Each step is equal-sized. Sure, for the people higher up this ladder, their kids are more apt to get more education, better health insurance. But that doesn't mean there are classes."

Many other researchers disagree. "Class awareness and the class language is receding at the very moment that class has reorganized American society," said Michael Hout, a professor of sociology at the University of California, Berkeley. "I find these 'end of class' discussions naïve and ironic, because we are at a time of booming inequality and this massive reorganization of where we live and how we feel, even in the dynamics of our politics. Yet people say, 'Well, the era of class is over.'"

One way to think of a person's position in society is to imagine a hand of cards. Everyone is dealt four cards, one from each suit: education, income, occupation and wealth, the four commonly used criteria for gauging class. Face cards in a few categories may land a player in the upper middle class. At first, a person's class is his parents' class. Later, he may pick up a new hand of his own; it is likely to resemble that of his parents, but not always.

Bill Clinton traded in a hand of low cards with the help of a college education and a Rhodes scholarship and emerged decades later with four face cards. Bill Gates, who started off squarely in the upper middle class, made a fortune without finishing college, drawing three aces.

Many Americans say that they too have moved up the nation's class ladder. In the Times poll, 45 percent of respondents said they were in a higher class than when they grew up, while just 16 percent said they were in a lower one. Over all, 1 percent described themselves as upper class, 15 percent as upper middle class, 42 percent as middle, 35 percent as working and 7 percent as lower.

"I grew up very poor and so did my husband," said Wanda Brown, the 58-year-old wife of a retired planner for the Puget Sound Naval Shipyard who lives in Puyallup, Wash., near Tacoma. "We're not rich but we are comfortable and we are middle class and our son is better off than we are."

THE AMERICAN IDEAL

The original exemplar of American social mobility was almost certainly Benjamin Franklin, one of 17 children of a candle maker. About 20 years ago, when researchers first began to study mobility in a rigorous way, Franklin seemed representative of a truly fluid society, in which the rags-to-riches trajectory was the readily achievable ideal, just as the nation's self-image promised.

In a 1987 speech, Gary S. Becker, a University of Chicago economist who would later win a Nobel Prize, summed up the research by saying that mobility in the United States was so high that very little advantage was passed down from one generation to the next. In fact, researchers seemed to agree that the grandchildren of privilege and of poverty would be on nearly equal footing.

If that had been the case, the rise in income inequality beginning in the mid-1970's should not have been all that worrisome. The wealthy might have looked as if they were pulling way ahead, but if families were moving in and out of poverty and prosperity all the time, how much did the gap between the top and bottom matter?

But the initial mobility studies were flawed, economists now say. Some studies relied on children's fuzzy recollections of their parents' income. Others compared single years of income, which fluctuate considerably. Still others misread the normal progress people make as they advance in their careers, like from young lawyer to senior partner, as social mobility.

The new studies of mobility, which methodically track peoples' earnings over decades, have found far less movement. The economic advantage once believed to last only two or three generations is now believed to last closer to five. Mobility happens, just not as rapidly as was once thought.

"We all know stories of poor families in which the next generation did much better," said Gary Solon, a University of Michigan economist who is a leading mobility researcher. "It isn't that poor families have no chance."

But in the past, Professor Solon added, "people would say, 'Don't worry about inequality. The offspring of the poor have chances as good as the chances of the offspring of the rich.' Well, that's not true. It's not respectable in scholarly circles anymore to make that argument."

One study, by the Federal Reserve Bank of Boston, found that fewer families moved from one quintile, or fifth, of the income ladder to another during the 1980's than during the 1970's and that still fewer moved in the 90's than in the 80's. A study by the Bureau of Labor Statistics also found that mobility declined from the 80's to the 90's.

The incomes of brothers born around 1960 have followed a more similar path than the incomes of brothers born in the late 1940's, researchers at the Chicago Federal Reserve and the University of California, Berkeley, have found. Whatever children inherit from their parents—habits, skills, genes, contacts, money—seems to matter more today.

Studies on mobility over generations are notoriously difficult, because they require researchers to match the earnings records of parents with those of their children. Some economists consider the findings of the new studies murky; it cannot be definitively shown that mobility has fallen during the last generation, they say, only that it has not risen. The data will probably not be conclusive for years.

Nor do people agree on the implications. Liberals say the findings are evidence of the need for better early-education and antipoverty programs to try to redress an imbalance in opportunities. Conservatives tend to assert that mobility remains quite high, even if it has tailed off a little.

But there is broad consensus about what an optimal range of mobility is. It should be high enough for fluid movement between economic levels but not so high that success is barely tied to achievement and seemingly random, economists on both the right and left say.

As Phillip Swagel, a resident scholar at the American Enterprise Institute, put it, "We want to give people all the opportunities they want. We want to remove the barriers to upward mobility."

Yet there should remain an incentive for parents to cultivate their children. "Most people are working very hard to transmit their advantages to their children," said David I. Levine, a Berkeley economist and mobility researcher. "And that's quite a good thing."

One surprising finding about mobility is that it is not higher in the United States than in Britain or France. It is lower here than in Canada and some Scandinavian countries but not as low as in developing countries like Brazil, where escape from poverty is so difficult that the lower class is all but frozen in place.

Those comparisons may seem hard to believe. Britain and France had hereditary nobilities; Britain still has a queen. The founding document of the United States proclaims all men to be created equal. The American economy has also grown more quickly than Europe's in recent decades, leaving an impression of boundless opportunity.

But the United States differs from Europe in ways that can gum up the mobility machine. Because income inequality is greater here, there is a wider disparity between what rich and poor parents can invest in their children. Perhaps as a result, a child's economic background is a better predictor of school performance in the United States than in Denmark, the Netherlands or France, one recent study found.

"Being born in the elite in the U.S. gives you a constellation of privileges that very few people in the world have ever experienced," Professor Levine said. "Being born poor in the U.S. gives you disadvantages unlike anything in Western Europe and Japan and Canada."

BLURRING THE LANDSCAPE

Why does it appear that class is fading as a force in American life?

For one thing, it is harder to read position in possessions. Factories in China and elsewhere churn out picture-taking cellphones and other luxuries that are now affordable to almost everyone. Federal deregulation has done the same for plane tickets and long-distance phone calls. Banks, more confident about measuring risk, now extend credit to low-income families, so that owning a home or driving a new car is no longer evidence that someone is middle class.

The economic changes making material goods cheaper have forced businesses to seek out new opportunities so that they now market to groups they once ignored. Cruise ships, years ago a symbol of the high life, have become the ocean-going equivalent of the Jersey Shore. BMW produces a cheaper model with the same insignia. Martha Stewart sells chenille jacquard drapery and scallop-embossed ceramic dinnerware at Kmart.

"The level of material comfort in this country is numbing," said Paul Bellew, executive director for market and industry analysis at General Motors. "You can make a case that the upper half lives as well as the upper 5 percent did 50 years ago."

Like consumption patterns, class alignments in politics have become jumbled. In the 1950's, professionals were reliably Republican; today they lean Democratic. Meanwhile, skilled labor has gone from being heavily Democratic to almost evenly split.

People in both parties have attributed the shift to the rise of social issues, like gun control and same-sex marriage, which have tilted many working-class voters rightward and upper income voters toward the left. But increasing affluence plays an important role, too. When there is not only a chicken, but an organic, free-range chicken, in every pot, the traditional economic appeal to the working class can sound off key.

Religious affiliation, too, is no longer the reliable class marker it once was. The growing economic power of the South has helped lift evangelical Christians into the middle and upper middle classes, just as earlier generations of Roman Catholics moved up in the mid-20th century. It is no longer necessary to switch one's church membership to Episcopal or Presbyterian as proof that one has arrived.

"You go to Charlotte, N.C., and the Baptists are the establishment," said Mark A. Chaves, a sociologist at the University of Arizona. "To imagine that for reasons of respectability, if you lived in North Carolina, you would want to be a Presbyterian rather than a Baptist doesn't play anymore."

The once tight connection between race and class has weakened, too, as many African-Americans have moved into the middle and upper middle classes. Diversity of all sorts—racial, ethnic and gender—has complicated the class picture. And high rates of immigration and immigrant success stories seem to hammer home the point: The rules of advancement have changed.

The American elite, too, is more diverse than it was. The number of corporate chief executives who went to Ivy League colleges has dropped over the past 15 years. There are many more Catholics, Jews and Mormons in the Senate than there were a generation or two ago. Because of the economic earthquakes of the last few decades, a small but growing number of people have shot to the top.

"Anything that creates turbulence creates the opportunity for people to get rich," said Christopher S. Jencks, a professor of social policy at Harvard. "But that isn't necessarily a big influence on the 99 percent of people who are not entrepreneurs."

These success stories reinforce perceptions of mobility, as does cultural myth-making in the form of television programs like "American Idol" and "The Apprentice."

But beneath all that murkiness and flux, some of the same forces have deepened the hidden divisions of class. Globalization and technological change have shuttered factories, killing jobs that were once stepping-stones to the middle class. Now that manual labor can be done in developing countries for $2 a day, skills and education have become more essential than ever.

This has helped produce the extraordinary jump in income inequality. The after-tax income of the top 1 percent of American households jumped 139 percent, to more than $700,000, from 1979 to 2001, according to the Congressional Budget Office, which adjusted its numbers to account for inflation. The income of the middle fifth rose by just 17 percent, to $43,700, and the income of the poorest fifth rose only 9 percent.

For most workers, the only time in the last three decades when the rise in hourly pay beat inflation was during the speculative bubble of the 90's. Reduced pensions have made retirement less secure.

Clearly, a degree from a four-year college makes even more difference than it once did. More people are getting those degrees than did a generation ago, but class still plays a big role in determining who does or does not. At 250 of the most selective colleges in the country, the proportion of students from upper-income families has grown, not shrunk.

Some colleges, worried about the trend, are adopting programs to enroll more lower-income students. One is Amherst, whose president, Anthony W. Marx, explained: "If economic mobility continues to shut down, not only will we be losing the talent and leadership we need, but we will face a risk of a society of alienation and unhappiness. Even the most privileged among us will suffer the consequences of people not believing in the American dream."

Class differences in health, too, are widening, recent research shows. Life expectancy has increased over all; but upper-middle-class Americans live longer and in better health than middle-class Americans, who live longer and in better health than those at the bottom.

Class plays an increased role, too, in determining where and with whom affluent Americans live. More than in the past, they tend to live apart from everyone else, cocooned in their exurban chateaus. Researchers who have studied data from the 1980, 1990 and 2000 censuses say the isolation of the affluent has increased.

Family structure, too, differs increasingly along class lines. The educated and affluent are more likely than others to have their children while married. They have fewer children and have them later, when their earning power is high. On average, according to one study, college-educated women have their first child at 30, up from 25 in the early 1970's. The average age among women who have never gone to college has stayed at about 22.

Those widening differences have left the educated and affluent in a superior position when it comes to investing in their children. "There is no reason to doubt the old saw that the most important decision you make is choosing your parents," said Professor Levine, the Berkeley economist and mobility researcher. "While it's always been important, it's probably a little more important now."

The benefits of the new meritocracy do come at a price. It once seemed that people worked hard and got rich in order to relax, but a new class marker in upper-income families is having at least one parent who works extremely long hours (and often boasts about it). In 1973, one study found, the highest-paid tenth of the country worked fewer hours than the bottom tenth. Today, those at the top work more.

In downtown Manhattan, black cars line up outside Goldman Sachs's headquarters every weeknight around 9. Employees who work that late get a free ride home, and there are plenty of them. Until 1976, a limousine waited at 4:30 p.m. to ferry partners to Grand Central Terminal. But a new management team eliminated the late-afternoon limo to send a message: 4:30 is the middle of the workday, not the end.

A Rags-to-Riches Faith

Will the trends that have reinforced class lines while papering over the distinctions persist?

The economic forces that caused jobs to migrate to low-wage countries are still active. The gaps in pay, education and health have not become a major political issue. The slicing of society's pie is more unequal than it used to be, but most Americans have a bigger piece than they or their parents once did. They appear to accept the tradeoffs.

Faith in mobility, after all, has been consciously woven into the national self-image. Horatio Alger's books have made his name synonymous with rags-to-riches success, but that was not his personal story. He was a second-generation Harvard man, who became a writer only after losing his Unitarian ministry because of allegations of sexual misconduct. Ben Franklin's autobiography was punched up after his death to underscore his rise from obscurity.

The idea of fixed class positions, on the other hand, rubs many the wrong way. Americans have never been comfortable with the notion of a pecking order based on anything other than talent and hard work. Class contradicts their assumptions about the American dream, equal opportunity and the reasons for their own successes and even failures. Americans, constitutionally optimistic, are disinclined to see themselves as stuck.

Blind optimism has its pitfalls. If opportunity is taken for granted, as something that will be there no matter what, then the country is less likely to do the hard work to make it happen. But defiant optimism has its strengths. Without confidence in the possibility of moving up, there would almost certainly be fewer success stories.

Janny Scott and David Leonhardt, "Shadowy Lines That Still Divide," *The New York Times* (May 15, 2005). Copyright © 2005 by *The New York Times* Co. Reprinted with permission.

2. A Statistical Portrait of the U.S. Working Class

Michael D. Yates

The biennial *State of Working America* (hereinafter *SWA*), written by economists at the Economic Policy Institute in Washington, D.C., is the best compendium and analysis of U.S. labor market statistics there is.[1] In one convenient book, there are data on the distribution of income and wealth, all aspects of wages and benefits, employment and unemployment, poverty, regional labor markets, and international labor comparisons. In addition to the data, there are explanations for all of the major labor market trends. Does the stagnating minimum wage contribute to poverty? Is rising wage inequality the result of the growing educational requirements of jobs? Are trade agreements such as the North American Free Trade Agreement (NAFTA) necessarily good for workers as mainstream economists keep telling us? Why do the wages and incomes of racial and ethnic minorities continue to lag behind those of whites? Does the labor market model of the United States, with its very limited regulation, deliver better results for workers than does the more institutionally constrained model of most European nations? Mishel, Bernstein, and Allegretto analyze their data using sophisticated statistical techniques to give us answers to these and many other questions. A review of this book, along with some critical commentary, will give readers a good idea of how workers in the United States have been faring and what they can reasonably expect in the future.

What do the data tell us about the state of the U.S. working class? Basically they tell us that, with one exception, workers in the United States have been taking a beating for the past thirty years. The single exception is roughly the period from 1995 to 2000. From 1995 to 2000, wages (unless otherwise indicated, wages will refer to "real" wages, a measure of the purchasing power of our wages) began to grow significantly after two decades of stagnation, especially for those workers at the bottom of the wage distribution. Poverty rates declined and unemployment rates fell to thirty-year lows. The gap between both black workers and Hispanics and whites declined, in terms of wages, family incomes, unemployment rates, and the incidence of poverty. However, this rebound in some of the most basic indicators of working-class well-being ended with the onset of recession in March 2001 and the beginning of what has accurately been described as a "jobless recovery" in November of that same year. During the recession and the recovery, unemployment rose and has stayed well above 5 percent up to the present. The gains made by minorities and those at the bottom of the income distribution have eroded. Most of the increases in total income have gone to the owners of capital; very little has found its way into the hands of workers. Most disturbingly, many months after the recovery began, employment remains stagnant and wages are once again falling behind the rise in prices.

Although the *SWA* contains labor market data covering the entire period after the Second World War, most of this volume concerns itself with the rapid economic expansion of the late 1990s, the down-turn of 2001, and the recovery since then. So it makes sense for this review to do the same.

The authors stress that when unemployment is very low, workers benefit greatly and those at the bottom of the income distribution benefit the most. They also say that high productivity growth is essential, but this seems a dubious proposition, especially given the tremendous disconnect between productivity gains and wages over the past thirty years. And even more so since the very meaning of the word "productivity" is ambiguous to say the least. Productivity is very difficult to measure unambiguously, especially when applied to the economy as a whole, and even if we could measure it, it would be hard to know what it means. If a given number of workers produce more output but at the expense of their health or at the expense of our environment, is the productivity gain an obviously good

Table 1.1 U.S. Unemployment Rates

Years Rate	Overall Rate	White Rate	Black Rate	Hispanic Rate
1973–79	6.5%	6.8%	12.5%	9.5%
1979–89	7.1	5.5	14.7	10.3
1989–2000	5.6	4.2	10.8	8.6
1995	5.6	4.9	10.4	9.3
1996	5.4	4.7	10.5	8.9
1997	4.9	4.2	10.0	7.7
1998	4.5	3.9	8.9	7.2
1999	4.2	3.7	8.0	6.9
2000	4.0	3.5	7.6	5.7
2001	4.7	4.2	8.6	6.6
2002	5.8	5.1	10.2	7.5
2003	6.0	5.2	10.8	7.7
2004	5.5	4.8	10.4	7.0

Sources: SWA, 222; Bureau of Labor Statistics (BLS), http://www.bls.gov. These are official unemployment rates, derived from a monthly survey of households. They include only those who are without jobs but are actively seeking work. They exclude so-called "discouraged workers," those who have given up looking for work for market-related reasons. They also exclude "involuntary part-time" workers, those who desire full-time work but cannot find it.

thing? Even if we suppose that it is possible to say that, all else remaining equal, workers are now producing greater output than they did before, what is it about the increase in productivity that compels the payment of higher wages? A society whose output per person has risen obviously has more output to go around, but why would workers automatically get any of the greater output? The abstract fantasies of mainstream economists tell us that higher productivity automatically raises wages, but these are fantasies not the real world.

Table 1.1 shows the unemployment data. Although unemployment rates fell between 1992 and 2000, it wasn't until the second half of the decade that they fell to levels not seen in decades. The national rate for 2000 was the lowest since 1969, and the 2000 rates for blacks and Hispanics were the lowest on record. (It must be noted that the black rate does not reflect the fact that more than one million black persons are in our jails and prisons. Many of these would be unemployed if they were not incarcerated. And many are in prison because employment was not available to them.) Such low rates meant that labor market shortages were the rule rather than the exception, and these shortages benefited workers. Employers had to raise wages to attract and keep employees. And because minority workers are always over-represented among those not working, they benefit the most from tight labor markets. However, note that with the onset of recession in 2001, minority unemployment began to rise again. Black unemployment rates have been double-digit since 2002.

Table 1.1 does not include separate unemployment rates for women. These have been very close to, and in some years below, those for men for more than a decade. Women used to have higher unemployment rates than men, but the decline of sectors of the economy dominated by male employment, especially manufacturing, has helped to make the rates converge. Also not shown in the table is "hidden unemployment" (see note at the bottom of table 1.1), which fell dramatically during the expansion as part-time workers were able to find full-time jobs and those who had dropped out of the labor force reentered it and found work. However, this too has increased considerably during the recession and jobless recovery (see 242–48).

The correlation between low unemployment rates and wage rates is shown in table 1.2, which includes data from earlier years for comparison purposes. The workers included comprise what we normally think of as the working class, except for public employees. We see from these data how real wages rose dramatically between 1947 and 1973, then declined over the next twenty-two years before rising again between 1995 and 2003. The annual growth rate between 1995 and 2000 was the highest since the post–Second World War "golden age," not coincidentally the period with the lowest unemployment rates since then too. After 1995–2000, wage growth slowed, as the economy entered recession and the jobless recovery. In 2004, the real wage declined, remarkable at a time when the economy is supposedly heating up.

The wage numbers in table 1.2 are averages for workers as a whole, so as with the overall unemployment rates, they tell us nothing about specific categories of workers. Nor do they tell us anything about wage inequality. Several facts stand out if we take a broader look at wages:

1. Wage rates vary tremendously by race and by gender (166–67). In 2003, the median hourly wage rate of black men was about 73 percent that of white workers (in table 1.2, the wage rate is a mean, which is the simple average of all wage rates. The median wage rate is the wage rate right in the middle of all wage rates ranked from highest to lowest; 50 percent are higher and 50 percent are lower than the median.) The Hispanic median was about 64 percent of the white median wage rate. For women, the percentages for blacks and Hispanics were 86 and 75 percent respectively. The growth of these median wage rates for black and Hispanic men and for black women grew faster than the white median wage during the 1995–2000 expansion, again showing how low unemployment rates typically benefit most those at the bottom. Interestingly if we look at median family incomes instead of wage rates, we find that blacks and Hispanics gained even more on whites during this period. This is because low unemployment rates and the corresponding tight labor markets allowed more minority family members to find employment and encouraged employers to increase hours of work. However, the recession and jobless recovery have in large part reversed these gains (48).
2. For a nation as rich as the United States, there are a very large number of low-paying jobs. One of the most interesting data sets in the *SWA* is that for the fraction of jobs which pay an hourly wage rate insufficient to support a family

Table 1.2 Real Hourly Wage Rates of All Private Production and Nonsupervisory Workers, 1947–2004 (in 2003 Dollars)

Year	Real Average Hourly Earnings
1947	$ 8.47
1967	13.30
1973	14.85
1979	14.86
1982	14.34
1989	14.04
1995	13.95
2000	14.95
2003	15.35
2004	15.27

Business Cycles	Average Growth Rate
1947–67	2.3%
1967–73	1.8
1979–89	0.0
1979–89	–0.6
1989–2000	0.6
1989–95	–0.1
1995–2000	1.4
2000–03	0.9
1979–2003	0.1

Source: SWA, 119. The 2004 number is courtesy of the authors.

of four at the poverty level of income with full-time, year-round work. In table 1.3 are some of the data for 2003. During the expansion of the 1990s, women gained against men and blacks gained against whites in terms of laboring at poverty-level employment. Hispanics, on the other hand, fell further behind whites, no doubt because of increases in immigration of relatively unskilled Hispanic workers.

3. There is a great deal of wage inequality in the United States, and it has been growing since the late 1970s (120–27). The *SWA* authors look at high, middle, and low wage earners. High wages are those in the 90th percentile (only 10 percent of all workers earn more than these workers); middle earners are those at the 50th percentile (the median wage earner); and low wage earners are those in the 10th percentile (only 10 percent of workers earn less than these workers). The gap between the top and the middle has been rising throughout this period. However, the gap between the middle and bottom narrowed during the 1990s and has stayed constant since then. In this connection, it can also be noted that the gap between workers with high and low amounts of schooling has grown considerably since the 1970s. Two important aspects of wage inequality are the decline in the real value of the minimum wage

Table 1.3 Poverty-Level Employment, 2003

Workers	Percent of Employment at or below the Poverty Wage
All workers	24.3%
Men	19.6
Women	29.4
Whites	20.4
Men	15.1
Women	26.0
Blacks	30.4
Men	26.2
Women	33.9
Hispanics	39.8
Men	35.7
Women	45.8

Source: SWA, 128–33.

and the runaway inflation of the salaries of top corporate officials. In terms of purchasing power, the federal minimum wage of $5.15 per hour is worth nearly 25 percent less today than it was in 1967 (200). Executive pay, on the other hand, has risen by leaps and bounds; if we limit ourselves just to salary and cash bonuses, CEO pay more than doubled between 1989 and 2003. The ratio of CEO pay to the wage of the average worker went from 24 in 1967 to 300 in 2000 (212–16). Certainly this increase must call into question the alleged connection between productivity increases and wages, unless we are to believe that the productivity of CEOs rose more than ten times faster than that of the average worker over this period.

During the 1995–2000 expansion, employment grew by amounts large enough to push the unemployment rate down to levels not seen in a long time, and these low rates helped workers to improve their economic circumstances (224–31). But once recession hit in March 2001, the economy began to shed jobs and continued to do so long into the recovery. While employment has rebounded in recent months, President George W. Bush's first term has witnessed the poorest job performance since the presidency of Herbert Hoover. There are a few more jobs now at the end of his first term than there were at the beginning, but this is only due to an increase in public employment; private sector employment is lower. The data are quite remarkable. Between 2001 and the present, manufacturing shed jobs for forty-one consecutive months. Overall, 1.1 million jobs were lost during the first twenty-one months of the recovery! Employment growth has been weaker in this recovery than in any recovery since the Second World War. This is the second straight recovery (the last one was in 1991) in which many jobs were shed even as the economy was growing, but it is much worse in terms of both jobs lost and the time it has taken for employment to expand.

There is now tremendous slack in our labor markets even though the unemployment rate has fallen over the past three years and even though it didn't reach levels typical of post–Second World War contractions. Evidence of labor slack can be seen in several statistics (237–55). First, the average duration of unemployment and long-term unemployment have been high even as the recovery has picked up steam. The average duration of unemployment in February of 2004 was 20.3 weeks, the highest since July 1983. However, the unemployment rate for the first date was 5.6 percent, while for the latter date it was 9.4 percent. Such a high average duration of unemployment with a relatively low unemployment rate is very unusual and a sure sign of labor market distress for workers. The long-term unemployed are those who have been searching for work for twenty-seven weeks or longer. In 2003, the long-term unemployed comprised 22.1 percent of all unemployed, again a very high number given the rate of unemployment. Even by the end of 2004, the long-term unemployed made up 20.2 percent of all unemployed, very much higher than in almost every recovery year for the past forty years. The long-term unemployed also include many workers with a college education, workers of prime working age, and workers in white collar and professional employment. Between 2000 and 2003, the highest growth in long-term unemployment occurred among those with a bachelor's degree or higher, those forty-five and older, those in management and professional occupations, those in industries such as information and professional and business services, men, and whites. The last recession and the current recovery have seen labor market difficulties for a wide range of workers, again something quite unusual by historic standards.

A second sign of labor market slack is the decline in labor force participation rates, that is, the share of the working-age population actually in the labor force (the labor force consists of those employed and those unemployed). A decline in this means that people are dropping out of the labor force, an unhealthy sign during a recovery. At the end of 2004, the labor force participation rate was 66 percent, down one percentage point from what it was at the last business cycle peak in March 2001. Had the rate been the same in December of 2004 as it was in March of 2001, nearly 3,000,000 more persons would have been in the labor force. If we assume that these people dropped out of the labor force because they couldn't find jobs and imagined them rejoining the labor force now, the unemployment rate would be nearly 7.5 percent.

If we shift our attention away from wages to income and the connected concept of wealth, two facts stand out. First, poverty, defined here as income below a certain threshold, is extensive in the United States (309–20, 324–28). The poverty threshold is very low, equal to three times a minimum food budget set by the Department of Agriculture. In 2003, it was $18,660, before taxes. The incidence of poverty overall in 2003 was 12.5 percent, which equates to just over 35,000,000 persons. Naturally, there is great variability in the incidence of poverty among groups. In 2003, the poverty rates for whites, blacks, and Hispanics were 10.5, 24.4, and 22.5 percent respectively. The overall rate for children under eighteen years of age was 19.8 percent; for whites, blacks, and Hispanics the rates were 14.3,

34.1, and 29.7 percent respectively. All of these rates shifted down dramatically during the 1995–2000 expansion, most of all for blacks and Hispanics. The overall rate was 11.3 percent in 2000, while that for blacks was 22.5 percent and that for Hispanics, 21.5 percent. These latter rates fell so much that the gap between minority and white rates closed to its lowest levels on record. Unfortunately, these positive trends have been reversed. Of course, in any discussion of poverty, we must realize that the official poverty thresholds are completely inadequate as measures of economic hardship. Many economists believe that thresholds twice the official one would better show how many people are in difficult economic circumstances. If we used such a threshold, the incidence of poverty would rise about two and one-half times; more than 88,000,000 would be classified as poor.

Second, both income and wealth are horribly unequally distributed (58–72, 277–307). The rich are definitely getting richer, both absolutely and relatively, and the poor are getting poorer in both senses as well. The economic pie has steadily gotten bigger, but the share going to those at the bottom has actually shrunk, as most of the gains from greater productivity have gone to the owners of capital. Families have been able to bring home higher incomes each year, but this has mainly been due to greater hours of work and more family members working. However, during the last recession, median family incomes fell for whites, blacks, and Hispanics and it may now be true that we are reaching limits to the ability of families to increase hours and send more members into the workplace. As with wage rates, the 1995–2000 expansion saw faster increases in family income for blacks and Hispanics than for whites. But since then, minorities have suffered much sharper losses than have whites. And today, as in the past, the ratios of black and Hispanic family income to white family income remain well below 65 percent.

Incomes have been becoming more unequal for more than three decades, and even the rapid growth of the 1995–2000 period, which, as we have seen benefited working people in several ways, failed to reverse this trend. Table 1.4 and figure 1.1 provide some stark testimony to growing inequality. The table shows how the total increase in incomes between 1979 and 2000 was distributed among various income classes. The richest 1 percent of all households, whose income is mainly from capital (or capital income disguised as wages), grabbed an astonishing 38.4 percent of all of the income produced over a twenty-one-year

Table 1.4 Distribution of Income Growth to Income Group, 1979–2000

Income Group (Households)	Share of Income Growth, 1979–2000
Poorest 20%	0.8%
Middle 20%	5.1
Richest 20%	74.0
80–95%	21.5
95–99%	14.1
Richest 1%	38.4

Source: SWA, 62.

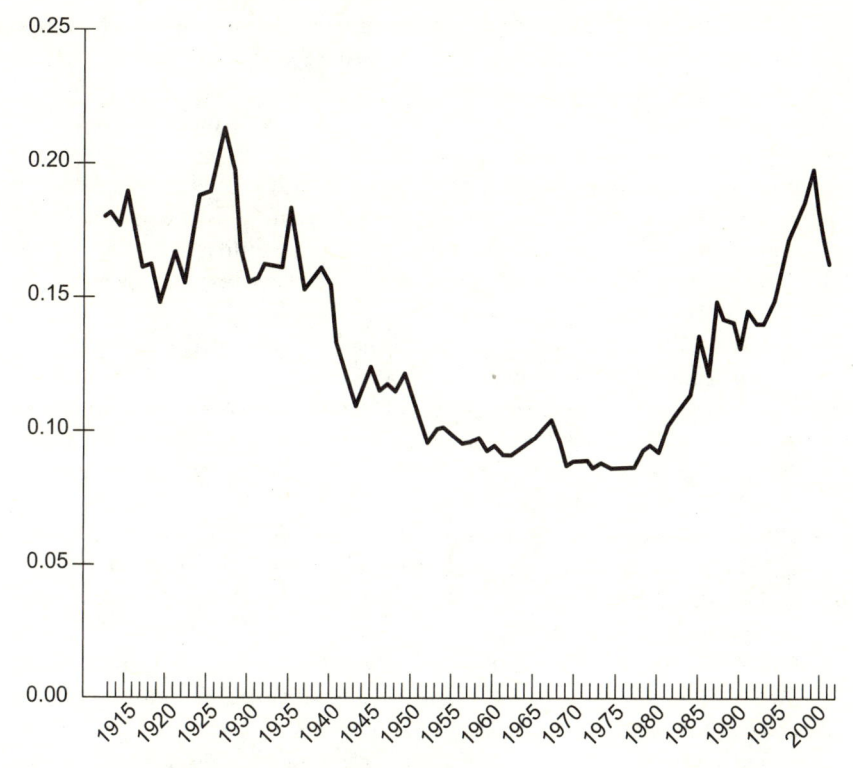

Figure 1.1 Income Share of the Top 1 Percent

period. The poorest 20 percent of households took home a mere 0.8 percent of the total income. Consider that in 2003 there were 111,278,000 households in the United States. One percent of this number is 1,112,780 households. These very rich households got a share of the income increase forty-eight times higher (38.4 divided by 0.8) than the 22,255,600 families which comprise the poorest 20 percent of households.

Figure 1.1 shows the share of total household income going to the richest 1 percent of households from 1913 to 2002. This chart graphically shows what has been happening in the United States. In the 1920s, capital reigned supreme, and workers were on the defensive, suffering a string of setbacks from which it was routinely predicted they would never recover. Yet they did recover and then some during the Great Depression, the Second World War, and the years immediately following the war. This upsurge corresponds roughly with the downward trend on the graph from the onset of the depression to the middle of the 1970s. The upward swing on the graph marks the attack on labor by capital which commenced at the end of the "golden age." The graph slopes down when the stock market bubble collapsed in 2001, but it is again on the upswing as markets have recovered and capital continues to usurp the fruits of workers' labor.

The distribution of wealth (the money value of all of an entity's assets) is much more unequally distributed than income. The concept of net worth is useful here. This is the difference between total assets and total debt. Among the many statistical nuggets about wealth provided in *SWA*, here are some of particular interest:

- In 2001, the richest 1 percent of all households had 33.4 percent of all net worth. The bottom 90 percent had 28.5 percent. This is somewhat of an understatement for today since it reflects the losses suffered by the very rich in the recent stock market collapse, losses which have been largely reversed in the last two years.
- In 2001, 17.6 percent of all households had zero or negative net worth, and 30.3 percent had net worth less than $10,000.
- Wealth is racially divided. 13.1 percent of white households had zero or negative net worth in 2001, while this was true for 30.9 percent of black households. The median financial wealth (holdings of stocks, bonds, cash, and the like) of blacks was a paltry $1,100; for whites it was $42,100.
- The rich are asset heavy, especially with respect to financial assets (those which yield income), and debt poor, while the opposite is true for those with the lowest incomes. In 2001, the richest 1 percent of households owned 44.8 percent of all common stock (excluding stock owned through pensions); the poorest 80 percent owned 5.8 percent. This suggests that the poorest 10 or 20 percent own a minuscule share of stock. Even including stocks held through various pension arrangements, in 2001, those households with yearly incomes less than $15,000 held 1.1 percent of all stocks, while those with annual incomes equal to or greater than $250,000 owned 40.6 percent of all stock. Debt, on the other hand, bears down most heavily on the poor. In 2001, debt service payments made up 40 percent or more of yearly household income for 27 percent of those households with less than $20,000 in income. For households with yearly income between $90,000 and 100,000, the percentage was 2 percent. Of the former group, 13 percent were sixty days or more late paying their bills; for the latter group the rate was 1.3 percent.

It is important to note that there has been a tremendous inflation in asset prices over the past decade, first in stock prices and now in real estate. There is no question that the late 1990s saw a stock market bubble, and we are now witnessing a real estate bubble. However, asset price inflation greatly benefits the very rich. They own most of the assets whose prices rise, and they can use the rising prices to buy other assets solidifying their control over both the economy and the political system. Since this asset price inflation is part and parcel of modern monopoly capitalism and the political decisions that are its handmaiden (both bubbles were encouraged by Alan Greenspan and the Federal Reserve System), it can be seen as a subtle form of class struggle, one barely perceived by most of us.

What have been the causes of the trends so well illustrated in the *SWA?* The authors offer a number of explanations, supported by sophisticated statistical analyses. While mainstream economists like Harvard's Martin Feldstein throw up their hands, mystified by the great rise in income and wage inequality, the *SWA* authors show us that the reasons for this are not hard to find at all. The tax system has become more regressive; tax rates have been lowered for the top income recipients and the largest corporations. This has channeled money from the poor to the rich, increasing inequality. The Bush tax cuts, for example, have transferred "0.8 percent of total, after-tax household income from the bottom 99 percent to the top 1 percent" (3).

Unions have become noticeably weaker; in 2004 union workers comprised only 12.5 percent of employed workers. Just twenty-one years before, density was 20.1 percent. In the private sector, union density in 2004 was 7.9, its lowest level since the early 1900s. Even in the public sector, density is down to 36.4 percent, from 37.2 percent in 2003. In Indiana and Missouri, new Republican governors have ordered an end to collective bargaining for state workers.

Union workers make much higher wages and more and better fringe benefits than do nonunion workers (189–98). In 2003, the union wage premium (the difference between union and nonunion wages after controlling for a variety of worker characteristics such as amount of schooling) was 15.5 percent (for black workers it was 20.9 percent and for Hispanics 23.2 percent). Therefore, as the labor force is increasingly made up of relatively more nonunion workers, average wages will fall. But in addition, unions benefit blacks and Hispanics more than whites, blue-collar more than white-collar workers, less-educated more than more-educated workers, and those at the bottom of the wage distribution more than those at the top. So as unions become less common, the wage gap between whites and minorities increases, as do those between blue- and white-collar workers, high school and college graduates, and low- and high-wage workers.

Another factor responsible for growing inequality is the decline in the purchasing power of the minimum wage noted above. This has happened because Congress has made the political decision not to increase the minimum wage over long periods of time. Then any rise in prices reduces the buying power of a fixed minimum wage. The major impact of this is on poor women, since women represent nearly 60 percent of all minimum wage workers as well as nearly 60 percent of all workers earning no more than one dollar an hour above the minimum wage (201). If the minimum wage were increased, both groups of workers would benefit as employers were forced to keep their wage structures in balance. The failure of the minimum wage to grow has greatly exacerbated inequality at the bottom of the wage distribution. Consider the wage gap between the poorest workers and those in the middle, that is between those workers earning a wage at the 10th percentile of the wage distribution and those at the 50th (median) percentile. *SWA* estimates that a falling real minimum wage is responsible for most of the growth in this gap, much more than can be accounted for by changes in the skill requirements of jobs or any failure of poor workers to increase their schooling. Overall, the authors estimate that the decline in union power and the fall in the real minimum wage are responsible for about one-third of the growth in wage inequality (5).

Mainstream economists have argued that one important source of inequality is a technologically driven increase in the skill requirements of jobs. Workers who get large amounts of schooling will have these skills; those who don't will not. Thus, technology will widen the gap between skilled and unskilled workers, or what amounts to the same thing, the gap between more and less educated workers. The authors of *SWA* demolish this argument (205–12). The details are too complicated for quick explanation. Suffice it to say that during the 1990s when technology presumably sped up and there was an accelerated introduction of computers into workplaces, nearly all types of wage inequality slowed down. Yet those at the very top of the wage distributions—mainly high-level corporate executives—are pulling away from everyone else, and it seems implausible that technology could be the cause of this. The wages of CEOs and their immediate subordinates have risen whether productivity increases (presumably driven by technology according to the mainstream) have been high or low, in corporations both low and high tech, in businesses doing well and in those not doing so well.

Any argument that we will be entering a period in which high skill will be necessary for most jobs does not stand up to the facts. As I said in these pages last April:

Nearly 30 million persons labor as teaching assistants, food preparers and servers, counter attendants, cashiers, counter and rental clerks, bookkeepers, customer service reps, stock clerks and order fillers, secretaries, general office clerks, assemblers, sorters, helpers, truck drivers, packers and packagers, and laborers. The Bureau of Labor Statistics estimates that the ten occupations with the largest job growth between 2000 and 2010 will be food preparation and service workers, customer service representatives, registered nurses, retail salespersons, computer support specialists, cashiers, general office clerks, security guards, computer software engineers, and waiters and waitresses. Of these, nurses and software engineers are the only obviously "good" jobs, and even these are rapidly being rationalized or outsourced by cost-conscious managers.

The *SWA* authors perform an interesting analysis in which they take the occupational structure of 2002 and compare it with BLS projections for 2012 (216–18). Assuming that the BLS estimates are correct, they show that there will be very minimal occupational "upgrading," and this will require only slightly greater educational attainment and wage rate. For example, the BLS data show that in 2002, 26.9 percent of jobs required a college education, but this will rise to just 27.9 percent by 2012. Hardly anything to write home about. It may be that skill requirements of any given job might rise (as opposed to rising skill requirements due to a change in the occupational structure), but history doesn't lend much evidence for this possibility.

The emphasis by mainstream economists on technology as a causal factor in the conditions of workers is matched by their fixation on "free" trade as something which is of obvious benefit to working people (178–89). I put the word free in quotes because much trade among nations is anything but free, such as trade in the services of doctors and lawyers and materials and methods that are patented or copyrighted. But if we look at the impact of the North American Free Trade Agreement and others like it, we see clearly that "free" trade has been a disaster for workers. The political decisions which ended capital controls and pushed through these trade agreements have led to large increases in imports of manufactured consumer goods and capital goods used in manufacturing; they have promoted the shifting of U.S.-based production overseas to low-wage venues in Mexico and China; they have given employers a gigantic club with which to threaten workers and obtain wage concessions from them; and they have given rise to the phenomenon of outsourcing both unskilled and skilled jobs. The consequences have been very large losses of manufacturing employment, lower wages for workers with less skill and schooling, and high unemployment for highly skilled workers such as computer programmers. The authors estimate that trade-related impacts on workers have been responsible for another one-third of the growth in wage inequality. They don't have estimates of the amount of outsourcing of jobs. However, in a recent study done for the U.S.-China Economic and Security Review Commission, researchers Kate Bronfenbrenner and Stephanie Luce found that in the first quarter of 2004 alone as many as 100,000 jobs (suggesting about 400,000 per year) were outsourced. Their absolute rock-bottom estimate was 25,000, and this was more than five times higher than the estimate of the Bureau of Labor Statistics.

To say that the jobs of U.S. workers are being outsourced to lower wage countries is not to say that U.S. workers should be privileged over those in other countries. Workers everywhere are subject to the same forces. NAFTA has provided few benefits and lots of harm to Mexican workers, and the cheap U.S. corn flooding Mexican markets is wreaking havoc on Mexican peasants, forcing them to abandon the land and seek employment in the cities of Mexico and the United States. Jobs are now being outsourced from Mexico to China, and should wages rise enough in China, jobs will be outsourced from there too.

Mishel, Bernstein, and Allegretto offer by way of conclusion the observation that the economy today is at a crossroads. It can take a path leading back toward the kind of "virtuous cycle" which existed in the long post–Second World War boom and in the shorter expansion at the end of the 1990s. Or it can continue on the path set in motion after the long boom and the shorter expansion ended. Let us look at each of these paths.

The *SWA* authors correctly point out how beneficial low unemployment rates are for working people. As we have already noted, they refer to the 1995–2000 period throughout the book, pointing out the gains made by workers. They even compare it favorably to the long post–Second World War (1947–73) boom in which workers saw both their real wages double and fringe benefits expand in scope and increase in amounts, and in which all income groups from the bottom to the top shared in roughly equal degree the tremendous rise in productivity. They are hopeful that the economy can return to the growth trajectory exhibited in the 1995–2000 period.

I am more pessimistic about this. The authors might have delved into the mini-boom of the late 1990s a little more deeply as have other economists such as Robert Pollin and David Kotz. In referring to the 1995–2000 period, the SWA authors tell us what they mean by a "virtuous cycle" (19–34). As the economy begins to expand, certain conditions must exist for the expansion to continue, to become self-reinforcing. The key is for the income generated by the expansion to be broadly shared. As they put it, " ... broad-based income gains generate equally broad consumption, triggering greater confidence among investors and producers. This confidence in turn feeds greater investment and sustains further growth. At the same time, these growing incomes boost government coffers, leading to a better fiscal position and other associated benefits, from reassuring financial markets to providing government with more resources to meet social needs" (21). The "virtuous cycle" is helped along by "strong labor market institutions" such as labor unions and rising minimum wages.

The most virtuous of "virtuous cycles" was the long economic boom from the end of the Second World War until the middle of the 1970s. The pent-up domestic demand from the war (buttressed by large savings, the growth of credit purchases, and public subsidization of housing and schooling—limited, however, to whites) and enormous demand for U.S. capital exports by war-ravaged Europe tightened labor markets and made business expectations about the future very positive. This caused an increase in capital spending, which in turn tightened labor markets further. Wages rose both because of strong demand for labor and because relatively strong labor unions forced businesses to share some of the increases in revenues. All of this made workers more confident about the future and more willing to spend money. The automobile industry boomed, and this greatly increased capital spending in a host of areas from steel, oil, and glass to road, home, restaurant, and motel construction. Meanwhile the rudiments of a social safety net were in place, including social security and unemployment compensation. Government spending continued upward as military spending never fell back to what it was before the war, and enormous highway building and other government-financed construction projects grew in size. Hence a virtuous cycle of investment and employment growth, wage and consumer spending growth, higher tax revenues and government spending, optimistic expectations about the future all around, all of these leading to the whole process beginning anew. Capital controls and limited international competition kept most of the gains inside the country.

Of course, the postwar boom came to an end as all booms must, for reasons expounded by the editors of this magazine for many years. And I do not mean to imply that the "golden age" was in all ways good for workers. But even so, it is difficult to see how the 1995–2000 expansion can be compared to that of the "golden age." It is true that there were significant increases in capital spending and then in consumer spending. But it is also true that much of the investment spending as the expansion proceeded was due to the overly optimistic expectations generated by the stock market bubble. As even those who should have known better began to suggest that the expansion might go on indefinitely, businesses got caught up in a spending frenzy lest they fall behind their competitors. What this investment spending did mainly was create a lot of excess capacity throughout the economy, and excess capacity cannot rise without sooner or later bringing an end to an investment boom. Consumption spending was fueled by both the inflation in stock prices—through the "wealth effect" by which households spend more because they have more wealth, that is, a greater sense of economic security—and borrowing (itself pumped up by the greater paper wealth which could be used as collateral for loans). When the stock bubble burst in 2000, it wasn't long before investment and consumer spending stopped rising. What is more, the higher incomes brought about by the expansion were not at all equitably shared, so there could not be the kind of broad-based working-class spending that marked the "golden age."

The federal government received an enormous tax revenue windfall as the rise in stock prices brought in billions of dollars in capital gains taxes. But the government did not use its revenues to increase the amounts of money spent on the social welfare programs that would make workers healthier, better educated, and more productive, things which would reap many future benefits. As Pollin points out, spending on education, for example, failed to keep up with the growth of the economy as a whole. Instead draconian crime bills were enacted and poor women were denied welfare.

Two final points can be made here. First, there were not the institution forces at work which were there during the golden age. The labor movement continued to shed members and lose both economic and political power throughout nearly the entire expansion. This denied workers the larger share of the economic growth they would have had had they been able to count on strong unions. The declining political power of unions meant that they could not effectively pressure the government to raise the minimum wage and do all of the other things that both increase the security of workers and their disposable incomes. Luckily there was an earned income tax credit which does help poor working people to help maintain and improve slightly their standard of living. Second, today a lot of any increase in incomes leaks out of the domestic economy in the form of spending on imports. The thorough deregulation of the economy continued throughout the 1990s, especially through the passage of NAFTA. This set the stage for massive movements of capital overseas and the outsourcing of both unskilled and skilled jobs.

What all of this amounts to is that it is hard to argue that there was anything close to a "virtuous cycle" during the boom of the late 1990s. A good indication of this is the speed with which things deteriorated for workers once the boom ended. And as we have seen, the current expansion, now three years old, has seen little in the way of recovery for workers. Real wages are falling, and employment is just now getting back to where it was when Bush took office. As the authors of *SWA* make crystal clear, most of the gains of the current recovery have gone to capital not labor:

> [In the corporate sector of the economy] inflation-adjusted capital income grew 32.2 percent over the recession and jobless recovery, while real compensation [wages plus benefits] was up only 1.2 percent. Thus, the vast majority (84.6 percent) of the real income growth in the corporate sector since the first quarter

of 2001 has accrued to capital income, a hugely disproportionate share when considering that capital income comprised just 16.6 percent of total corporate income when the recession started in early 2001. (31)

So where does all of this leave us? Whither the workers of the United States? We have seen that with the exception of a brief period at the end of the 1990s and the beginning of the new century, it is clear that workers have become increasingly insecure in their employment and in their lives when they become unemployed. And it is also clear that the late 1990s expansion was not fueled by a "virtuous cycle," but by a stock market bubble and a large volume of consumer debt. Once the bubble ended, the downward trend in worker well-being continued where it had left off before the expansion began. With the country bogged down in war in Iraq, Bush tax cuts guaranteeing enormous budget deficits and higher interest rates into the indefinite future, no obvious demand stimulus on the horizon, a mountain of debt limiting long-term growth of consumption, a record trade imbalance which has made the country thoroughly dependent on the willingness of foreigners to buy government bonds, and the continued outsourcing of jobs, it is difficult to see anything but a bleak future for workers. What is more, structural changes in the way the labor markets function appear to be creating a greater disconnect between the growth of the nation's output and the expansion of employment.

The state of working America is in large part a function of the class struggle. Although wages, hours, employment, unemployment, and productivity might appear to be determined by what happens in the impersonal marketplace and by the independent impact of technological changes, in reality all of these are shaped by the struggle between workers and employers as this occurs in both workplaces and in the larger political arena. If the statistics which define the economic conditions of working people show deterioration, then this is evidence that employers have increased their power. If this is happening at the same time that the economic conditions of capitalists are improving, then it is certain that this is so. We can probe the data further to see if we can tell why workers are losing power, and this in turn can help us to develop strategies and tactics to help workers regain what they have lost and to push ahead. What this long review of *The State of Working America* makes clear is that the rebuilding of power of the U.S. working class is really the only thing which can give workers any sense of hope that the future will be in any way better than the past thirty years. And this rebuilding must be on an entirely different basis than in the past. It must have a radical vision, which understands that this system has had more than enough time to fulfill its promises and admits that it cannot do so. And U.S. labor must, above all, ally itself with workers in the rest of the world, especially in the poor countries. For example, in addressing the outsourcing of jobs and immigrant labor, labor must never scapegoat workers in other countries. Instead of demanding protection from outsourcing, it must demand expanded unemployment compensation, full pay while retraining, and a public commitment to full employment. Instead of feeding anti-immigrant hysteria, it must support immigrant rights, show solidarity with workers' movements in the countries from which immigrants come, and take the lead in demanding a complete revamping of U.S. foreign policy.

NOTE ON SOURCES

The page numbers in parentheses are for page references in *The State of Working America, 2004–2005*. Unless otherwise noted, all other data have been taken from the Bureau of Labor Statistics (www.bls.gov) or the Bureau of Census (www.census.gov). The references to works by Pollin and Kotz are Robert Pollin, *Contours of Descent: U.S. Economic Fractures and the Landscape of Global Austerity* (New York: Verso, 2003), and David Kotz, "Neoliberalism and the U.S. Economic Expansion of the '90s," *Monthly Review*, April 2003. The study by Bronfenbrenner and Luce is Kate Bronfenbrenner and Stephanie Luce, *The Changing Nature of Corporate Global Restructuring: The Impact of Production Shifts in the U.S., China, and around the Globe*, report submitted to the U.S.-China Economic and Security Review Commission, October 14, 2004. The article from which I quoted myself is "Workers Looking for Jobs, Unions Looking for Members," *Monthly Review*, April 2004. On Martin Feldstein's inability to analyze income inequality, see Michael Yates, "The Rich, the Poor, and the Economists," available at http://www.monthlyreview.org/nftae02.htm.

NOTE

1. Lawrence Mishel, Jared Bernstein, and Sylvia Allegretto, *The State of Working America: 2004–2005* (Ithaca, N.Y.: Cornell University Press, 2005), 484 pages. Visit the EPI website, www.epinet.org, to learn more about their work.

3. THE OTHER AMERICA
AN ENDURING SHAME
Jonathan Alter

It takes a hurricane. It takes a catastrophe like Katrina to strip away the old evasions, hypocrisies and not-so-benign neglect. It takes the sight of the United States with a big black eye—visible around the world—to help the rest of us begin to see again. For the moment, at least, Americans are ready to fix their restless gaze on enduring problems of poverty, race and class that have escaped their attention. Does this mean a new war on poverty? No, especially with Katrina's gargantuan price tag. But this disaster may offer a chance to start a skirmish, or at least make Washington think harder about why part of the richest country on earth looks like the Third World.

"I hope we realize that the people of New Orleans weren't just abandoned during the hurricane," Sen. Barack Obama said last week on the floor of the Senate. "They were abandoned long ago—to murder and mayhem in the streets, to substandard schools, to dilapidated housing, to inadequate health care, to a pervasive sense of hopelessness."

The question now is whether the floodwaters can create a sea change in public perceptions. "Americans tend to think of poor people as being responsible for their own economic woes," says sociologist Andrew Cherlin of Johns Hopkins University. "But this was a case where the poor were clearly not at fault. It was a reminder that we have a moral obligation to provide every American with a decent life."

In the last four decades, part of that obligation has been met. Social Security and Medicare have all but eliminated poverty among the elderly. Food stamps have made severe hunger in the United States mostly a thing of the past. A little-known program with bipartisan support and a boring name—the Earned Income Tax Credit—supplements the puny wages of the working poor, helping to lift millions into the lower middle class.

But after a decade of improvement in the 1990s, poverty in America is actually getting worse. A rising tide of economic growth is no longer lifting all boats. For the first time in half a century, the third year of a recovery (2004) also saw an *increase* in poverty. In a nation of nearly 300 million people, the number living below the poverty line ($14,680 for a family of three) recently hit 37 million, up more than a million in a year.

With the strain Katrina is placing on the gulf region (and on families putting up their displaced relatives), it will almost certainly increase more.

The poverty rate, 12.7 percent, is a controversial measurement, in part because it doesn't include some supplemental programs. But it's the highest in the developed world and more than twice as high as in most other industrialized countries, which all strike a more generous social contract with their weakest citizens. Even if the real number is lower than 37 million, that's a nation of poor people the size of Canada or Morocco living inside the United States.

Their fellow Americans know little about them. In the last decade, poverty disappeared from public view. TV dislikes poor people, not personally but because their appearance is a downer and—according to ratings meters—causes viewers to hit the remote. Powerful politicians aren't much friendlier: poor folks vote in small numbers. Republicans win little of their support and Democrats often take it for granted.

Until Katrina, the pressure was off. After President Clinton signed welfare reform in 1996, the chattering classes stopped arguing about it. With welfare caseloads cut in half—more than 9 million women and children have left the rolls—even many liberals figured the trend lines were headed in the right direction. The real-world challenges of welfare reform explained in Jason DeParle's landmark 2004 book, "American Dream," went unheeded, as Clinton initiatives and the boom of the 1990s pulled 4.1 million of the working poor out of poverty. (Good times don't always have that effect. The Reagan boom of the 1980s did the same for only 50,000.) Meanwhile crime plummeted in cities across the country, down to levels not seen since the 1950s. Few noticed that progress in fighting poverty stalled with the economy in 2001.

President Bush, preoccupied with terrorism and tax cuts, made no mention of it. His main involvement with poverty issues has been on education, where he sharply increased aid to poor schools as part of his No Child Left Behind initiative. Democrats have offered little on education beyond opposition to NCLB. They've shown more allegiance to the teachers unions (whose contracts are models of unaccountability) than to poor kids. Bush's other antipoverty idea was to bolster so-called faith-based initiatives by shifting a little federal funding of social programs to religious groups. Post-Katrina, this will likely be extended. But it's a Band-Aid, not an antipoverty strategy. The last notable poverty expert working in the White House, John Dilulio, departed in 2001 after explaining that the administration had no interest in real policy analysis.

The president has made a point of hiring more high-ranking African-Americans than any of his predecessors. But his identification with blacks is a long way from, say, LBJ's intoning, as he did in 1965, "Their cause must be our cause, too.... And we shall overcome." Bush rarely meets with the poor or their representatives. His mother made headlines when she visited the Houston Astrodome and said: "So many of the people in the arenas here, you know, were underprivileged anyway. So this is working very well for them"—as if sharing space with 10,000 strangers was a step up.

Who are the poor? With whites making up 72 percent of the population, the United States contains more poor whites than poor blacks or Hispanics. In fact, the Center on Budget and Policy Priorities reports that the increase in white poverty in nonurban areas accounts for most of the recent uptick in the poverty rate. But only a little more than 8 percent of American whites are poor, compared with 22 percent of Hispanics and nearly a quarter of all African-Americans (in a country that is 12 percent black). This represents a significant advance for blacks in recent decades, thanks to the growth of the black middle class, but it's still a shamefully high number. By contrast, immigration has sent poverty among Hispanics up, though it has not been as intractable for them across generations.

After 40 years of study, the causes of poverty are still being debated. Liberals say the problem is an economic system that's tilted to the rich; conservatives blame a debilitating culture of poverty. Clearly, it's both—a tangle of financial and personal pain that often goes beyond insufficient resources and lack of training. Family issues are critical. Married-couple families are significantly less poor than female-headed households. While hunger, crime, drugs and overt racial discrimination have eased, other problems connected with poverty may have worsened: wage stagnation, social isolation and a more subtle form of class-based racism. Each can be found in New Orleans, pre-Katrina.

The primary economic problem is not unemployment but low wages for workers of all races. With unions weakened and a minimum-wage increase not on the GOP agenda, wages have not kept pace with the cost of living, except at the top. (In 1965, CEOs made 24 times as much as the average worker; by 2003, they earned 185 times as much.) Since 2001, the United States has lost 2.7 million manufacturing jobs. New Orleans's good jobs left much earlier, replaced by employment in the restaurant and tourism industry, which pays less and usually carries no health benefits. Medicaid covers poor children but few poor adults, who put off seeing the doctor, cranking up the cost. For the poor, the idea of low-wage jobs' covering the basic expenses of living has become a cruel joke.

Consider the case of Delores Ellis. Before Katrina turned her world upside down, the 51-year-old resident of New Orleans's Ninth Ward was earning the highest salary of her life as a school janitor—$6.50 an hour, no health insurance or pension. Pregnant at 17 and forced to drop out of high school, she went on welfare for a time, then bounced around minimum-wage jobs. "I worked hard all my life and I can't afford nothing," Ellis says. "I'm not saying that I want to keep up with the Joneses, I just want to live better."

Ellis is hampered by cultural habits, too. Like almost all poor evacuees interviewed by *Newsweek,* she has no bank account. Before the storm, she did own a stereo, refrigerator, washer and dryer, two color TVs and a 1992 Chevy Lumina with more than 100,000 miles on it. This, too, is common among the poor; like more comfortable Americans, they spend on consumer goods beyond their means. But these are often their only assets. The reason that more African-Americans didn't heed warnings to leave New Orleans before the hurricane hit goes beyond the much-publicized lack of cars. They were reluctant to abandon their entire net worth to looters. John Edwards, who has spent much of the year since he lost the vice presidency studying the problems of "the two Americas," says that establishing thousands of bank accounts is critical—not just for Katrina evacuees, but for others in poverty.

Isolation is the second big factor that makes poverty even worse. While racial segregation in housing is at its lowest levels since 1920, Sheryll Cashin, author of "The Failures of Integration," has found that only 5 to 10 percent of American families live in stable, integrated communities. More than half a century after *Brown v. Board of Education,* public schools are still almost totally segregated—the result of where people choose to live, not law. Blacks and whites increasingly go to school with more integrated Hispanics, but not with each other. One big change is that blacks seem only a little more interested in integration than whites.

But there's a steep price to this voluntary segregation. While overt discrimination is dwindling—in part because perpetrators can be successfully sued for practicing it—it still exists. A 1999 University of Pennsylvania study showed that telephone callers using "black English" were offered fewer real-estate choices. At a deeper level, Harvard's Glenn C. Loury has identified what he calls "discrimination in contact." Informal contacts between people across racial lines break down wariness and lead to the connections that help people find jobs. When perfectly legal social segregation prevents blacks from having such informal networks, they slip back.

This isolation has hampered many Katrina evacuees and other inner-city blacks. Joycelyn Harris has spent her whole life in the Ninth Ward. One of 11 children, she dropped out of school at the age of 12 and went on to have five children of her own, later working at Burger King and as a hotel chambermaid. She and her boyfriend, Kenneth Anthony, fled the city last week with nothing but $9 in their pockets and the clothes on their backs. They lived for a time in a New Orleans housing project isolated by two industrial canals and railroad tracks. "Sometimes I wanted to back out, but you can't," says Anthony, who has lived in four different housing projects. "I felt like I was incarcerated."

In the last decade, the government has torn down more than 70,000 units of public housing nationwide, including where Harris and Anthony once lived. But too often, the people who resided there are left to fend for themselves. While everyone agrees that housing vouchers are a good idea, the waiting list to use them for public housing is five years.

Following the Gateraux model in Chicago, the Clinton administration launched a "scatter-site" housing program in four cities that found homes for the poor in mixed-income neighborhoods. While the move doesn't much benefit adults, their children—confronted with higher expectations and a less harmful peer group—do much better. "It really helped in Atlanta," says Rep. John Lewis, a hero of the civil-rights movement. Bush and the GOP Congress killed the idea, as well as the Youth Opportunity Grant program, which had shown success in partnering with the private sector to help prepare disadvantaged teens for work and life. They tried to cut after-school programs—proven winners—by 40 percent, then settled for a freeze.

The third problem exacerbating poverty is what some call racism. Others argue the word is too inflammatory for a more subtle but no less debilitating effect.

Racism was clearly present in the aftermath of Katrina. Readers of Yahoo News noticed it when a pair of waterlogged whites were described in a caption as "carrying" food while another picture (from a different wire service) of blacks holding food described them as "looters." White suburban police closed at least one bridge to keep a group of blacks from fleeing to white areas. Over the course of two days, a white river-taxi operator from hard-hit St. Bernard Parish rescued scores of people from flooded areas and ferried them to safety. All were white. "A n--ger is a n--ger is a n--ger, he told a *Newsweek* reporter. Then he said it again.

Was the slowness of Washington's rescue efforts also a racial thing? In 2004, Bush moved huge resources into Florida immediately following hurricanes there. No one was stranded. The salient difference was not race but politics. Those hurricanes came just before an election.

Obama, the only African-American in the US. Senate, says "the ineptitude was colorblind." But he argues that while—contrary to rapper Kanye West's attack on Bush—there was no "active malice," the federal response to Katrina represented "a continuation of passive indifference" on the part of the government. It reflected an unthinking assumption that every American "has the capacity to load up their family in an SUV, fill it up with $100 worth of gasoline, stick some bottled water in the trunk and use a credit card to check into a hotel on safe ground." When they did focus on race in the aftermath, many Louisianans let their fears take over. Lines at gun stores in Baton Rouge, La., snaked out the door. Obama stops short of calling this a sign of racism. For some, he says, it's a product of "sober concern" after the violence in the city; for others, it's closer to "racial stereotyping."

Harvard's Loury argued in a 2002 book, "The Anatomy of Racial Inequality," that it's this stereotyping and "racial stigma," more than overt racism, that helps hold blacks in poverty. Loury explains a destructive cycle of "self-reinforcing stereotypes" at school and work. A white employer, for instance, may make a judgment based on prior experience that the young black men he hires are likely to be absent or late for work. So he supervises them more closely. Resenting the scrutiny, the African-Americans figure that they're being disrespected for no good reason, so they might as well act out, which in turn reinforces their boss's stereotype. Everybody goes away angry.

Such problems are often less about race than class, which has become a huge factor within the black community, too. It's hard for studious young African-Americans to brave the taunts that they're "acting white." The only answer to that is a redoubled effort within the black community to respect academic achievement and a commitment by white institutions to use affirmative action not just for middle-class minorities but for the poor it was originally designed to help.

Beyond the thousands of individual efforts necessary to save New Orleans and ease poverty lie some big political choices. Until Katrina intervened, the top priority for the GOP when Congress reconvened was permanent repeal of the estate tax, which applies to far less than 1 percent of taxpayers. (IRS figures show that only 1,607 wealthy people in Louisiana, Alabama and Mississippi even pay the tax, out of more than 4 million taxpayers—one twenty-fifth of 1 percent.) Repeal would cost the government $24 billion a year. Meanwhile, House GOP leaders are set to slash food stamps by billions in order to protect subsidies to wealthy farmers. But Katrina could change the climate. The aftermath was not a good omen for the Grover Norquists of the world, who want to slash taxes more and shrink government to the size where it can be "strangled in the bathtub."

What kind of president does George W. Bush want to be? He can limit his legacy to Iraq, the war on terror and tax cuts for the rich—or, if he seizes the moment, he could undertake a midcourse correction that might materially change the lives of millions. Katrina gives Bush an only-Nixon-could-go-to-China opportunity, if he wants it.

Margaret Schuber, who evacuated to Atlanta, was a middle-school principal in Jefferson Parish before retiring recently. "I have lived in the city all my life and I didn't realize there were so many people suffering socioeconomically. If you believe in the idea of community, then we all bear responsibility." Schuber is concerned that so many energetic young people aren't planning to return. She's going back to volunteer in the schools. "We all need to do what we can to turn things around," she says.

The Hard Numbers

More than 37 Million Americans live in poverty, Individuals under 65 earning less than $9,800 a year are considered poor.

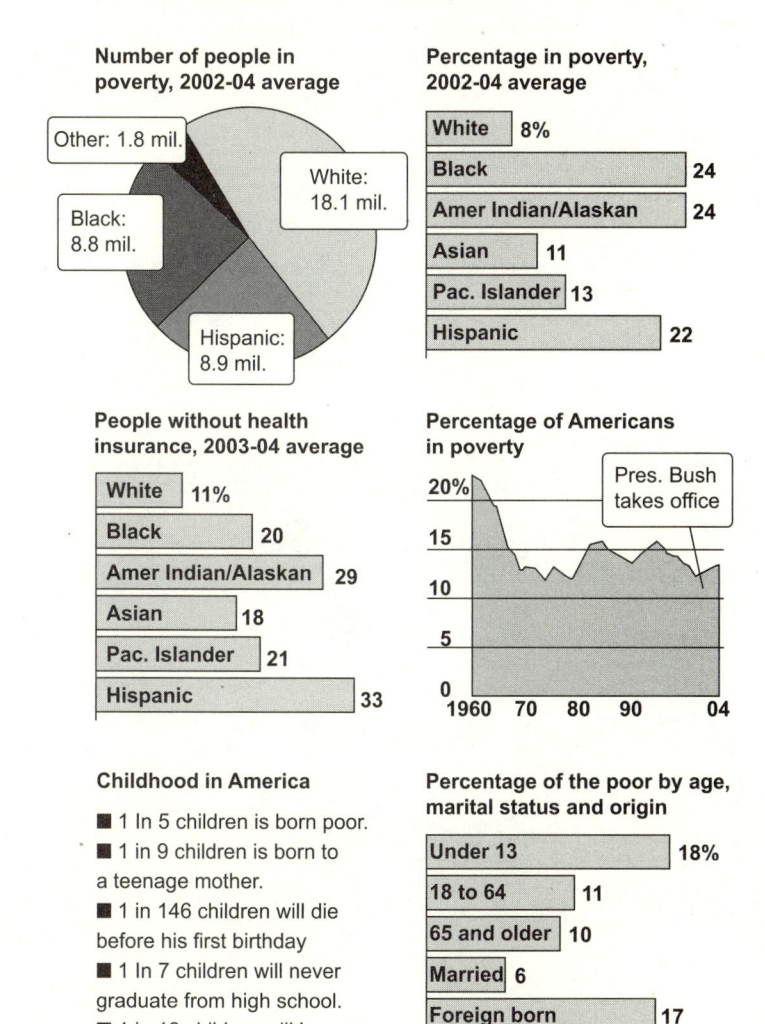

Number of people in poverty, 2002-04 average

- Other: 1.8 mil.
- Black: 8.8 mil.
- White: 18.1 mil.
- Hispanic: 8.9 mil.

Percentage in poverty, 2002-04 average

Group	%
White	8
Black	24
Amer Indian/Alaskan	24
Asian	11
Pac. Islander	13
Hispanic	22

People without health insurance, 2003-04 average

Group	%
White	11
Black	20
Amer Indian/Alaskan	29
Asian	18
Pac. Islander	21
Hispanic	33

Percentage of Americans in poverty

(graph from 1960 to 2004, ranging 0-20%; marker: "Pres. Bush takes office")

Childhood in America

- 1 In 5 children is born poor.
- 1 in 9 children is born to a teenage mother.
- 1 in 146 children will die before his first birthday
- 1 In 7 children will never graduate from high school.
- 1 in 13 children will be arrested before the age of 17.

— CHILDREN'S DEFENSE FUND

Percentage of the poor by age, marital status and origin

Group	%
Under 13	18
18 to 64	11
65 and older	10
Married	6
Foreign born	17
Navive	12

Sources: Children's Defense Fund, Censusscope.org, Annie E. Casey Foundation, GNOCDC.ORG, U.S. Census Bureau.

Note: Whites are non-Hispanic. Hispanic can be any race. Values may be based on individual income or consumption levels

America was built and saved by the Margaret Schubers of the world. Now we need them again, not just in the midst of an emergency but for the hard work of redemption.

Note

Joseph Contreras and Sarah Childress in New Orleans, Jessica Silver-Greenberg and Anne Underwood in New York, and Pat Wingert in Washington contributed to the writing of this reading.

Chapter 2
The Inequality Gap

One way to conceptualize social class in the United States is to divide income categories into fifths: the bottom 20 percent, the second 20 percent, the middle 20 percent, the fourth 20 percent, and the top 20 percent. These quintiles can be compared to see whether the incomes represented within them are increasing at about the same rate and the income gap remains constant or, conversely, whether the rates vary and the gap is either widening or closing. From the end of World War II until the beginning of the 1980s, the income gap remained fairly stable as the incomes across all five groups increased at about the same rate. Since that time, however, the globalizing economy and deindustrialization, among other factors, have caused an increase in the income gap. As shown in Table 2.1, the U.S. Census Bureau notes that, in 2003, the share of combined income in the lowest quintile was 3.4 percent of the total, compared to 49.8 percent for the highest quintile. Put another way, if the combined income in the United States was $100, the people in the bottom 20 percent would share $3.40 while those in the top 20 percent would split $49.80. Moreover, since the late 1960s the income share for the bottom quintile has consistently decreased while the top quintile has consistently increased.

The Center on Budget and Policy Priorities (CBP) released a report in 2006 stating that the income gap between the rich and the poor in America is widening, and has been since the 1980s. Since that period, the rate of

Table 2.1 Percentage Distribution by Aggregate Income

Year	Lowest 20 percent	Highest 20 percent
1970	4.1%	43.3%
1980	4.3%	43.7%
1990	3.9%	46.6%
2000	3.6%	49.6%
2003	3.4%	49.8%

Table adapted from U.S. Census Bureau, "Income, Poverty, and Health Insurance Coverage in the United States: 2003," *Current Population Reports,* P60–226 (August 2004).

increase in the earnings of the top 20 percent has outdistanced the rate of increase in those of the other 80 percent of wage earners, causing the income gap to widen. Additionally:

- Average income for the bottom 20 percent of individuals in the United States was $14,114 in 1980–1982 and $16,778 in 2001–2003—an increase of 18.87 percent (compared to 22.22 percent for the second quintile) (CBP, 2006).
- Average income for the middle 20 percent of individuals in the United States was $36,657 in 1980–1982 and $46,875 in 2001–2003—an increase of 27.87 percent (compared to 35.94 percent for the fourth quintile) (CBP, 2006).
- Average income for the top 20 percent of individuals in the United States was $109,195 in 1980–1982 and $201,707 in 2001–2003—an increase of 84.72 percent (CBP, 2006).
- Today, the average salary for the top 100 CEOs is $37.5 million dollars a year—more than 1,000 times as much as the average worker earns (*The Economist*, 2004).
- The inequality gap is growing not only between the top and the bottom quintiles but also between the middle class and the upper class (CBP, 2006).

This widening income gap has serious implications for society. The most obvious consequence is embodied in the everyday problems facing individuals in the lower classes. Further, as the gap increases it becomes more difficult to overcome; those most profoundly affected by the ravages of poverty are the least likely to find an avenue out. The following selections describe the problems of the growing gap between poor and rich, and what that means for society.

REFERENCES

CBP (Center on Budget and Policy Priorities). 2006. Available online at http://www.cbpp.org/1-26-06sfp.htm.

The Economist. 2004. "Meritocracy in America: Ever Higher Society, Ever Harder to Ascend" (December 29), Washington, D.C. Available online at http://www.economist.com/world/na/displayStory.cfm?story_id=3518560.

U.S. Census Bureau. 2004. "Income Inequality (Middle Class)—Narrative." Available online at http://www.census.gov/hhes/income/midclass/midclsan.html.

U.S. Census Bureau. 2004. "Income Inequality—Table 1." Available online at http://www.census.gov/hhes/income/incineq/p60tb1.html.

U.S. Census Bureau. 2004. "Income, Poverty, and Health Insurance Coverage in the United States: 2003," *Current Population Reports,* P60–226 (August).

4. Tilting the Tax System in Favor of the Rich

The New York Times

The progressive tax system, which was set up to ensure that rich people shoulder a bigger share of the government's bills than the not-so-rich, is in trouble.

Wealthy individuals and large corporations have been steadily, and successfully, prevailing upon their congressional allies to rewrite the tax code, shifting more of the burden onto others.

Among their recent victories:

- Shrinking the estate tax
- Rolling back taxes paid by investors and corporations
- Using revenues from payroll taxes on workers to mask the cost of tax cuts for the rich

Congress came back from its summer recess this year planning to hand America's wealthiest families their biggest tax victory in years: permanent repeal of the estate tax.

Hurricane Katrina interfered with those plans. Even die-hard tax slashers realized that after a national-televised tragedy in which thousands of poor people were unable to get out of harm's way, the timing was not right for a multi-billion-dollar tax cut on America's largest fortunes. But when the memories of Katrina fade, opponents of the estate tax will no doubt try again to get rid of it.

Opponents of the estate tax use inflammatory sound bites like "death tax" or "double tax" to make it look like they are concerned about eliminating injustices. But their real aim is to take another giant step in the direction of abolishing taxes on investments—especially capital gains on stocks, bonds and real estate. Because investors are disproportionately wealthy, repealing or reducing investment taxes produces a windfall for those at top. That further erodes the tax system's progressivity—the principle that one's share of the tax burden should rise with one's ability to pay.

In addition to being unfair, estate tax repeal is unaffordable. The first 10 years of repeal would cost the Treasury $745 billion, and nearly $1 trillion when interest is factored in, according to Congress's Joint Committee on Taxation. That's far more than the entire projected budget for homeland security. The advocates of repeal don't talk about how this enormous decline in government revenue would be made up.

But since the federal government was already deeply in debt before Katrina—and paying to rebuild will only add to the red ink—the cost of estate tax repeal would eventually have to be covered by cutting government programs, raising other taxes, or some combination of the two.

It is not only the poor who lose out. The have-nots will pay for high-end tax cuts mainly through reduced government services. But the broad middle class will pay for them both in the form of higher future taxes and reduced government programs.

Against this backdrop, Katrina's interruption of the drive to repeal the estate tax presents an opportunity. Advocates for middle-class and poor Americans now have a chance to expose what is truly at stake at a time when Americans just saw up close what limited government, and the growing chasm between rich and poor, can mean.

Katrina was a moment of clarity for much of the country. This should extend to the tax code. What should be repealed is not the estate tax, but years of tax policies that have shielded too much of wealthy people's money from taxes, and shifted too much of the burden onto everyone else.

THE ZEAL FOR REPEAL: THE DRIVE TO DO AWAY WITH THE ESTATE TAX

Until Katrina struck, estate tax repeal was going to be one of the first items Congress took up when it returned from recess. Given the many pressing issues facing the nation—from chemical plant security to fixing the immigration system—it is clear that the people pushing repeal onto the national agenda have a tremendous amount of clout.

Who are they? The Bush administration, Republican members of Congress, and—not surprisingly—some of America's wealthiest families. Among them: the Marses of Mars candy bars, the Waltons of Wal-Mart, the Gallos of Gallo wine and the Tysons of chicken fame. These enormously wealthy families, who would stand to gain the most if the estate tax is eliminated, have largely stayed in the background.

Opponents of the estate tax have argued that it is a burden on large numbers of ordinary Americans—which it is not. And they have made their case by drumming away at a few sound bites—notably that the estate tax is a "death tax," or a "double tax." They have done an impressive job of staying on message, but their arguments are flimsy to the point of being fraudulent.

Calling the estate tax a "death tax" implies that the tax, like death, applies to everyone. It doesn't. "The death tax label added moral momentum to the case for repeal, turning the taxman into a pimp for the grim reaper," write Michael J. Graetz and Ian Shapiro in their book "Death by a Thousand Cuts: The Fight Over Taxing Inherited Wealth." This year, the tax applies only to estates valued at more than $1.5 million ($3 million for married couples), about the top two percent of estates annually. By 2009, only estates worth more than $3.5 million will face the tax ($7 million for couples)—less than one half of one percent of Americans.

Repeal advocates like to argue that the estate tax will hit farms and small businesses hard. Congress's own budget agency is the latest in a long line of researchers to debunk those claims.

The important point about the estate tax is that it is primarily the tax system's way of taxing wealth that has never been taxed. When people die, they generally leave behind assets like stocks, bonds and real estate that have increased in value since they were purchased. In general, that appreciation is taxed when an asset is sold. But if these assets still belong to a person at the time of his or her death, there should still be a way to tax the value of the appreciation. The estate tax captures some of that untaxed profit.

The estate tax is clearly not an act of governmental viciousness. Nor is it a morbid way to feast off the deceased. It is just the opposite—a big favor, or "death subsidy," in the form of lifelong tax deferral on profits as they compound over time.

The claims that the estate tax is a "double tax" are also misleading. There are a wide array of taxes that could be considered "double," depending on when you start counting. A worker's wages may be taxed by both the federal and state governments. Or the same worker may pay income tax on a dollar of income, and then a sales tax when the same money is spent. Unlike the investor sitting on an appreciated stock or bond, the worker doesn't get to postpone paying those taxes until after he or she has died.

The estate tax is primarily the government's way of ensuring that the wealthiest Americans ultimately—that is, after they die—pay their fair share. The real advocates of unfairness in this debate are the supporters of repeal, who want the rich to be exempted from tax on their appreciated assets. The people who would benefit from repeal, of course, would be those inheriting assets. Where there are winners, however, there are also losers.

The estate tax is still the government's most progressive tax. In 2004, for instance, the top 1 percent of households paid 23 percent of all federal taxes but 83 percent of estate taxes. If the estate tax were repealed, leaving heirs with bigger untaxed fortunes, the tax burden would shift to the less wealthy. Or else the shortfall in tax revenue would lead to cuts in government programs, which also would hurt the less well-off.

All this explains the zeal behind the repeal movement. Opponents of the estate tax know that they are waging an ideological battle—a battle against progressive taxation.

THE UNTAXING OF INVESTMENTS: THE WAR ON CAPITAL GAINS TAXES

The people who stand to gain from estate tax repeal are by and large the same people who benefit most from the ongoing campaign to cut or eliminate capital gains taxes—another tax that falls most heavily on the rich.

Hurricane Katrina prompted Congress to delay its plan to extend special tax breaks for capital gains, just as it did plans for repealing the estate tax. With the nation's attention focused on the poor storm victims of New Orleans, it would have been a problematic time to push through a capital gains tax whose benefits would go overwhelmingly to people who make more than $200,000—about the top 3 percent of the income scale, while adding some $23 billion a year to the deficit.

The delay, however, does not mean that the cause has been abandoned. Ending the tax on investments, particularly capital gains, will no doubt remain a cherished goal of anti-tax conservatives.

In a nutshell, the argument against taxing investment gains is that doing so reduces the incentive for saving and investment, which in turn reduces job creation and wages. According to this theory, a tax on the wealthy ends up hurting everyone. In effect, these critics of the capital gains tax are saying that the main aim of the tax system should be economic growth, even if pursuing it means making the tax system more regressive. Economic growth, so the logic goes, will boost overall tax revenues, more than making up for the drag of regressive taxes.

The problem with this variation on the trickle down theory is that after centuries of debate and research, there is still no consensus on the relationship between capital gains tax cuts, investment, and economic growth. The growth that does occur when investment taxes are low generally flows to wealthy investors. And despite all the claims to the contrary, tax cuts have never been proven to pay for themselves.

This impasse leads to a fairness argument: Since the evidence is inconclusive that capital gains taxes have much of a negative effect, it seems unfair to largely exempt capital gains from tax while taxing wages and salaries. Perhaps more important, if the aim of the system is to distribute the tax burden based on ability to pay, capital gains must be taxed—even if doing so has a negative impact on saving and investment. In a progressive system, maintaining a degree of fairness is one of the core principles.

Opponents of capital gains taxes have already been remarkably successful. Through a combination of exempting some gains from taxation and reducing the rates, they have managed to whittle away at the taxes investors end up paying. Since the last big tax-code overhaul in the Reagan era, the tax rate on capital gains has dropped from a high of 28 percent in 1987 to just 15 percent in 2003. The 15 percent rate is ostensibly temporary, though Mr. Bush and his Congressional allies are fighting to make it permanent. By comparison, the top rate on income from employment is currently 35 percent.

The estate tax is another prime example. In 1980, the per-person amount of wealth exempt from the estate tax was $175,000. By 2009, the exemption is scheduled to rise to $3.5 million. And, of course, if the pro-repealers have their way, estates will never face taxation.

Then there is the problem with the alternative minimum tax, which was designed to ensure that wealthy taxpayers pay their fair share. The alternative tax was first enacted in 1969, when it was learned that many multimillionaires used tax shelters to avoid paying any income tax. For years, many investors had to pay the A.M.T. when the tax rate for capital gains was lower than the rate on income from working. Since 1990, however, taxpayers who use the special low rates on capital gains have generally not had to pay the A.M.T. That change alone now saves investors billions of dollars in taxes each year.

Rather than fix the A.M.T., some members of Congress have recently proposed abolishing it. That would be yet another blow to fairness.

Tax Avoidance Goes Global: Overseas Tax Shelters

Another way the tax burden on the wealthy has been reduced is the decline in taxes on corporations.

Corporate income tax payments are made with money that would otherwise be paid to the companies' stockholders and bondholders. So the growing number of "opportunities" for corporations to avoid taxes—with the sometimes tacit, sometimes explicit, approval of Congress—are actually opportunities for investors to save on taxes.

In the last 50 years, the corporate income tax has virtually disappeared. In 1954, corporate income taxes provided 30 percent of federal tax revenue, a share equal to 5.6 percent of the size of the economy. It's been mostly downhill since then. Since the 1980s, corporate income taxes have provided about 10 percent of federal revenues, a share equal to 1 to 2 percent of the economy. In 2004, a year of historically high business profits, corporate income taxes as a share of the economy came to 1.6 percent.

Corporate tax sheltering is now rampant. It "has become cheaper and spread by imitation, as more and more companies get away with it," writes Daniel N. Shaviro, a professor of taxation at New York University Law School and a visiting scholar at the American Enterprise Institute, in his recent book "Corporate Tax Shelters in a Global Economy."

Trying to minimize tax liability is not inherently abusive, Mr. Shaviro says, but "aggressive tax sheltering that crosses or even nears the boundaries of what is legally permitted can have negative effects on broader social norms of tax compliance."

On that point, there is no doubt. One of the biggest tactics for sheltering corporate income right now involves overseas profits. American companies are increasingly booking huge profits in foreign tax havens, where the money is out of the reach of the I.R.S. A study last year by Martin Sullivan, a former Treasury Department economist, showed that American multinationals reported a record $149 billion of profit abroad in 2002. Some of the companies have no legitimate business operations abroad. Many others have bona fide business interests, which are often coupled with aggressive tax avoidance strategies.

In 1998 and 1999, the I.R.S. tried to close a major loophole that allows American companies to shift their profits overseas. But a massive lobbying effort by business interests persuaded Congress to block the effort.

Rather than support efforts by the Treasury to enforce existing law, time and again Congress has intervened to help companies shelter their profits. The corporate tax bill signed into law by the president last year included $140 billion in new corporate tax cuts, including $43 billion specifically for companies with overseas operations.

This year, this kind of tax avoidance hit a new low. Congress declared a special one-year tax holiday for 2005, during which American companies can repatriate foreign profits at a tax rate of 5.25 percent—an 85 percent discount off the normal corporate rate. That means that companies are actually being rewarded for years of avoiding taxes by parking profits overseas. By year's end, an estimated $300 billion in profits may have found its way home at the reduced rate. Such a huge giveaway to corporations is good news for shareholders, but bad news for everyone else. The tax holiday is inflating revenue this year, but it is likely to reduce it in the future, because companies are rushing to bring home profits at this year's bargain-basement tax rate.

A thoughtful approach to corporate taxes in a global economy might reveal that an entirely new system is needed, with closer cooperation between countries to prevent artificial shifting of profits among them. But the powers that be are not having that debate. Rather, something completely predictable is happening—overt corporate giveaways, yet another form of shielding those at the top from taxes.

Higher Taxes on America's Paychecks: The Rise, and Rise, of Payroll Taxes

At the same time that the taxes investors pay—estate, capital gains and corporate—have gone down as a share of federal revenue, taxes that workers pay have grown. In 1980, 31 percent of federal revenues came from payroll taxes, which are paid by everyone who works for a living. In 2004, 39 percent did.

Payroll taxes are sharply skewed against the lowest wage earners. In 2004, the average payroll tax rate for workers making $50,000 to $75,000 was 12 percent. For someone making more than $1 million, it was just 1.5 percent.

The reason for this imbalance is that a large portion of the wages of highly salaried people are exempt from payroll taxes. This year workers and employers will each pay a 6.2 percent payroll tax, which is earmarked for social security, on all workers' wages up to $90,000. Wages above $90,000 are not subject to the tax. (Workers and employers will also each pay a 1.45 percent payroll tax on all wages, with the proceeds going to Medicare.) The hit is even bigger than it seems. Although workers pay half and employers pay half, most economists agree that workers ultimately bear most or all of the employer's share in the form of lower wages and salaries.

The tax system is now so out of whack that the vast majority of Americans now pay more in regressive payroll taxes than they do in progressive income taxes.

Regressive as they are, payroll taxes are actually becoming more so. The amount of income that the tax is applied to has not kept up with the income gains of the highest-paid workers. In 1983, only 10 percent of total wages escaped the payroll tax. Today, 15 percent does—wages earned by those with the highest salaries.

It gets worse still. Payroll taxes have long exceeded the amount needed to pay for current Social Security benefits, creating a surplus in the Social Security trust fund. (The surplus is currently $173 billion annually). At the same time, however, the rest of the government is running a deficit, currently $504 billion, caused in large part by various tax cuts on investment. The "official" deficit is therefore $331 billion. ($173 billion trust fund surplus minus $504 billion budget shortfall.) In effect, the surplus—which comes from taxes paid by working people at the middle and lower rungs of the income ladder—is being used to mask the true cost of today's deficit-financed tax cuts on estates, capital gains and corporations.

It wasn't supposed to be this way. Excess payroll tax revenues were intended to build up a cushion to pay Social Security benefits to baby boom retirees. The payment of those benefits—akin to a "return" on one's taxes—would erase the painful regressivity of the tax.

If current high-end tax cuts continue, however, the deficits they provoke will make all government programs vulnerable to cutbacks, including Social Security, even though workers have been paying high payroll taxes for decades precisely to avoid that outcome.

In this way, tax cuts for the rich are fomenting a crisis for everyone else. The Bush tax cuts are especially damaging because of their size, and because they are occurring just as baby boomers begin to retire. If the Bush tax cuts were allowed to expire, their revenue would be far more than enough to close the long-term funding gap in Social Security, without cutting benefits. But the Bush administration wants to make them permanent.

Saving the Beast

There are two things going on when taxes on the rich are cut as drastically as they are being cut right now. The tax burden is shifted downward and lower tax revenues "starve the beast"—conservative-speak for forced reduction in government programs.

The non-rich are hit twice. They are forced to bear more of the nation's tax burden, and they lose needed government programs.

Congress is poised, despite Katrina, to cut back on an array of government programs—because the taxes have been rigged in a way that means we can no longer afford them. It has aimed its scalpel at programs that serve the poor, like Medicaid and food stamps, and ones that Americans of all incomes rely on—infrastructure spending, environmental protection and, yes, disaster relief. And as recent history and budget trends suggest, Social Security and Medicare are also at risk of deep cuts in the not too distant future unless the tax system is restored to sanity.

In 2001, President Bush endorsed starving the beast when he described a probable decline in federal revenue as "incredibly positive news" because it would "put a straitjacket" on government spending. Or, as Grover Norquist, a prominent leader of the anti-tax, anti-government movement put it in 2001—in a phrase that has chilling reverberations after Katrina—the goal is to get government "down to a size where we can drown it in a bathtub."

Americans have never truly bought into that philosophy—despite all of the talk about the popularity of cutting taxes. Polls show that respondents have a knee-jerk preference for lower taxes. But they also show an increased willingness to pay up when the alternatives—less effective government and growing inequality—are pointed out to them.

The speed with which Congress tabled its tax-cutting agenda after Katrina—temporarily, at least—indicates that lawmakers know that such actions do not reflect the will of the people.

Katrina has changed the calculus on tax cuts, by reminding Americans of the importance of government in their lives—and by implication, of the importance of taxes. Before Mr. Bush even took his first trip to flood-ravaged New Orleans, he said in an interview that the Gulf Coast could be rebuilt without raising taxes. Perhaps Mr. Bush's comment was a tacit way of trying to convince the public that a major issue underlying the Katrina disaster—who should pay for government and how much—has been resolved.

It hasn't.

5. Income and Inequality
Millions Left Behind
Woodrow Ginsburg

Income and Inequality

In spite of the ten-year growth of the economy, relatively low unemployment for many of those years, the absence of inflation pressures, and other positive economic trends, the United States still suffers from an extreme and growing inequality in income distribution and distressingly high poverty.

Applying the test of whether an economic system raises earnings of most of its citizens—an appropriate measure of success or failure—the American system has been "a clear failure in the past two decades," noted by renowned Massachusetts Institute of Technology (MIT) economist Lester Thurow.

A similar assessment was made by the well-known Harvard economist Benjamin M. Friedman in his recent book, *The Moral Consequences of Economic Growth*. Friedman noted with deep concern that American middle-class living standards have been stagnating for most of the past thirty years (with the brief exception of the late 1990s) and the decline in the past five years means that more than half of the population is not getting ahead economically. Such a trend puts our democracy at serious risk. American citizens must feel that their standard of living, or at least that of their children, is improving. That sense does not prevail today.

This failure results in the United States suffering greater economic inequality than all other industrial countries. It jeopardizes equal opportunity. It gives huge economic and political power to big corporations and to the wealthy. And it erodes the sense of community and common purpose essential for democracy.

There has been a major shift for the worse in the years after 1980. From 1950 to 1980 the economy expanded rapidly, with broad and progressive sharing of its tremendous gains to more and more Americans, including those at the bottom of the economic ladder. But, starting in 1980, an unprecedented regressive shift in the distribution of earnings and wealth began—a shift that has led to the current gross inequities that beset our nation. Here are the details of that shift:

The Post-War Years, 1950–1980

The income of Americans during the post-war years of 1950–1980 doubled and income inequality was significantly lessened. Income distribution in the United States became less unequal and fairer. From 1980 through 2001, however, those progressive income trends not only came to a halt, but reversed, and inequality worsened sharply. The trend was particularly steep from 1979 through 1992 when an incredible 98% of the gain in total household income was garnered by the wealthiest 20% of households. The other 80% of households in this period shared the remaining 2% gain in total household income.

Many factors were responsible for the trend. The most important were regressive government policies such as the Reagan tax cuts of 1981, deep cuts in many social and economic programs benefiting middle and low income Americans, the anti-union policies of the Reagan and Bush Administrations which restrained wage increases and the failure to adjust the federal minimum wage.

From 1950 to 1980 real income (income adjusted for inflation) increased *for all groups*—from the poorest fifth (quintile) to the richest fifth. The gain for the lowest fifth was 144.1%; for the second fifth, 99.2%; for the middle and fourth fifths slightly over 100 (107.6% and 114.1%); and for the top fifth, 97.6%. Figure 2.1, "Growing Together," shows this distribution.

The Reagan–Bush I Years, 1980–2001

In sharp contrast to trends in the 1950–1980 period, the shortsighted policies of the Reagan and Bush Administrations produced an entirely different pattern of income distribution for 1980–2001. This inequitable pattern is reflected in the changes in the figures for family income in figure 2.2, "Growing Apart." The wealthiest fifth of families, ranked by income, increased their income by *59.3%;*

54 Chapter 2 / The Inequality Gap

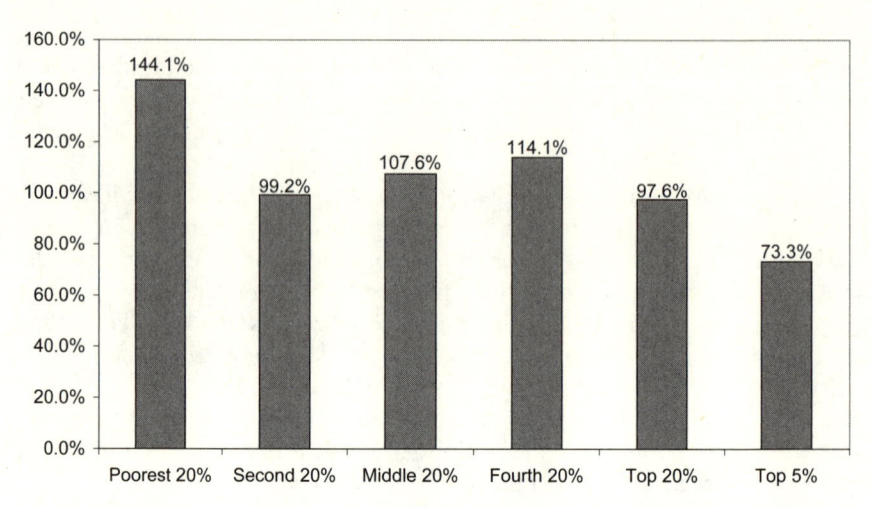

Figure 2.1 1950–1980—Growing Together: Change in Real Family Income by Quintile

- Poorest 20%: 144.1%
- Second 20%: 99.2%
- Middle 20%: 107.6%
- Fourth 20%: 114.1%
- Top 20%: 97.6%
- Top 5%: 73.3%

far outstripping the increases for all other groups. Income for the poorest 20% gained only *7.5%*. The second fifth of families gained only *14.3%*, while the middle 20% of families had an income increase of *20.1%*.

More wage earners per family and more hours of work each year were largely responsible for the income growth that did occur. In 1997, a married couple in the middle 20% of families worked 256 more hours than in 1989! But those factors were not sufficient to offset other factors that limited income increases for most families and worsened income distribution in the 1980–2001 period.

Because of the extremely uneven distribution of the nation's economic growth from 1980 through the early 1990s, income inequality widened so greatly that the current gap between the richest and the poorest is larger than it has been since the Depression years of the 1930s.

Income Trends for Whites, Blacks and Hispanics

As a result of economic expansion, particularly from 1995–99, median family income for all families reached $54,061 in 2004.

Beneath the overall average, however, Census figures show that the income of minority families lagged behind Whites. Median income for Black families in 2004 was $35,853, up a substantial 19.4% from 1990. However, Black family income was still *41%* below White family income. Similarly, Hispanic family income was *42%* below White family income.

Table 2.1 presents income figures for Whites, Blacks, and Hispanic families for 1950–2004.

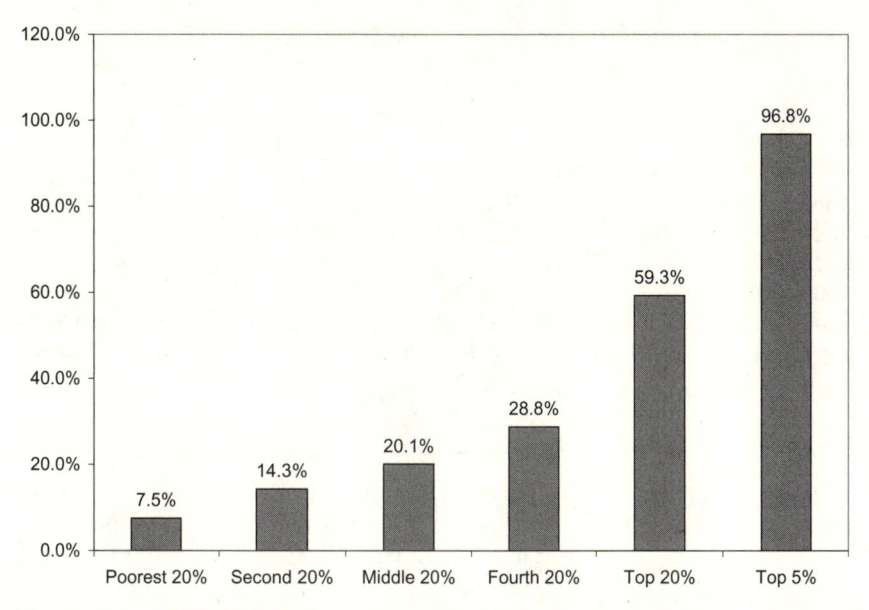

Figure 2.2 1980–2001—Growing Apart: Change in Real Family Income by Quintile

Poorest 20%	Second 20%	Middle 20%	Fourth 20%	Top 20%	Top 5%
7.5%	14.3%	20.1%	28.8%	59.3%	96.8%

Family Income Shares

This trend of the unequal distribution of the nation's wealth for 1980–2004 is also clearly reflected in the shares of total income received by families ranked by income and for the richest 5% of families.

Table 2.2 shows the richest fifth of families had almost half (47.9%) of total income in 2004—far larger than their 40.9% share in 1970. At the other end of the income ladder, the poorest 20% of families experienced a sharp shrinkage in their share from 5.4% in 1970 to 4.2% in 2004—close to the smallest share in the

Table 2.1 Median Real Family Income 1950–2004 by Race and Hispanic Origin (in 2004 dollars)

Group	1950	1970	1980	1990	2004	Percent change 1950–1980	1980–2004
White	$22,892	$43,122	$47,560	$51,734	$54,067	107.8%	13.7%
Black	$12,419	$26,453	$27,519	$30,023	$35,853	221.6%	30.3%
Hispanic	n/a	n/a	$31,952	$32,837	$35,401	n/a	10.8%

Table 2.2 Share of Total Income Received by Each Fifth of Families 1950–2004

	1950	1970	1980	1990	2004	1950–1980 Change	1980–2004 Change
Poorest Fifth (20%)	4.5%	5.4%	5.3%	4.6%	4.2%	+17.8%	−20.8%
Second Fifth (20%)	12.0%	12.2%	11.6%	10.8%	9.6%	−3.3%	−16.4%
Middle Fifth (20%)	17.4%	17.6%	17.6%	16.6%	15.4%	+1.2%	−12.5%
Fourth Fifth (20%)	23.4%	23.8%	24.4%	23.8%	23.0%	+4.3%	−6.1%
Top Fifth (20%)	42.7%	40.9%	41.1%	44.3%	47.9%	−3.8%	+16.1%
Top 5%	17.3%	15.6%	14.6%	17.4%	20.9%	−15.6%	+43.8%

post-war period. Put in other terms, the wealthiest fifth of the families had an 11 times bigger share of total national income than the poorest fifth of families—one of the highest rich-poor ratios in U.S. history. During the decades of the 1950s and 1970s, the rich-poor ratio ranged from 7.5:1, to 8.5:1.

This inequality can also be seen in the actual income figures in table 2.3. For the top 5%, average family income in 2004 was *$294,257—up $142,246—or 93.6%* from 1980. Table 2.2 shows the top 5% group had 20.9% of total income in 2004, somewhat less than the share of the entire lower 3/5ths of all families ranked by income.

An alternative picture of this gross inequality is portrayed in Table 2.4 which shows the shifts of the shares of family income for the poorest 20% of families, the middle 60%, the highest 20%, and the top 5% of families during the years from 1950 to 2004.

Senator Charles Schumer (D-NY) in a forum on income inequality a few years ago noted, "The main cause of American's anxiety is the growing gap between the haves, the have-nots and those in the middle who feel they have to run faster and faster merely to stay in place."

As table 2.4 shows, the income share for the middle class—the second, third and fourth quintiles combined—declined from *53.6%* in 1980 to *48.0%* in 2004. In the same 20-year period, the top 20% of families and the wealthiest 5%, enjoyed substantial increases in their share of total income. For the top 20%, the increase was 16.1% from 1980 to 2004 and for the top 5%, a 43.8% jump.

We see in table 2.3, during the two decades from 1980 to 2000, the two highest income families arranged by quintiles—the fourth quintile and the wealthiest 20% of families—had income gains of 29.2% and 61.0% respectively.

At the other end of the income ladder, the poorest 20% of families had income gains of 11.3%; the second quintile, gains of 16.9% and the middle 20%, gains of 21.6%.

Note how much smaller these changes were compared to the three decades earlier, when expansion was more equitably shared. Then, the poorest 20% had

Table 2.3 Average Real Family Income 1950–2004 by Fifths (20%) and Top 5% of Families

Quintile	1950	1970	1980	2000	2004	Percent Change 1950–1980	Percent Change 1980–2000	Percent Change 2000–2004
Poorest 20%	$5,774	$12,908	$13,920	$15,490	$14,209	+141.1%	+11.3%	−8.30%
Second 20%	$15,317	$28,542	$30,302	$35,417	$33,802	+97.5%	+16.9%	−4.60%
Middle 20%	$22,210	$41,269	$45,777	$55,664	$54,244	+106.1%	+21.6%	−2.60%
Fourth 20%	$29,684	$55,669	$63,510	$82,037	$81,024	+114.0%	+29.2%	−1.20%
Fifth 20%	$54,505	$95,729	$106,931	$172,123	$168,733	+96.2%	+61.0%	−2.00%
Top 5%	$88,334	$145,769	$152,011	$305,005	$294,257	+72.1%	+100.6%	−3.50%

Table 2.4 Family Share of Total Income 1950–2004 (Shrinking Share of Middle Class)

Group of Families	1950	1970	1980	1990	2004	1950–1980 Change	1980–2004 Change
Lowest 20%	4.5%	5.4%	5.3%	4.6%	4.2%	+17.8%	–20.8%
Middle 60%	53.8%	53.6%	53.6%	53.6%	48.0%	+1.5%	–10.5%
Highest 20%	42.7%	40.9%	41.1%	44.3%	47.7%	–3.8%	+16.1%
Top 5%	17.3%	15.6%	14.6%	17.4%	20.9%	–15.6%	+43.8%

income gains of 141.1%, the second, 97.5% and the middle quintile, 106.1%. The years under the Bush II Administration (through 2004) reflect deteriorating living standards across the board.

It is important to note here that Census Bureau data understates the income received by many Americans. This becomes clear when income information published by the Congressional Budget Office (CBO) is examined. That agency in 1947 began publishing income and tax statistics that include, among other items, capital gains and earned income tax credits. Such income data supplements the money income figures of the Census Bureau.

For the well to do, the omission of capital gains in Census data seriously understates their income. Further, the Census includes only the first one million dollars of earnings from a person's primary employment. Incomes above the one million amount are not included in the Census data but they are included by the CBO.

As calculated by CBO, the shares of national income show a greater inequality than the Census data. For the wealthiest 20%, CBO projects for 1999 a 50.4% share, while the Census data for 1998 show a 47.3% share.

The CBO also publishes after-tax income data. These figures demonstrate the impact of tax legislation in the past two decades on American families. After-tax income for the 20% of the families at the middle of the income distribution rose only 8% in the 22 year period, 1977–1999. In the same period, after-tax income for the richest 20% of families rose 43%! The comparable figure for the poorest 20% of families shows a 9% decline.

Wealth Inequality

This severe inequality of income is surpassed by the even greater concentration of the nation's wealth. Based on research by Edward N. Wolff, a leading expert on wealth in the United States, holdings of the wealthy have grown steeply during the past three decades. In 1976, the richest 10% of families held 50% of the country's wealth; by 1995, they held 70% of all wealth. In 1995, the top 20% of families owned 84% of wealth, with the remaining 80% of families holding only *16%*

of the nation's wealth. This extremely inequitable distribution of wealth is much greater than the distribution of income. In 2004, the richest 20% of families had almost 50% of total income, while leaving the remaining 50% of income to be shared by 80% of families.

Inequality: USA vs. Other Industrial Nations

Income inequality in America is far greater than in other major industrial nations. Numerous studies have documented this situation. One frequently cited study is the Luxembourg Income Study[1] that compared the income gap between the rich and the poor in the United States with that of ten industrial European countries, Canada, and Australia.

The study also contains a series of other income figures. One set compares the median income of the poorest 10% of families with the overall median income in that country. Here are some key findings:

- The poorest 10% of families in the U.S. had income equal to 36% of median income. At the other end of the income ladder, the wealthiest 10% of families had income equal to 208% of the median.

The statistics in the other countries showed that income for the poorest 10% of families averaged *51% of the median,* and for the richest 10% of families, 186%. In other words, the poorest American lived on only about one third of the average family income. In other countries, families in similar economic conditions lived on income of about half of the income of the average family.

- In Sweden, the Netherlands, and Finland, the poorest families had incomes equal to 57% of the median income in those countries. The country with the highest percentage was Belgium with a 58% figure; the United Kingdom had the lowest figure of 44%. These figures are for the early 1990s.

More recent data compiled by the Organization for Economic Cooperation and Development (OECD) shows that, from 1991 to 1995, earning inequality in the U.S. continued to rise more rapidly than in other countries. As the OECD staff wrote: "The United Kingdom and the United States stand out as the only countries where there has been a pronounced rise in earnings inequality."[2]

Table 2.5 provides the evidence to support that statement. The OECD found the gap between the income of the wealthiest and poorest 30% of families was greater in the U.S. than in 11 other industrialized nations.

Table 2.5 shows that the wealthiest 30% of families in America held 52.5% of disposable income while the poorest 30% held only 11.8%—a 4.5 to 1 ratio. In contrast, in Finland the ratio was 2.7 to 1. Details of inequality in other industrialized countries show similar smaller gaps between their wealthiest and poorest citizens than in the U.S.

Table 2.5 Share of Disposable Income Held by the Wealthiest and Poorest 30% in Major Countries

Country	Wealthiest 30%	Poorest 30%
Denmark	48.3%	13.8%
Sweden	45.8%	15.8%
Finland	45.6%	17.0%
Norway	46.1%	16.3%
Netherlands	46.3%	15.8%
Germany	48.9%	14.7%
Canada	49.2%	14.3%
France	49.0%	15.6%
Belgium	48.3%	15.5%
Australia	49.3%	13.8%
Italy	53.2%	12.0%
United States	52.5%	11.8%

Source for statistics: OECD Reports: Income Distribution and Poverty in 13 OECD Countries; 2000

Another illustration of the sharp differences between the United States and foreign countries is the compensation of Chief Executive Officers (CEOs). American CEOs' compensation does not reflect stock options, various insurance plans, and other special privileges. A report of the Center for American Progress on CEO pay "Supersize This: How CEO Pay Took Off While America's Middle Class Struggled" (May 2005) showed that pay for CEOs in foreign countries averaged 33% of the pay for American CEOs. Table 2.6 shows foreign CEO pay as a percent of United States CEO pay in a number of major countries.

Notes

1. Luxembourg Income Study, Human Capital Program at European Commission, June 1994.
2. Public Broadcast System Transcript of May 17, 2003 Citing World Bank and OECD Sources.

Table 2.6 Foreign Chief Executive Officers

Country	Pay as a percent of U.S. CEO pay
Japan	20%
France	33%
United Kingdom	37%
Germany	42%
Canada	40%

6. The Perks of Privilege
Clara Jeffery

In 1985, the *Forbes* 400 were worth $221 billion combined. Today, they're worth $1.13 trillion—more than the GDP of Canada.

There've been few new additions to the *Forbes* 400. The median household income has also stagnated—at around $44,000.

Among the *Forbes* 400 who gave to a 2004 presidential campaign, 72% gave to Bush.

In 2005, there were 9 million American millionaires, a 62% increase since 2002.

In 2005, 25.7 million Americans received food stamps, a 49% increase since 2000.

Only estates worth more than $1.5 million are taxed. That's less than 1% of all estates. Still, repealing the estate tax will cost the government at least $55 billion a year.

Only 3% of students at the top 146 colleges come from families in the bottom income quartile; only 10% come from the bottom half.

Bush's tax cuts give a 2-child family earning $1 million an extra $86,722—or Harvard tuition, room, board, and an iMac G5 for both kids.

A 2-child family earning $50,000 gets $2,050—or 1/5 the cost of public college for one kid.

This year, Donald Trump will earn $1.5 million an hour to speak at Learning Annex seminars.

Adjusted for inflation, the federal minimum wage has fallen 42% since its peak in 1968.

If the $5.15 hourly minimum wage had risen at the same rate as CEO compensation since 1990, it would now stand at $23.03.

A minimum wage employee who works 40 hours a week for 51 weeks a year goes home with $10,506 before taxes.

Such a worker would take 7,000 years to earn Oracle CEO Larry Ellison's yearly compensation.

Ellison recently posed in *Vanity Fair* with his $300 million, 454-foot yacht, which he noted is "really only the size of a very large house."

Only the wealthiest 20% of Americans spend more on entertainment than on health care.

The $17,530 earned by the average Wal-Mart employee last year was $1,820 below the poverty line for a family of 4.

Five of America's 10 richest people are Wal-Mart heirs.

Public companies spend 10% of their earnings compensating their top 5 executives.

One thousand seven hundred thirty board members of the nation's 1,000 leading companies sit on the boards of 4 or more other corporations—including half of Coca-Cola's 14-person board.

The bidder who won a round of golf with Tiger Woods for $30,100 at a 2004 Buick charity auction could deduct all but about $200.

Tiger made $87 million in 2005, all but $12 million from endorsements and appearance fees.

The 5th leading philanthropist last year was Boone Pickens, in part due to his $165 million gift to Oklahoma State University's golf program.

Within an hour, OSU invested it in a hedge fund Pickens controls. Thanks to a Katrina relief provision, his "gift" was also 100% deductible.

Last year 250 companies gave top execs between $50,000 and $1 million worth of wholly personal flights on corporate jets.

This perk is 66% more costly to companies whose CEO belongs to out-of-state golf clubs.

The U.S. government spends $500,000 on 8 security screeners who speed execs from a Wall Street helipad to American's JFK terminal.

United has cut the pensions and salaries of most employees but promised 400 top executives 8% of the shares it expects to issue upon emerging from bankruptcy.

United's top 8 execs will also get a bonus of between 55% and 100% of their salaries.

In 2002, "turnaround artist" Robert Miller dumped Bethlehem Steel's pension obligation, allowing "vulture investor" Wilbur L. Ross to buy steel stock and sell it at a 1,000 percent profit.

In 2005, Delphi hired Miller for $4.5 million. After Ross said he might buy Delphi if its labor costs fell, Miller demanded wage cuts of up to 63 percent and dumped the pension obligation.

Ten former Enron directors agreed to pay shareholders a $13 million settlement—which is 10% of what they made by dumping stock while lying about the company's health.

Poor Americans spend 1/4 of their income on residential energy costs.

Exxon's 2005 profit of $36.13 billion is more than the GDP of 2/3 of the world's nations.

CEO pay among military contractors has tripled since 2001. For David Brooks, the CEO of bulletproof vest maker DHB, it's risen 13,233%.

At the $10 *million* bat mitzvah party Brooks threw his daughter last year, guests got $1,000 gift bags and listened to Aerosmith, Kenny G., Tom Petty, Stevie Nicks, and 50 Cent—who reportedly sang, "Go shorty, it's your bat mitzvah, we gonna party like it's your bat mitzvah."

For performing in the Live 8 concerts to "make poverty history," musicians each got gift bags worth up to $12,000.

Oscar performers and presenters collectively owe the IRS $1,250,000 on the gift bags they got at the 2006 Academy Awards ceremony.

A dog food company provided "pawdicures" and other spa treatments to pets of celebrities attending the 2006 Sundance Film Festival.

One of Madonna's recent freebies: $10,000 mink and diamond-tipped false eyelashes.

Paris Hilton, who charges clubs $200,000 to appear for 20 minutes, stiffed Elton John's AIDS benefit the $2,500-per-plate fee she owed.

According to *Radar* magazine, Owen Wilson was paid $100,000 to attend a Mercedes-Benz-sponsored Hamptons polo match. When other guests tried to speak with him, he reportedly said, "That's not my job."

THE PERKS OF PRIVILEGE: SOURCES

Increasing worth of the *Forbes* 400: "The *Forbes* 400", Forbes.com, September 20, 2005

Forbes 400 lack of new additions: "Don't Blink. You'll Miss the 258th-Richest American," *The New York Times,* September 25, 2005; "Income Stable, Poverty Rate Increases, Percentage of Americans Without Health Insurance Unchanged," U.S. Census Press Release, August 30, 2005

Forbes 400 gave to Bush: "Bush Wins-Among Rich Listers," Forbes.com, October 11, 2004

Rising number of American millionaires: "Millionaires Once Again on the Rise," TNS Financial Services, September 2, 2005

Food stamps: "Food Stamp Program Monthly Data," USDA Food and Nutrition; "Food Stamp Program FAQs," USDA Food and Nutrition.

A World of Difference: "Towers Perrin: Managing Global Pay and Benefits," 2005–2006.

Cost of repealing the estate tax: Stuart Kantor, Urban Institute; "Estimated Budget Effects of the Revenue Provisions Contained in the President's Fiscal Year 2006 Budget Proposal," Joint Committee on Taxation, March 9, 2005

Top Colleges and income class: "Socioeconomic Status, Race/Ethnicity and College Admissions," Anthony Carnevale and Stephen Rose, The New Century Foundation, March 2003.

Bush's Tax Cuts and 2-child families: "Table T05–0277 Current-Law Distribution of Individual Income and Payroll Tax Burden," Urban-Brookings Tax Policy Center Microsimulation Model, 2005.

Cost of Harvard, public colleges, iMacs: "America's Best Colleges 2006: Harvard University At a Glance," "Tuition Increases Slow at Public Colleges, According to the College Board's 2005 Reports on College Pricing and Financial Aid," October 18, 2005; "iMac G5."

Donald Trump earns $1.5M an hour: "Donald J. Trump Gets $1.5 Million for Speech: His New Rate is $25,000 a minute to speak—Highest ever paid," October 19, 2005.

Minimum wage has fallen: "History of Federal Minimum Wage Rates under Fair Labor Standards Act, 1938–1996," U.S. Department of Labor.

Minimum wage vs. CEO compensation since 1990: "Executive Excess 2005," United for a Fair Economy.

Minimum wage earner working full-time makes $10,506: "History of Federal Minimum Wage Rates under Fair Labor Standards Act, 1938–1996," U.S. Department of Labor.

Larry Ellison compensation: Wikipedia, "Larry Ellison."

Larry Ellison's $300 million yacht: "The Good Life Aquatic," *Vanity Fair,* May 2005.

"Wealthiest 20% spend more on entertainment than health care: Consumer Expenditures in 2003," U.S. Bureau of Labor Statistics, June 2005.

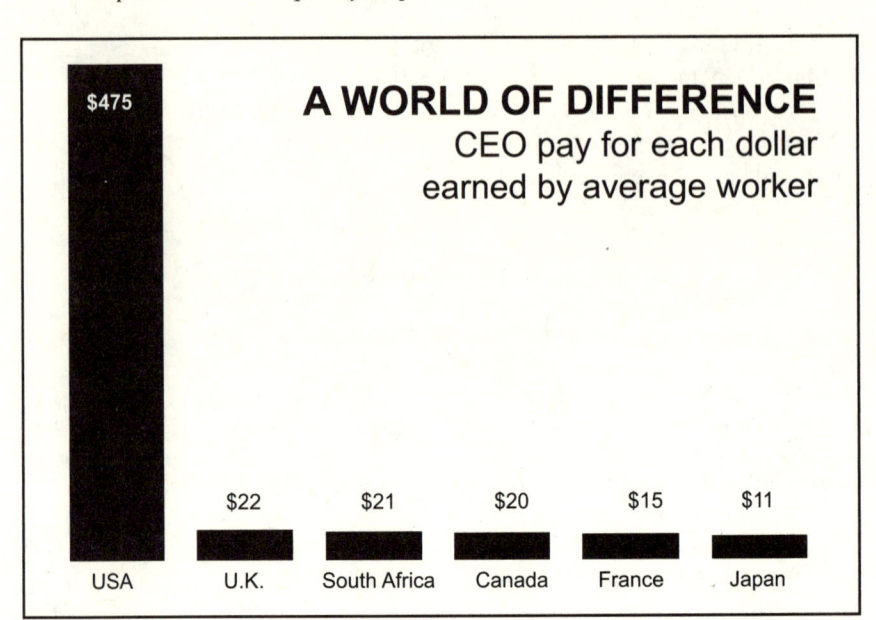

A WORLD OF DIFFERENCE
CEO pay for each dollar earned by average worker

USA	$475
U.K.	$22
South Africa	$21
Canada	$20
France	$15
Japan	$11

Average Wal-Mart employee: Dan Fogelman, Wal-Mart spokesman, March 17, 2005; "2005 Federal Poverty Guidelines," U.S. Department of Health and Human Services.

"Five of America's top ten richest Wal-Mart heirs: The 400 Richest Americans," *Forbes*, September 22, 2005.

A New Gilded Age: Emmanuel Saez, Professor of Economics, UCBerkeley, "Income Inequality in the United States, 1913–1998" with Thomas Piketty, Quarterly Journal of Economics, 118(1), 2003, 1–39 (Longer updated version, November 2004, Oxford University Press).

Public companies spend 10%: Bebchuk, Lucian and Yaniv Grinstein. "The Growth of Executive Pay," 2005.

1,730 corporate board members on other boards: "The Corporate Library."

A round of golf with Tiger Woods: "Round with Tiger fetches $30,100 for charity," PGATOUR.com, June 7, 2004; Al Abrams, Media Director, Buick Open.

Tiger's made $87 million: "Forbes Top Celebrities"; "On Tour Stats," Official Site for Tiger Woods.

Boone Pickens and Oklahoma State: "Billionaire gives a big gift but still gets to invest it," *The New York Times*, February 24, 2006; "The 2005 Slate 60", Slate.com, February 20, 2006.

Boone Pickens and the tax deductibility of his gift: "Billionaire gives a big gift but still gets to invest it," *The New York Times*, February 24, 2006.

250 companies gave execs personal flights: Strauss, Gary. "The corporate jet: Necessity or ultimate executive toy?" *USA Today*, April 26, 2005, and "Morgan Stanley Proxy Statement," February 2006.

Flights 66% more expensive: Yermack, David. "Flights of Fancy: Corporate Jets, CEO Perquisites, and Inferior Shareholder Returns," March 2005.

Airport screeners for Wall Street execs: "Company offers helicopter flights to JFK gate," Associated Press, February 8, 2006; Jennifer Marty-Peppin, Transportation Security Administration, Public Affairs Manager.
United Airlines execs get shares: "Gee, bankruptcy never looked so good," *The New York Times,* January 15, 2006; Jean Medina, United Airlines, Public Affairs.
United Airlines execs get bonuses: "Gee, bankruptcy never looked so good," *The New York Times,* January 15, 2006; Jean Medina, United Airlines Public Affairs.
Robert Miller and Bethlehem Steel: "Whoops! There goes another pension plan," *The New York Times,* September 18, 2005.
Robert Miller and Delphi: "Whoops! There goes another pension plan," *The New York Times,* September 18, 2005; "Miller says Delphi can no longer afford jobs banks, some plants," Associated Press, September 24, 2005; "Delphi Corp.'s [sic] files for bankruptcy," Associated Press, October 9, 2005.
Former Enron directors pay shareholders $13 million settlement: University of California, Office of the President "Press release" and "Former Enron directors, officer agree to pay $168 million to settle class-action fraud suit," *Power Markets Weekly,* January 17, 2005.
Poor Americans spend a quarter of income on energy: "FY 2006 Energy Bills Forecast: The Impact on Low-Income Consumers," Economic Opportunity Studies.
Exxon's 2005 profit: "ExxonMobil Corporation Estimated Fourth Quarter 2005 Results," *Business Wire,* January 30, 2006; "Total GDP 2004," World Development Indicators database, World Bank.
CEO pay among military contractors: "Executive Excess 2005: Defense Contractors Get

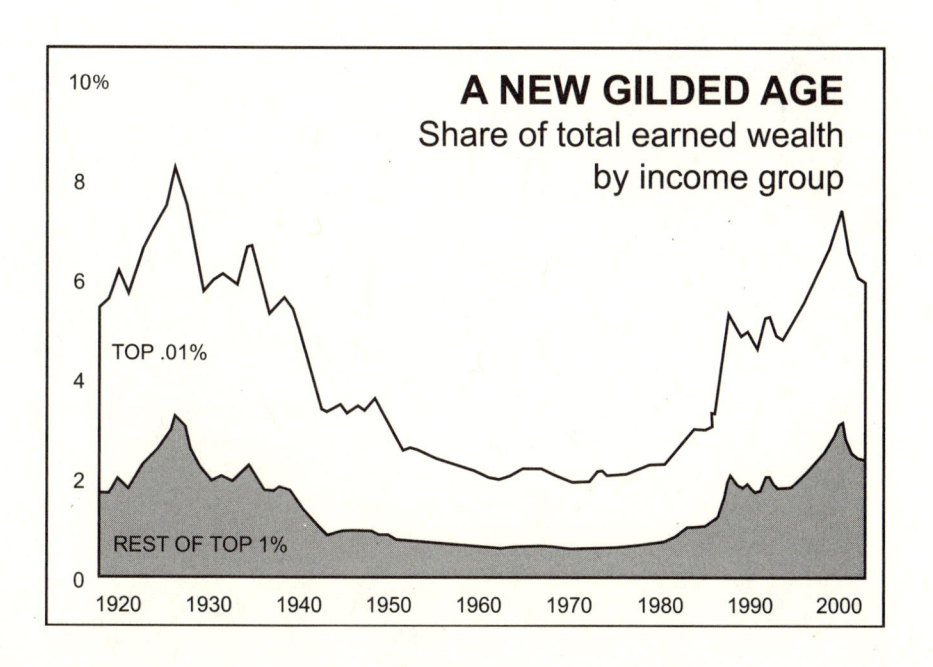

A NEW GILDED AGE
Share of total earned wealth by income group

More Bucks for the Bang," United for a Fair Economy, Institute for Policy Studies, August 30, 2005.
Brooks' Bat Mitzvah party: *New York Daily News* Lloyd Grove, February 28, 2006.
Live 8 concerts: *Philadelphia Inquirer* June 30, 2005. Nicole Cashman, Cashman and Associates.
Oscar performers and presenters: "Academy Awards Show Presenters and Performers," Academy of Motion Picture Arts and Sciences; "Oscar Gifts Taxable, I.R.S. Reminds Stars," *The New York Times,* March 5, 2006; H&R Block representative, San Francisco.
Pawdicures at Sundance: "The coifed, the primped, and the pampered."
Madonna's freebies: Gina Brooke, Artistic Director, shu uemura.
Paris and Elton: "Showbiz Tonight", CNN Transcripts, October 19, 2005; "Elton Bans Hilton from Future Oscar Parties", IMDB News, March 13, 2006.
Owen Wilson rented: "A-List Party Rentals," *Radar Magazine, Nov/Dec 2005.*

CHAPTER 3

THE DISAPPEARING MIDDLE

The middle class consists of individuals who fall into the third or middle quintile of the stratification system. As noted in the last section of readings, regarding the inequality gap, the percentage of aggregate incomes is declining for this middle quintile. Despite the shrinkage, a majority of Americans, when asked to locate themselves in the class structure, have traditionally included themselves as members of the middle class. This next section of readings seeks to answer the question "Are people simply identifying with other classes, or is the middle class truly shrinking?" Evidence from NOW (2004) suggests the latter. This organization has found evidence that the United States is undergoing an "income squeeze" and that the shape of the income distribution in America is changing; in short, the middle class is disappearing.

John Kerry, the Democratic candidate for president in the 2004 election, stated that current economic policies were hurting the middle class, that wages were falling, and that "the middle class [was] shrinking" (Annenberg, 2004a). The Annenberg Political Fact Check group, an organization that verifies claims by politicians, initially believed that the data Kerry cited to support his contention were "dubious." Some suggested that Kerry's statement was likely untrue because the numbers he depended on were gathered during a period of recession (see Annenberg 2004a for a full discussion). One month after this statement, however, the Annenberg group noted that it had found support for Kerry's claim and that, in fact, the middle class was shrinking (Annenberg, 2004b).

Citing Census Bureau figures (U.S. Census Bureau, 2004), the Annenberg group calculated that the middle class had decreased by 1.2 percent between 2000 and 2003 whereas the lower social classes increased by 1.5 percent. In addition, median income dropped 3.4 percent during the same period (Annenberg, 2004b). Thus, the evidence indicated not only that the middle class was shrinking but also that those moving out of the middle class were moving down rather than up.

Paul Krugman (2005) put the question of a shrinking middle class differently. Specifically, he asked whether the middle class was the model of American society that people believed it was, or whether it was an historic aberration. Krugman argued that the economic and political conditions that allowed the middle class to thrive in the 1950s and 1960s—"compression of incomes, strong labor unions, and progressive taxation" (Krugman, 2005, para. 6) no longer exist, and, indeed, that the political conditions currently in place are specifically working against a middle class.

Not only is the middle class shrinking, but individuals who are still classified as "middle class" are having a difficult time maintaining the middle-class lifestyle (NOW, 2002). A combination of factors ranging from stagnant wages and company downsizing to rapidly increasing housing costs and high levels of debt (e.g., credit card debt and student loans) has indeed rendered the middle class more elusive, a trend that is likely to continue into the foreseeable future. The following readings address this issue of the disappearing middle class.

REFERENCES

Annenberg Political Fact Check. 2004a. "Kerry's Dubious Economics" (August 3). Available online at http://www.factcheck.org/article228.html.

Annenberg Political Fact Check. 2004b. "Update on Kerry's 'Shrinking Middle Class'—Still Shrinking in 2003" (September 1). Available online at http://www.factcheck.org/article249.html.

Krugman, Paul. 2005. "Losing Our Country," *New York Times* (June 10).

NOW: Politics and Economy. 2002. "Middle Class Squeeze: The Changing Shape of the Income Distribution." Public Broadcasting Service. December 13, 2002. Available online at http://www.pbs.org/now/politics/middleclass.html.

NOW: Politics and Economy. 2004. "Who Is the Middle Class?" Public Broadcasting Service (June 25). Available online at http://www.pbs.org/now/politics/middle-classoverview.html.

U.S. Census Bureau. 2004. "Income Stable, Poverty Up, Numbers of Americans With and Without Health Insurance Rise, Census Bureau Reports" (August 26). Available online at http://www.census.gov/Press-elease/www/releases/archives/income_wealth/002484.html.

7. Our Society's Middle Is Shrinking from View

Louise Auerhahn

If the Silicon Valley economy was a carnival, the barker would be saying, "Step right up, ladies and gents! Right before your eyes—see the incredible shrinking middle class! Catch a glimpse before it's gone!"

In the last two decades, Silicon Valley's economy has rushed through a roller coaster ride of ups and downs. But one disturbing trend has remained constant; the middle class has grown steadily smaller. Even worse, the "new economy," both pre- and post-crash, is characterized by increasing inequality and by massive and perpetual insecurity.

When the valley's economy tumbled in 2001, numerous middle-class families were pushed over the edge. Since then, real median household income in the county has declined from $81,665 in 2000 to $76,544 in 2003. The proportion of adults in poverty climbed by 40 percent.

These are not mere cyclical setbacks; they represent a fundamental shift in the U.S. economy. In the early 1980s, American families began to notice that good middle-class jobs were becoming harder to find. Economists confirmed that, after decades of increasing prosperity, income inequality had begun to grow dramatically; the rising tide was no longer lifting all boats.

The 1990s saw the emergence of an "hourglass economy," with rapidly increasing numbers of low-wage and high-wage jobs, but few in the middle" especially in Silicon Valley. In Santa Clara County, the number of both low-income and high-income families grew between 1990 and 2000, while middle-class households (incomes between $15,000 and $100,000) declined.

For the families falling to the bottom or teetering on the edge, the hourglass economy was a disaster. But policy-makers found it hard to see it as such in the face of the overall prosperity of the dot-com boom. True, the hourglass shape of the economy was worrisome, but at least we could console ourselves with the thought that some families were making it to the top in spectacular fashion.

Is that still the case? Since 2000, income inequality in Santa Clara County has continued to increase, with the middle class continuing to shrink. But now, instead of growth at the top and bottom of the income distribution, only the bottom is growing.

With a shrinking or stagnant upper class, a disappearing middle class and an ever-increasing low-wage service sector, income distribution now resembles not so much an hourglass as an old-fashioned Victorian gown: small on top, cinched down to nearly nothing in the middle, and ballooning out at the bottom.

In just three years, the number of Santa Clara households with incomes below $15,000 has grown by 30 percent, and the number between $15,000 and $35,000 has grown by 25 percent. That means 26,000 more households have fallen into the bottom of the Victorian gown. By comparison, the proportion of households earning between $35,000 and $50,000 has stagnated, rising by just 6 percent, about 3,000 households. Households bringing in $50,000 to $100,000 have dropped by 9 percent, with 17,000 households falling out of this category. And at the top of the scale, households earning $100,000 and above have decreased by 4 percent.

So what does it mean for us to be living in a Victorian-gown economy? It means the loss of necessities many of us took for granted—health coverage, time to spend with our families, a home we could pay off without breaking the bank. It means constant insecurity, being forever one job loss or health crisis away from losing everything we've worked for. It means that the American Dream is fast becoming the privilege of a few.

Three economic and political shifts are responsible for the disappearing dream. One, low-wage work is booming, while middle-class jobs with health benefits are vanishing, often being outsourced. Two, the cost of living is accelerating, especially for housing and health care. And three, federal and state administrations are chipping away at the safety net: gutting health programs, reducing child care, and now, attempting to privatize Social Security. We are witnessing the repeal of the New Deal.

Fortunately, we still have a chance to stop the growth of the Victorian gown. Fighting the offshoring of jobs, demanding that businesses pay a living wage, supporting health insurance for working families—these and many more efforts are all part of a growing movement to change the direction of our economy.

In the Great Depression, Americans strove together to build the political and economic structures that produced record growth and a thriving middle class. By applying Silicon Valley's ingenuity and collaborative spirit, we can do so again. Our goal should be nothing less than an economy in which shared prosperity, not massive inequality, is the main attraction.

Note

Louise Auerhahn is associate policy director for Working Partnerships USA. She wrote this article for the *Mercury News*.

8. The Vanishing Middle-Class Job
As Income Gap Widens, Uncertainty Spreads
Griff Witte

Scott Clark knows how to plate a circuit board for a submarine. He knows which chemicals, when mixed, will keep a cell phone ringing and which will explode. He knows how to make his little piece of a factory churn hour after hour, day after day.

But right now, as his van hurtles toward the misty silhouette of the Blue Ridge Mountains, the woods rising darkly on either side and Richmond receding behind him, all he needs to know is how to stay awake and avoid the deer.

So he guides his van along the center of the highway, one set of wheels in the right lane and the other in the left. "Gives me a chance if a deer runs in from either direction," he explains. "And at night, this is my road."

It's his road because, at 3:43 a.m. on a Wednesday, no one else wants it. Clark is nearly two hours into a workday that won't end for another 13, delivering interoffice mail around the state for four companies—none of which offers him health care, vacation, a pension or even a promise that today's job will be there tomorrow. His meticulously laid plans to retire by his mid-50s are dead. At 51, he's left with only a vague hope of getting off the road sometime in the next 20 years.

Until three years ago, Clark lived a fairly typical American life—high school, marriage, house in the suburbs, three kids and steady work at the local circuit-board factory for a quarter-century. Then in 2001 the plant closed, taking his $17-an-hour job with it, and Clark found himself among a segment of workers who have learned the middle of the road is more dangerous than it used to be. If they want to keep their piece of the American dream, they're going to have to improvise.

Figuring out what the future holds for workers in his predicament—and those who are about to be—is key to understanding a historic shift in the U.S. workforce, a shift that has been changing the rules for a crucial part of the middle class.

This transformation is no longer just about factory workers, whose ranks have declined by 5 million in the past 25 years as manufacturing moved to countries with cheaper labor. All kinds of jobs that pay in the middle range—Clark's $17 an hour, or about $35,000 a year, was smack in the center—are vanishing, including computer-code crunchers, produce managers, call-center operators, travel agents and office clerks.

The jobs have had one thing in common: For people with a high school diploma and perhaps a bit of college, they can be a ticket to a modest home, health insurance, decent retirement and maybe some savings for the kids' tuition. Such jobs were a big reason America's middle class flourished in the second half of the 20th century.

Now what those jobs share is vulnerability. The people who fill them have become replaceable by machines, workers overseas or temporary employees at home who lack benefits. And when they are replaced, many don't know where to turn.

"We don't know what the next big thing will be. When the manufacturing jobs were going away, we could tell people to look for tech jobs. But now the tech jobs are moving away, too," said Lori G. Kletzer, an economics professor at the University of California at Santa Cruz. "What's the comparative advantage that America retains? We don't have the answer to that. It gives us a very insecure feeling."

The government doesn't specifically track how many jobs like Clark's have gone away. But other statistics more than hint at the scope of the change. For example, there are now about as many temporary, on-call or contract workers in the United States as there are members of labor unions. Another sign: Of the 2.7 million jobs lost during and after the recession in 2001, the vast majority have been restructured out of existence, according to a study by the Federal Reserve Bank of New York.

Each layoff or shutdown has its own immediate cause, but nearly all ultimately can be traced to two powerful forces that reinforce each other: global competition and rapid advances in technology.

Economists and politicians—including the presidential candidates—are locked in a vigorous debate about the job losses. Is this just another rocky stretch of the U.S. economy that, if left alone, will foster new industries generating millions of as-yet-unimagined jobs, as it has during other times of upheaval? Or is the workforce hollowing out permanently, with those in the middle forced to slide down to low-paying jobs without benefits if they can't get the education, credentials and experience to climb up to the high-paying professions?

Over the next several months, *The Washington Post,* in an occasional series of articles, will explore the vast changes facing middle-income workers and the consequences for businesses and society.

Some of the consequences are already evident: The ranks of the uninsured, the bankrupt and the long-term unemployed have all crept up the income scale, proving those problems aren't limited to the poor. Meanwhile, income inequality has grown. In 2001, the top 20 percent of households for the first time raked in more than half of all income, while the share earned by those in the middle was the lowest in nearly 50 years.

Within the middle class, there has been a widening divide between those in its upper reaches whose jobs provide the trappings of the good life, and those in the lower rungs whose economic fortunes are less secure.

The growing income gap corresponds to a long-term restructuring of the workforce that has carved out jobs from the center. In 1969, two categories of jobs—blue-collar and administrative support—together accounted for 56 percent of U.S. workers, according to an analysis by economists Frank Levy of MIT and Richard J. Murnane of Harvard. Thirty years later the share was just 39 percent.

Jobs at the low and high ends have replaced those in the middle—the ranks of janitors and fast-food workers have expanded, but so have those of lawyers and doctors. The problem is, jobs at the low end don't support a middle-class life. And many at the high end require special skills and advanced degrees. "However you define the middle class, it's a lot harder now for high school graduates to be in it," Levy said.

College graduates aren't immune, either. In places like Richmond, the overall health of the economy masks layoffs that have snared not only blue-collar workers like Clark, but also thousands of office workers at companies like credit card giant Capital One Financial Corp. and high-tech retailer Circuit City Stores Inc. Those cutbacks have educated even those with bachelor's degrees in the new ways of a volatile economy.

A University of California at Berkeley study last year found that as many as 14 million jobs are vulnerable to being sent overseas. Many economists, though, say offshoring is more opportunity than threat because it allows companies to make and sell goods for less, and offer even better jobs than those that are lost. "Offshoring can't explain job loss. It can only explain job switch," said David R. Henderson, a Hoover Institution economist.

Henderson says the middle class is thriving, and by many measures, he's right. As a group they're earning more money than they have before, and their ranks have swollen with members who can afford the DVDs, SUVs and MP3s now seen by many families as part of the essential backdrop to modern life. Whereas Census numbers show the median household earned $33,338 in 1967 when adjusted for inflation, that number was up by $10,000 in 2003.

But when compared with those at the top, the middle has lost much ground. And many in the middle have dropped well behind their peers.

The gaps are likely to widen, according to Robert H. Frank, a Cornell economist. He said that as more people worldwide become available to do routine work for less money and as computers take on increasingly complex functions, the demand for those Americans whose skills are easily duplicated could drop. "The new equilibrium," Frank said, "may be a little meaner and more unpleasant than it was before."

BELIEVING IN MA BELL

In the Washington area, the federal government and its contractors have cushioned the impact of the change in the workforce. But you don't have to travel far for evidence of the shift: Just two hours south on I-95, to Richmond.

From a distance, like many parts of the United States, Richmond looks like a place where the middle class should thrive. As its economy evolved over the past century from agriculture to manufacturing to services and, finally, to technology, it hung on to some aspects of each phase. That diversity keeps the jobless rate below the national average. Paychecks for professionals are growing. Major corporations such as Philip Morris USA are adding staff. A biotech park has taken root in downtown. Two new malls recently opened in the suburbs.

And yet, for some who lack the right skills to match employers' demands, Richmond has less to offer than it used to.

"I think we're tending not to see any growth in the middle," said Michael Pratt, a Virginia Commonwealth University economics professor, "but I don't know anywhere in America where you are."

It wasn't always that way.

When Fred Agostino moved to suburban Richmond to head the Henrico County Economic Development Authority in the mid-1980s, employers wanted semi-skilled workers they could train for half a day and hire for life at a decent wage with benefits. Now companies looking to relocate to Richmond just want to know what percentage of the local population has a PhD. "They have to have educated, skilled, world-class people," Agostino said.

Meanwhile, the lifetime jobs were cut short.

The Viasystems Inc. circuit board factory was once known as "Richmond Works," and it provided good pay for people who didn't get past high school—like Scott Clark. He was also among the 2,350 people who lost their jobs in 2001, when the plant shut for good.

Today Clark is a driver-for-hire, willing to work virtually any schedule, and drive any route for less than anyone else. His old factory job was outsourced to workers in China, Canada or Mexico. But now he benefits from outsourcing, doing work that once might have been someone else's full-time job with benefits. A former proud union man, he has become part of the steady exodus from the labor movement, which now represents just under 13 percent of the workforce. Instead, he's part of another nearly 13 percent of the workforce that has grown, not shrunk—those who do jobs that are temporary, contract or on-call.

At least the work's not going anywhere. A real person in America, he reasons, has to drive American roads to get things from one place to another. There's security in that.

Clark used to feel the same security about work at the factory. When he started there in the mid-1970s, it was a new Western Electric plant, part of the Ma Bell family. When managers called him for an interview and he got the job, he could hardly believe it: "I said, 'It's funny you called me. My girlfriend's got college, and you ain't called her.' They said, 'What kind of college?' I said, 'She's taking biology and chemistry and all that stuff.' Before I got home, they called her and I had to turn around and bring her back up."

His girlfriend, Kathy, dropped out of school immediately. They started work the same day in 1976, making less than $10 an hour between them. Marriage followed.

Clark, a big, profane man, makes his way through Virginia yelling at other drivers, yelling at talk radio, and, occasionally, singing along to a sweet, sad bluegrass tune.

He doesn't have much patience for politicians. When Sen. John F. Kerry (Mass.), the Democratic presidential nominee, comes on the radio to talk about the economy, proclaiming, "I believe in building up our great middle class," Clark sneers, "Yeah, right." When President Bush's voice echoes through the cab a little later, Clark dubs him "a liar."

Clark has few nice things to say about corporations, either, but he concedes that the factory—for most of his years there—was run pretty well. He enjoyed the work, putting copper plating on circuit boards that would power phones, computers and even a few submarines for the Navy. Working in the chemical division was a dirty job. But because it was dirty, managers stayed away. Amidst the fumes, working long into the night on the second shift, the workers forged deep friendships. Clark and three buddies played the lottery religiously, with a vow that if one hit the jackpot, they would split the winnings and all retire on the spot.

"It was a real close-knit group of people," said Kathy Clark, who also worked the second shift for years. "We grew up there. We had our families there."

"You Could Work for Nothing"

But in 1996, the plant was sold by Lucent Technologies Inc., which had inherited it from AT&T Corp. Although the union made a bid, the victor was a startup called Viasystems.

Many of the workers, Scott Clark included, had a feeling Viasystems was not invested in the plant for the long term. The reality was hard to ignore: By 2001, few companies still made circuit boards in the United States. They could earn a bigger profit producing them where business costs were lower, and where the workers would not demand overtime or sick leave. Scott Clark was not surprised on the day Viasystems announced the factory would shut down.

"They point-blank told us.... 'You could work for nothing and we would still close this plant,'" Kathy Clark said.

On the plant's final day, the workers were told to throw their ID passes and beepers into a box in the auditorium. Scott Clark wouldn't do it. Instead he broke into a meeting of managers, and placed his pass on the table. "When I walked into this plant, they handed me that pass," he told them. "They were proud to give it to me, and I was proud to take it." Now he was giving it back. He turned, and left the plant for the last time.

A handful of employees stayed behind to remove the machines so they could either be shipped overseas or sold for scrap. In the end, Richmond Works was just a shell. The building still sits vacant off the side of Interstate 64 just outside Richmond, a 700,000-square-foot tan tombstone in a weedy field.

Kathy Clark was unemployed for a year after the plant closed. Scott Clark lost time to training as he began his second career on the road. With their savings all but evaporated, the Clarks have spent the past two years starting over.

Working 15-hour days, Scott Clark has been pulling in good money. He won't say exactly how much for fear that competitors will undercut him, but in the Richmond area, he said, a courier can make $800 a week for doing routes less time-consuming than his. That's more than his base pay at the factory, though his new job lacks any benefits and he has to pay for the van and the gas. Kathy Clark, meanwhile, got a full-time job this summer after two years of temp work. But they still have a lot of ground to make up. Had the plant stayed open, they would have been ready for retirement in just a few more years. Now, "I feel like I'm 18 years old again," said Kathy Clark, as she sat in a rocking chair in her living room, strands of light gray overtaking the dark brown of her short hair.

The Clarks know they have it better than many of their friends from the plant. They have frequent, impromptu reunions at Wal-Mart, where the talk inevitably turns to who has found work and who hasn't.

Raffael Toskes Sr. has, but only for $11 an hour. He rides around each day in an armored car, a gun strapped to his side. "I consider myself a middle-class person," said Toskes, who made $17 an hour at the plant. "But right now, I'm probably a lower-middle-class person."

Lawrence Provo has given up on trying to find a job. He was out of work for nearly two years after the plant closed. "That was probably the worst time in the world to become unemployed. Everybody was downsizing. Everybody was laying off," he said.

Provo and his wife cut back on expenses and sold their car, furniture and jewelry. They even sold their home, and moved in with Provo's mother-in-law. But it was not enough. They had come to rely on his factory wage, and now their debts spiraled into the tens of thousands. They declared bankruptcy, joining a record 1.6 million who filed last year.

Provo finally got a job through a temp agency for $8.50 an hour, less than $18,000 a year and a little more than a third of his pay at Viasystems. He was just getting his life back together when, in November last year, his heart failed him. "My doctor told me, 'You've got a choice: You can work or you can live,'" he said.

Robert Boyer retrained in computers after the plant closed. But tech companies told him they wanted five years' experience, not a certificate from a six-month course. So he works for $11.50 an hour at Home Depot, using the wisdom of four decades as plant electrician to help customers pick light bulbs for their remodeled kitchens.

Boyer turns angry at any suggestion that the jobs picture is not that bad. "When these guys get on the boob tube and say there's jobs out there, you just gotta go out there and get them, it makes me want to go out there and grab them by the throat and say, 'Where? Where are the jobs at?'"

Slipping Away at Circuit City

Ask Richmond's leaders, and they'll say the jobs are in infotech, biotech, nanotech and other kinds of tech yet to be conceived. "People have the impression that Richmond is a good-old-boy town. And we do have some old money here. But that money is going to build the new economy," said Robert J. Stolle, executive director of the Greater Richmond Technology Council. "Tech is the backbone of the Richmond economy."

One homegrown company seems to capture in its name Richmond's most deeply held ambitions: Circuit City. Born in 1949 to sell television sets to the masses, its existence attests to the enduring strength of the middle class. And all those sales of computers and video games have created a lot of jobs. With a local staff of 3,072, the chain is one of the Richmond area's largest employers.

But the work has a tendency to disappear. In the eight years after he moved to Richmond to take an offer at Circuit City, Chuck Moore lost his job in that company three times, proving that a white collar and a college degree are no protection from the forces that have shifted the ground under blue-collar workers like Clark.

At 35, Moore spent the first nine months of 2004 desperate for a job as he watched his grip on the middle class slipping away. His story complicates the idea that to be comfortable in America today, all you need is a little more education.

Moore's roots are solidly blue-collar: His father worked as an electrician for the same company for 40 years. His stepfather drove a truck. His brother went to work at the Georgia Pacific plant. His mother still manages the local Shoney's. No one in his family had ever graduated from college.

For nine years after his high school graduation, he and his wife, Terry, worked full time to pay for Chuck to complete his degree at the Savannah College of Art and Design. With a knack for electronics and an artistic eye, he wanted to animate movies or video games. "I thought that walking out that door with that degree in my hand, I wouldn't have to look. I would have people coming to me," Moore said.

But while Moore was in school—designing animation by day, manning a hotel desk by night—the technology had continued to improve and so had employers' capacity to hire artists anywhere on earth. A bachelor's degree might have been enough before; now you needed a master's or even a doctorate.

Moore started looking for computer jobs instead. He and Terry both had luck at Circuit City.

Moore's first job disappeared when the company closed a tech support center and began moving its call center operations to India. His second job—designing ads for the recruitment division—evaporated when the tech bubble burst. His last job there ended in January when the database he built to manage marketing projects worked so well that the company no longer needed the help of a human.

Until this past weekend, his job search had gone like this: 320 résumés sent out, six calls back. Three interviews. No offers. At first, he had put his old salary on his résumé: $40,000. Later he switched to, "negotiable."

"I've already been willing to go down 10 [thousand dollars]. And if it goes much longer, I might have to go down 15. For a guy with a bachelor's degree to take $25,000, I might as well be working at McDonald's," Moore said in August. "There's something not right about that."

Yet on Saturday, when an animal hospital offered him work as a veterinary assistant—for half what he had been making in his old job and no benefits—he accepted immediately. He starts today, cleaning out kennels and, he hopes, learning how to use the X-ray machines or work in the lab so he can add to his repertoire of skills.

Moore has thought of going back for his master's degree. But that's hardly an option when he has a 3-year-old son, not to mention a mortgage and student loans.

Instead, to help make ends meet, he's been teaching computer basics at J. Sargeant Reynolds Community College, where his students can identify with their teacher's plight. One is a 20-year Army veteran who found that the best he could do without college was become a salesman at Lowe's, the home improvement store. He was taking Moore's class so he could go to a four-year college in the fall.

"The job market for people like me is not that good," said the man, Albert DiCicco. "Maybe it is for people with bachelor's degrees."

Lately, DiCicco's predicament has been on the mind of Federal Reserve Chairman Alan Greenspan.

In June, Greenspan warned that a shortage of highly skilled workers and a surplus of those with fewer skills has meant wages for the lower half of the income scale have remained stagnant, while the top quarter of earners sprints away. Greenspan said the skills mismatch "can and must be addressed, because I think that it's creating an increasing concentration of incomes in this country and, for a democratic society, that is not a very desirable thing to allow to happen."

But it already has happened. The gap between the wages of a 30-year-old male high school graduate and a 30-year-old male college graduate was 17 percent as of 1979, according to analysis by Harvard's Murnane and MIT's Levy in their book, "The New Division of Labor." Now it tops 50 percent, with an even larger differential for women. Real wages for both high school graduates and high school dropouts have actually fallen since the 1970s. Meanwhile, wages for college graduates—who make up only about a quarter of the adult population—have soared upward.

The trend seems poised to continue. The list of the 30 jobs the Labor Department predicts will grow the most through 2012 includes high-paying positions such as postsecondary teachers, software engineers and management analysts. But nearly all require a college degree. There are also plenty of jobs that demand no college—including retail sales and security guard—but they pay a low wage.

And yet, as Moore's situation shows, a college diploma offers a porous shield when demand for a certain skill evaporates. College graduates have, in recent years, become an increasingly large percentage of the long-term unemployed. When they find new work, their salary cuts have been especially deep.

The optimists among economists—and there are many—point to trends that could help mitigate the pain of job losses and lead to future growth. One is the coming mass retirement of baby boomers, which could leave plenty of openings for those trying to break into the workforce. Economists tend to believe, too, that trade and technology will ultimately create new efficiencies that produce far more jobs than they destroy and leave everyone, on average, better off.

A Tough Climb

Scott Clark isn't sure if he will emerge better off. Spending day and night in the cab of a van was not exactly how he planned to live out his fifties and sixties, but he'll get by. He's even managed to save enough money to begin cutting his hours from 15 down to 11.

It's the end of the day now and as Clark battles the Richmond evening rush hour, his thoughts are turning to home. He's already fulfilled his part of the American dream, doing better than his parents did. "Everybody tells me I'm low class," Clark says, chuckling faintly. "But we're middle class. We're definitely middle class."

Yet his kids—his son is 26 and his twin daughters are 21—still live at home because they can't afford places of their own. None of them went to college, although his daughters had 3.8 grade-point averages in high school and his son aced the SATs. They're saving to go back to school—eventually. In the meantime, they work. His son lays carpet and his daughters stock shelves in a warehouse.

Will they be able to move up the economic ladder, just like he did? Clark ponders the question. After a long day, he is showing the strain, getting sleepy with his regular bedtime of 6:30 p.m. fast approaching.

"I really don't know. It's just too uncertain. It really is. There's nothing there," he says, turning completely serious for the first time all day. "There's nothing you can just count on. I wish there was."

CHAPTER 4

SOCIAL MOBILITY

Social mobility is the epitome of the American Dream—people starting with nothing who rise out of their poverty to eventually "make it." In truth, however, the rate of upward mobility in the United States is similar to that in other industrialized nations: It does not usually happen (Rothstein, 2000).

According to a report in *The Economist,* changes between the social class of fathers and that of sons have slowed in the past several decades. Researchers considering intergenerational movement in 1998 concluded that nearly 70 percent of males were either worse off or at the same level at which their fathers had been twenty years earlier (*The Economist,* 2004). Moreover, the greatest upward mobility was exhibited in higher social classes—affluent young men surpassing their fathers' economic status. The research was silent regarding women.

The Center on Budget and Policy Priorities (CBP, 2006), in addressing the question of social mobility, specifically considered whether low-income families have the potential to move out of poverty and move up the economic ladder. Their report indicated that most low-income families can expect to remain poor for long periods. In fact, the report found that in the 1990s, 75 percent of individuals in the bottom quintile remained there throughout consecutive years. Approximately half the individuals in the lowest quintile did move up over a ten-year period but, with few exceptions, only to the next lowest quintile; therefore, the poverty status of those who moved up did not change dramatically. Overall, income mobility in the United States declined in the 1980s and 1990s (CBP, 2006).

Rothstein (2000) echoed the findings of the Center on Budget and Policy Priorities, noting that social mobility has declined since the 1970s. Consider that in 1970, 28 percent of those in the lowest quintile stayed at the bottom; in the 1980s, the number of people remaining in the bottom quintile rose to 32 percent; and in the 1990s, 36 percent of those who began in the lowest class stayed in the lowest class (*The Economist,* 2004). If these trends continue, the first decade of the new century could see 40 percent of people in the United States located in the bottom tier.

Interestingly, the lack of social mobility is concealed, inasmuch as general economic changes make it appear that people have moved up in social standing when in fact they have remained at the same level as their parents (Rothstein, 2000). Thus, people may fail to recognize that they are not enjoying the promises of the American Dream. The readings for this section address issues related to social mobility in the twenty-first century.

REFERENCES

CBP (Center on Budget and Policy Priorities). 2006. Available online at http://www.cbpp.org/1-26-06sfp.htm.

Rothstein, Richard. 2000. "Offering Students a Hand to Move Up," Economic Policy Institute. Available online at http://www.epinet.org/content.cfm/webfeat_lessons20001004.

The Economist. 2004. "Meritocracy in America: Ever Higher Society, Ever Harder to Ascend" (December 29), Washington, D.C. Available online at http://www.economist.com/world/na/displayStory.cfm?story_id=3518560.

9. THE DEATH OF HORATIO ALGER
OUR POLITICAL LEADERS ARE DOING EVERYTHING
THEY CAN TO FORTIFY CLASS INEQUALITY

Paul Krugman

The other day I found myself reading a leftist rag that made outrageous claims about America. It said that we are becoming a society in which the poor tend to stay poor, no matter how hard they work; in which sons are much more likely to inherit the socioeconomic status of their father than they were a generation ago.

The name of the leftist rag? *Business Week,* which published an article titled "Waking Up From the American Dream." The article summarizes recent research showing that social mobility in the United States (which was never as high as legend had it) has declined considerably over the past few decades. If you put that research together with other research that shows a drastic increase in income and wealth inequality, you reach an uncomfortable conclusion: America looks more and more like a class-ridden society.

And guess what? Our political leaders are doing everything they can to fortify class inequality, while denouncing anyone who complains—or even points out what is happening—as a practitioner of "class warfare."

Let's talk first about the facts on income distribution. Thirty years ago we were a relatively middle-class nation. It had not always been thus: Gilded Age America was a highly unequal society, and it stayed that way through the 1920s. During the 1930s and '40s, however, America experienced what the economic historians Claudia Goldin and Robert Margo have dubbed the Great Compression: a drastic narrowing of income gaps, probably as a result of New Deal policies. And the new economic order persisted for more than a generation: Strong unions; taxes on inherited wealth, corporate profits and high incomes; close public scrutiny of corporate management—all helped to keep income gaps relatively small.

The economy was hardly egalitarian, but a generation ago the gross inequalities of the 1920s seemed very distant.

Now they're back. According to estimates by the economists Thom Piketty and Emmanuel Saez—confirmed by data from the Congressional Budget Office—between 1973 and 2000 the average real income of the bottom 90 percent of American taxpayers actually fell by 7 percent. Meanwhile, the income of the top 1 percent rose by 148 percent, the income of the top 0.1 percent rose by 343 percent and the income of the top 0.01 percent rose 599 percent. (Those numbers exclude capital gains, so they're not an artifact of the stock-market bubble.) The distribution of income in the United States has gone right back to Gilded Age levels of inequality.

Never mind, say the apologists, who churn out papers with titles like that of a 2001 Heritage Foundation piece, "Income Mobility and the Fallacy of Class-Warfare Arguments." America, they say, isn't a caste society—people with high incomes this year may have low incomes next year and vice versa, and the route to wealth is open to all. That's where those commies at *Business Week* come in: As they point out (and as economists and sociologists have been pointing out for some time), America actually is more of a caste society than we like to think. And the caste lines have lately become a lot more rigid.

The myth of income mobility has always exceeded the reality: As a general rule, once they've reached their 30s, people don't move up and down the income ladder very much. Conservatives often cite studies like a 1992 report by Glenn Hubbard, a Treasury official under the elder Bush who later became chief economic adviser to the younger Bush, that purport to show large numbers of Americans moving from low-wage to high-wage jobs during their working lives. But what these studies measure, as the economist Kevin Murphy put it, is mainly "the guy who works in the college bookstore and has a real job by his early 30s." Serious studies that exclude this sort of pseudo-mobility show that inequality in average incomes over long periods isn't much smaller than inequality in annual incomes.

It is true, however, that America was once a place of substantial intergenerational mobility: Sons often did much better than their fathers. A classic 1978 survey found that among adult men whose fathers were in the bottom 25 percent of the population as ranked by social and economic status, 23 percent had made it into the top 25 percent. In other words, during the first thirty years or so after World War II, the American dream of upward mobility was a real experience for many people.

Now for the shocker: The *Business Week* piece cites a new survey of today's adult men, which finds that this number has dropped to only 10 percent. That is, over the past generation upward mobility has fallen drastically. Very few children of the lower class are making their way to even moderate affluence. This goes along with other studies indicating that rags-to-riches stories have become vanishingly rare, and that the correlation between fathers' and sons' incomes has risen in recent decades. In modern America, it seems, you're quite likely to stay in the social and economic class into which you were born.

Business Week attributes this to the "Wal-Martization" of the economy, the proliferation of dead-end, low-wage jobs and the disappearance of jobs that provide entry to the middle class. That's surely part of the explanation. But public policy plays a role—and will, if present trends continue, play an even bigger role in the future.

Put it this way: Suppose that you actually liked a caste society, and you were seeking ways to use your control of the government to further entrench the advantages of the haves against the have-nots. What would you do?

One thing you would definitely do is get rid of the estate tax, so that large fortunes can be passed on to the next generation.

More broadly, you would seek to reduce tax rates both on corporate profits and on unearned income such as dividends and capital gains, so that those with large accumulated or inherited wealth could more easily accumulate even more. You'd also try to create tax shelters mainly useful for the rich. And more broadly still, you'd try to reduce tax rates on people with high incomes, shifting the burden to the payroll tax and other revenue sources that bear most heavily on people with lower incomes.

Meanwhile, on the spending side, you'd cut back on healthcare for the poor, on the quality of public education and on state aid for higher education. This would make it more difficult for people with low incomes to climb out of their difficulties and acquire the education essential to upward mobility in the modern economy.

And just to close off as many routes to upward mobility as possible, you'd do everything possible to break the power of unions, and you'd privatize government functions so that well-paid civil servants could be replaced with poorly paid private employees.

It all sounds sort of familiar, doesn't it?

Where is this taking us? Thomas Piketty, whose work with Saez has transformed our understanding of income distribution, warns that current policies will eventually create "a class of rentiers in the U.S., whereby a small group of wealthy but untalented children controls vast segments of the US economy and penniless, talented children simply can't compete." If he's right—and I fear that he is—we will end up suffering not only from injustice, but from a vast waste of human potential.

Goodbye, Horatio Alger. And goodbye, American Dream.

Note

Paul Krugman, an economics professor at Princeton and a columnist at the *New York Times*, is the author, most recently, of *The Great Unraveling: Losing Our Way in the New Century* (Norton).

10. Rags to Riches?
The American Dream is Less Common in the United States than Elsewhere

Bernard Wasow

How many times have you heard "you can be what you want to be if only you work for it"? The American dream has brought millions to our shores, legally or surreptitiously, in search of upward economic mobility. And, over the decades, millions of children of immigrants or of working-class Americans have prospered and advanced in our competitive economy.

But how easy is it for the children of poor parents to become prosperous? Recent evidence shows that there is much less mobility in the United States than most people assume. Horatio Alger notwithstanding, rags to rags and riches to riches are now the norm in this country to a greater degree than in many other developed nations. Our current education system, antidiscrimination laws, and other public policy tools that aim to give the children of poor parents a fair shot at a high income are not getting the job done. We may all believe in the American Dream, but we have a lot of work to do if we are to make that dream a reality.

Studies show that life chances differ profoundly depending on the circumstances into which a child is born (see figure 4.1). Only a small share of the children of the poor end up earning high incomes—most remain in or near poverty.

The columns in figure 4.1 show the income quintile (five groups in 20 percent increments) that people end up in as adults if they were born into the bottom 20 percent of the income distribution. Of those born into the bottom fifth of the income distribution, 42 percent end up where they started—at the bottom. Another 24 percent of those born into the bottom fifth move up slightly to the next-to-bottom quintile (still below the average). Only 7 percent of those born into the bottom fifth end up in the top tier—providing the relatively rare rags-to-riches stories that Americans celebrate.

Conversely, nearly 40 percent of those who are born into the top quintile remain there, while barely 6 percent of those born into the top 20 percent end up in the bottom fifth. So a person born into the top quintile is more than five times as likely to end up at the top as a person born into the bottom quintile.

Research also shows that sons and their fathers might have very different incomes some years (as one would expect if there were a lot of income mobility), but the more years one averages, the more closely sons' incomes match their fathers' incomes. Father or son may have a few unusual years, but if one averages fifteen years of a father's income, there is a close association with his son's income (also averaged for several years). Figure 4.2 shows how the association rises as the comparison period is extended.[1]

How can we explain the close association of fathers' and sons' incomes? There seems to be little economic mobility in the United States. But could this interpretation be wrong?

- Maybe the obstacles to mobility are unrelated to economic and social forces. The lack of movement across income levels might be attributable to inheritance of intelligence, with capable families ending up at the top and weak performers at the bottom.

Alternatively, perhaps mobility is limited by social and economic obstacles:

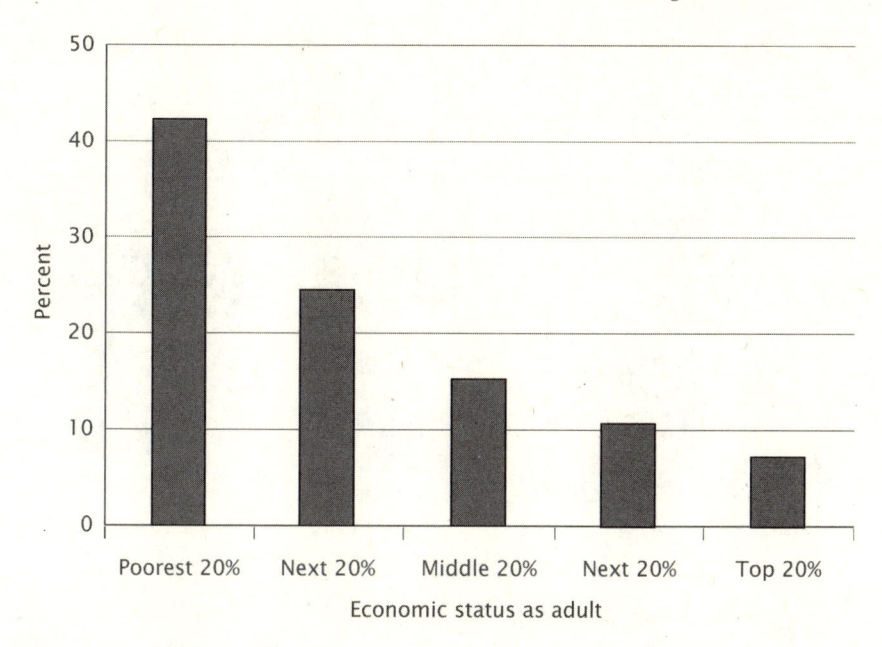

Figure 4.1 Where Those Born into the Poorest 20 Percent of the Population End Up as Adults

Note: The study followed more than 6,000 individuals, including parents and children, where the children were born between 1942 and 1972 and were observed both as children or young adults in a household they did not head and then later as adult heads of households or adult spouses.

Source: Data from Thomas Hertz, "Rags, Riches and Race: The Intergenerational Economic Mobility of Black and White Families in the United States," in *Unequal Chances: Family Background and Economic Success,* ed. Samuel Bowles, Herbert Gintis, and Melissa Osborne (New York: Russell Sage Foundation and Princeton University Press, forthcoming), Table 10, available at http://academic2.american.edu/~hertz/ HERTZ%20Rags%20Riches%20and%20Race%20April%202003. pdf.

- Maybe the children of the poor (at every level of ability) obtain less and inferior schooling compared to the children of the rich.
- Maybe wealth passed on during life and at death gives the children of rich parents their advantage.
- Maybe social networks and other aspects of social class drive opportunity toward children of people in similar social circumstances.

Economists have employed sophisticated techniques to try to disentangle many of these possible explanations as to why people tend to remain at income levels comparable to those of their parents. But the best research explains remarkably little about the strong association between fathers' and sons' incomes.

88 Chapter 4 / Social Mobility

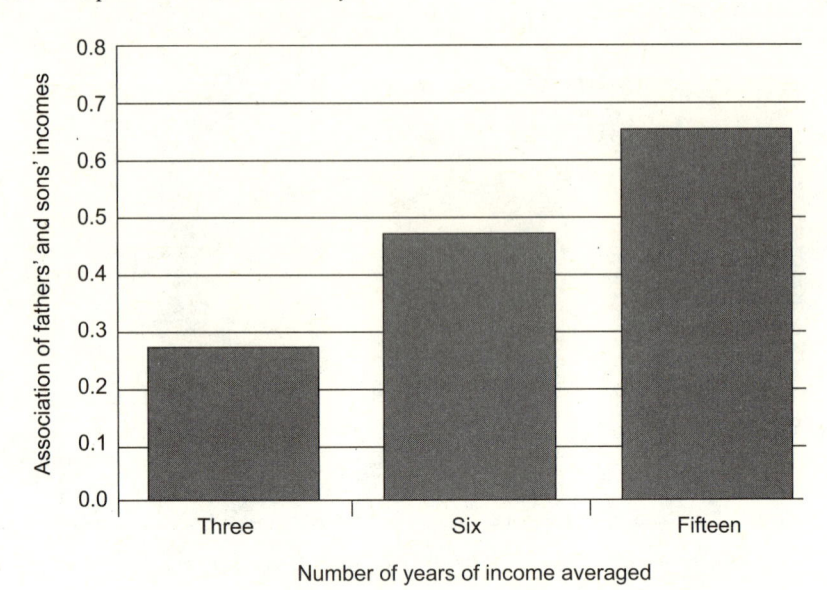

Figure 4.2 The Longer We Look, the More Sons Look Like Their Fathers

Source: Results from calculations done in Bhakshar Mazumder, "Earnings Mobility in the U.S.," in *Unequal Chances: Family Background and Economic Success,* ed. Samuel Bowles, Herbert Gintis, and Melissa Osborne (New York: Russell Sage Foundation and Princeton University Press, forthcoming).

Figure 4.3 shows the results of work by Samuel Bowles and Herbert Gintis, which concludes that similarities in intelligence can account for only about 4 percent of the similarities in income between fathers and sons. So the similarity in income of fathers and sons is not the result of the inheritance of intelligence. Race (also an inherited trait) accounts for only 7 percent of the correlation. Schooling and parents' wealth are more important, together accounting for 19 percent. Very likely, other sociological characteristics of class and culture are important, but, so far, research can account for only about one-third of the correlation between fathers' and sons' incomes. The evidence all points to the conclusion that economic mobility in the United States is limited for reasons we do not understand.

Perhaps most surprising is substantial evidence that citizens of other advanced countries are more likely to climb the economic ladder successfully than Americans. Figure 4.4 illustrates results from a variety of studies in other countries. As in the United States, different studies come up with different numbers because they use different data and, more important, because they average fathers' and sons' incomes over different periods of time. As Figure 4.2 illustrates, the association between fathers' and sons' incomes in studies conducted in the United States ranges from less than 0.3 to more than 0.6, where 0.6 implies a high association of fathers' and sons' incomes—that is, low economic mobility—while 0.3 implies

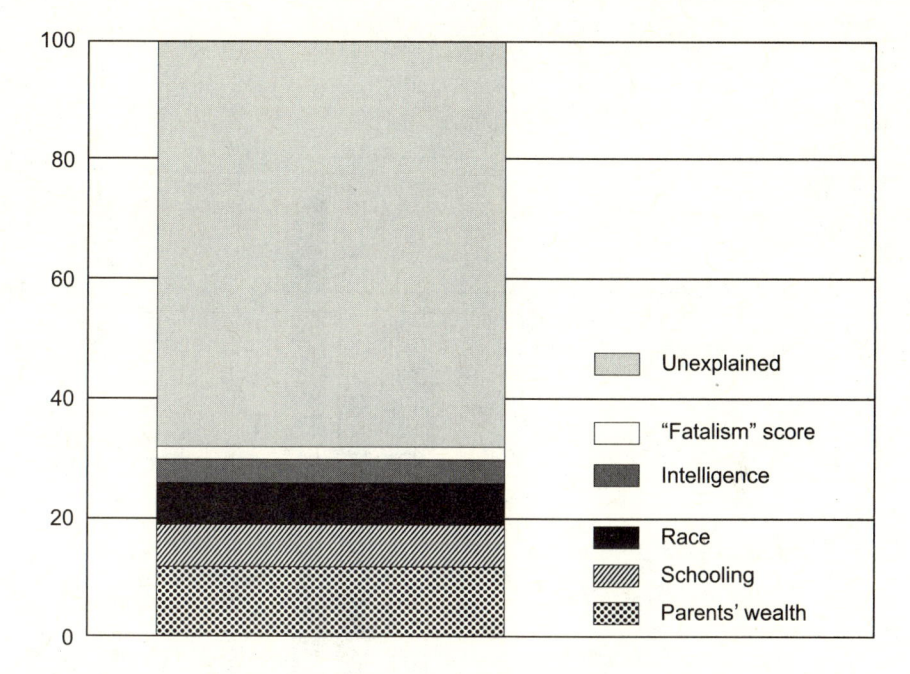

Figure 4.3 Causal Channels of Intergenerational Transmission of Income
Source: Data from Samuel Bowles and Herbert Gintis, "The Inheritance of Inequality," *Journal of Economic Perspectives* 16, no. 3 (Summer 2002): 3–30, Table 3.

somewhat greater mobility. One survey reported an average value in many U.S. studies of 0.43. In Figure 4.4, the studies for Scandinavia, Germany, and Canada suggest greater mobility than in the United States. These results are not conclusive because of differences among the studies in data sources and methods, but it is likely that economic mobility in the United States is lower than in the Scandinavian countries, Germany, and Canada.

In the end, we are left with a double challenge: Why is economic mobility in the United States so limited, and what policies can improve the prospect that people born into low-income families will be able to earn substantially more than their parents? This is an important question not only because we want a fair society but also because we want to make good use of the potential of all of our citizens.

Notes

Bernard Wasow is a Century Foundation Senior Fellow.
1. If the association were 1.0, a father and son would be expected to have the same income. An association of 0.0 would mean that the son's income bears no relationship to the father's. The closer the value is to 0.0, the greater the income mobility.

Figure 4.4 Mobility in Other Countries

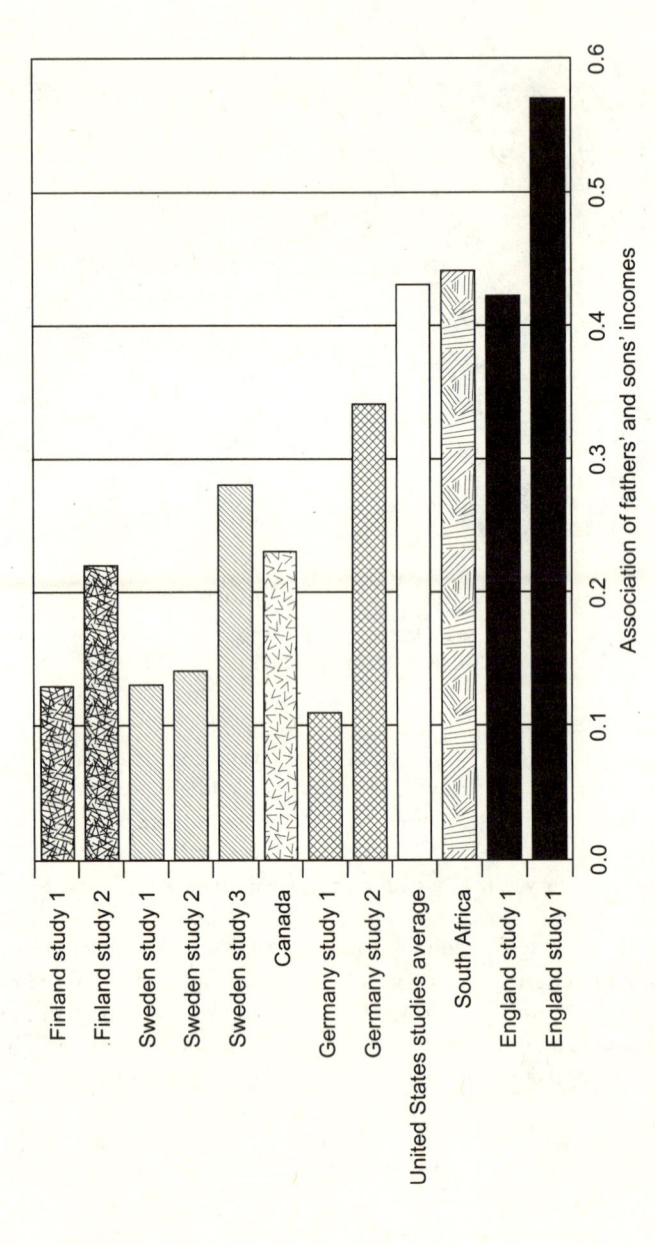

Source: Data from Gary Solon, "Cross-Country Differences in Intergenerational Earnings Mobility," *Journal of Economic Perspectives* 16, no. 3 (Summer 2002): 59–66, Table 1.

Part II
The Consequences of Class

CHAPTER 5
WORK

People with a good work ethic have long been considered on the path to upward mobility in the United States. The idea is that if you work hard you can have your own piece of the American Dream: a car, a home, a college education for your children, vacations, and security in retirement. For many, however, this outcome is elusive; hard work, by itself, is no longer a guarantee for achieving the dream.

The 1950s are often highlighted as epitomizing the modern, middle-class family, which consists of a male breadwinner and a female who stays home and cares for the children. This scenario has changed dramatically now that two-thirds of wives work outside the home for pay. Evidence suggests, however, that even two adults in the workforce are no longer always sufficient to meet the financial demands of owning a home, providing access to health care, sending children to college, and saving for retirement (Dugas, 2003).

In 2004, more than 28 million Americans earned less than $9.04 an hour or $18,800 a year (the poverty line for a family of four) (*BusinessWeek*, 2004). And among those, about 6.4 million worked at or below the minimum wage, holding menial, dead-end jobs that do not provide for retirement, health care, vacations, or insurance. In 2006, for the first time ever, full-time workers earning the minimum wage could not afford a one-bedroom apartment anywhere in the United States at market rates (vanden Heuvel, 2006). Moreover, the costs of utilities and transportation were making it increasingly difficult for one person, let alone a family, to survive. Those at the other income extreme made exorbitant salaries: $8,300 an hour for the chief executive officer of Halliburton and $13,700 an hour for the CEO of ExxonMobil (vanden Heuvel, 2006).

The first article in this section addresses the economic situation in the United States, focusing on jobs, taxes, and inequality. The second one describes America's low-wage workers.

References

BusinessWeek. 2004. "Working ... and Poor" (May 31).
Dugas, Christine. 2003. "Middle Class Barely Treads Water," *USA Today* (September 15). Available online at http://www.usatoday.com/money/perfi/general/2003-09-14-middle-cover_x.htm.
vanden Heuvel, Katrina. 2006. "$13,700 an Hour," *The Nation* (May 1): 5–6.

11. Still Not Getting By in Bush's America
Joel Wendland

According to recent statistics provided by the U.S. Census Bureau, the gap between the rich and poor since 1967 has grown by 75 percent. While the average total household income for families in the bottom 20 percent has grown by $2,500 since 1967, the top 20 percent have seen their incomes soar by about $62,000. According to the same report, the share of national income held by the bottom 20 percent fell to only 3.5 percent. In other words, approximately 26 million households combined to earn only 3.5 percent of the total income earned by people in the US. While income has sunk for the poor, the middle strata have seen their wages stagnate over the same period. Meanwhile healthcare costs, housing, education, gas and oil, and food have soared.

This growing disparity is of special concern as the jobs picture has looked bleak in the last three years. In the first two years of the Bush presidency, 2.6 million jobs were lost, nearly doubling the unemployment rate. While the Bush administration points to recent jobs creation to build a case for its reelection bid, over 1.5 million jobs remain unaccounted for. The jobs that have been created, says economist Art Perlo, may not even cover the number of people who entered the work force for the first time in the same period. This is certainly the case in recent months with only 112,000 jobs in June and 32,000 new jobs in July. At least 140,000 new jobs need to be added "each month just to absorb new workers," Perlo says.

Further, according to economists, 60 percent of the jobs that have been created pay less than the national average in wages, the vast majority are in the low-paying service sector, few provide benefits such as health care coverage, and as many as 1/5 are temp jobs. Currently, the national average of weekly wages is at its lowest point since the official end of the Bush recession in late 2001.

Many observers attribute this economic picture to job losses generated by outsourcing of work offshore. This is partially true, argues economist Doug Henwood of Left Business Observer in an interview with Political Affairs, but outsourcing, while a major problem for working people, accounts for only a relative handful of job losses in the last three years. The number of jobs that have been outsourced is in "the low six figures" in this period, but a normal economy in recovery should have created about 8 million jobs, says Henwood. The Bush economy has failed to do so.

In the wake of the long term trend of economic polarization, recent unemployment, and what the Bureau of Labor Statistics describes as underutilization (underemployment or having more than one job to earn a living wage), the Bush administration has followed a narrow, ideologically driven economic stimulus policy of tax cuts on top of tax cuts. In addition to the obvious problem of eliminating hundreds of billions of dollars from the treasury in the face of needed resources for the Iraq and Afghanistan misadventures and the transformation of large budget surpluses into enormous deficits, Bush tax policies have compounded economic problems for workers, suggests the findings of a recent Congressional Budget Office (CBO) report.

The budget crisis has first allowed the Bush administration to adopt its ideological imperative to cut government services. Among those have been important programs like veterans benefits, funding for public education, environmental protection and cleanup, child poverty programs, agricultural subsidy programs, medical research funding, and so on. In addition to this, Bush has eliminated hundreds of millions of dollars from worker training and relocation assistance funding for unemployed and displaced workers.

If that isn't enough, the direct result of the tax policies has been to intensify the polarization of wealth and poverty. According to the CBO, the top one percent of income earners, who average about $1.2 million each year, received 1/3 of the benefits from the tax cuts Bush pushed through Congress since 2001. Households in this income bracket received an average of $78,000 annually from the tax cut. The top 20 percent, averaging over $200,000, took in 2/3 of the total windfall from the tax cuts. The bottom 20 percent of wage earners averaged only about $250 in returns in the last three years. The tax benefit to the top 1 percent—the very richest of Americans—alone equals what it would cost for two wars in Iraq or what experts believe it would cost for two years to provide every American with health care coverage.

While Republicans claim that these statistics prove that the tax cuts benefited everyone, it is clear that Bush's tax policies have shifted the burden of financing federal spending to the working class. It is we who will have to pay for these tax policies: we will pay disproportionately to make up for the growing deficit with higher interest rates, higher tax rates, and more cuts in social services we all rely on.

Note

Joel Wendland is managing editor of Political Affairs, blogs at ClassWarNotes, and can be reached at jwendland@politicalaffairs.net.

12. AMERICA'S LOW-WAGE WORKERS
THE DEMOGRAPHY OF A CASTE
Beth Shulman

Who are America's low-wage workers? Many presume they are teenagers, illegal immigrants, or high school dropouts. These images perform a useful psychological function by allowing us to dismiss this phenomenon as one of societal outliers. Yet contrary to these stereotypes, America's low-wage workers are mostly white, female, high school educated, and with family responsibilities.

THE BASICS

Teenagers comprise only 7 percent of the low-wage workforce. Indeed, it is adults, a majority of whom have families, who labor in these jobs. And it is young adult non-college graduates who saw the most dramatic erosion of their wages over the last thirty years, with males earning 25 percent and women 13 percent less than their 1973 equivalents.

Nearly two-thirds of the low-wage workforce is white. Yet, blacks and Latinos are overrepresented in this group relative to their participation in the overall workforce. In fact, the proportion of minority workers in 2001 earning a low wage is substantial: 31.2 percent of blacks and 40.4 percent of Latinos in contrast to 20 percent of white workers.

Women make up 60 percent of the lower-paying workforce, even after a slight decline over the past two decades. Almost 30 percent of the female workforce is low-wage, in contrast to less than 20 percent of the male workforce. Of these women, three-fourths are white. Yet the proportion of minority women is significantly higher than white women: 35.8 percent and 46.6 percent of black and Latino women in contrast to 26.2 percent of white women.

This is not to downplay the number of men involved. In fact, men have increased their share of low-wage work over the past twenty years, reaching close to one-fifth of male workers. While they comprise 52 percent of the workforce, they still make up only 40 percent of the low-wage workforce. The statistical story for white men is similar. While white men have increased their share of the low-wage workforce over the past 20 years, they still hold fewer low-wage jobs proportionately than women and minorities. Women of color are four times more likely to hold a low-wage job than white men. White women are three times as likely as men to hold a low-wage job. And men of color are one and a half times as likely as white men to do so.

When it comes to education, it is not surprising that the low-wage workforce has less formal education than workers in more highly paid occupations. But contrary to the common belief that most low-wage workers lack a high school education, 40 percent have a high school diploma, 38 percent have at least some postsecondary education, and 5 percent have a college degree.

The low-wage labor force overall is better educated today than it was a generation ago. This mirrors the increase in education in the general labor force. The proportion of all workers with at least a college degree, for example, increased from 19 percent to 31 percent between 1979 and 2001. At the same time, the proportion of those without a high school degree fell from one in five to one in ten.

BEYOND THE BASICS — A STEEP HIERARCHY

It is no accident that women and minorities command a disproportionate share of low-paying jobs. Discrimination in the U.S. workplace has historically played a role in excluding them from higher-paying positions. While women and minorities made significant advances in the past generation with the creation of equal pay and equal opportunity legislation in the sixties and seventies, discrimination persists. With the same education, income continues to be lower for nonwhites and women.

Even within the low-wage sector, historically disadvantaged groups occupy the lowest rungs of the system. White males earn more than white females, and white females earn more than both black and Latino males and females with the same skills and jobs. And employers link race and gender with job suitability that locks in this stratification in the low-wage workforce.

So what is the situation for women workers today? Certainly, things have improved. The disparity between men's and women's wages dropped by 15 percent during the past thirty years. Yet women still have lower incomes and are more likely to work in low-wage jobs than men with similar qualifications. Nearly 60 percent of full-time female employees are paid less than $25,000 a year, and nearly 70 percent of the full-time female labor force is in low-paying occupational categories. While women had some success moving to traditionally male jobs in white collar and service occupations, they met with little such success in blue collar jobs including higher paying precision, production, and craft occupations.

Even within the low-wage sector, women are still concentrated in a number of low-status, low-paying jobs that are generally typecast as "female" jobs. Women, for example, make up close to 70 percent of the low-wage salesclerks and service workers. And native-born minority and immigrant women continue to disproportionately hold jobs in private households that are more likely to pay and provide the fewest benefits. This occupational segregation hurts women.

Female-dominated occupations pay less in spite of the fact that female-dominated occupations have more workers with college coursework. Women low-wage workers in general have higher levels of education than their male counterparts. Child-care workers, who are almost all female, make less than animal trainers, who are largely male. And these jobs provide less training and fewer advancement opportunities than male-dominated occupations. Women, in fact, represent 76 percent of the workers in jobs with the fewest advancement opportunities and only 5 percent of those in jobs with the most. It is not surprising that women are less likely to move out of low-earning jobs than men.

And low-wage occupations that employ mostly women have more part-time hours and temporary work than other jobs. Women comprise over 70 percent of the regular part-time workforce that constitute one-fifth of the overall workforce. Beyond regular part-time work, women make up 60 percent of the three million temporary-help industry jobs, including agency temps, direct-hire temps, on-call workers, and day laborers, a majority of which are low-wage.

Women with children face added barriers to getting better jobs. Today, 65 percent of married women with children under the age of six and 75 percent of women with school-age children (ages six to seventeen) work outside the home, triple and double the number, respectively, since 1960. Since 1979, the number of hours worked by couples with children increased by 600 hours, reflecting the overall increase in hours worked by women outside the home.

Despite the dramatic increase in the number of working mothers, the structure of America's workplaces and the family-support systems in place since the fifties have barely changed. Heidi Hartmann and Vicky Lovell with the Institute for Women's Policy Research (a leading research group on women's labor market issues) describe this stagnancy as "imposing an enormous disadvantage on women who wish to combine their labor market and caregiving work." This is in sharp contrast to Western Europe, where family policies such as family leave, child care, government-supported preschools, and increased workplace flexibility were introduced to accommodate the influx of working mothers to the workforce.

American workers get less government support for child care than any other country in the industrialized world, making child-care costs relative to women's earnings higher in the United States. Until passage of the Family and Medical Leave Act in 1993, the United States had no national maternity leave policy. Even now, it is tied with Switzerland in offering the shortest period of leave among the thirty democratic, industrialized nations comprising the Organization for Economic Cooperation and Development. It is one of the only OECD countries that does not offer some amount of pay during that period.

The American workplace is still organized around what American University law professor Joan Williams calls the "ideal worker." This is someone who can work forty hours a week, all year, with required overtime, and take little or no time off for childbearing or child rearing. Women who are still primarily responsible for caregiving and men who have child-care responsibilities cannot live up to this ideal. Instead of changing working conditions to adjust to the new reality, the U.S. workplace treats mothers like men without child-care responsibilities.

But without family-supportive policies and a restructured workplace, women, who continue to bear the primary responsibility for childcare and elder care and are more likely to be custodial single parents, are forced to reduce their work hours, take breaks from employment or avoid jobs that are likely to require work schedules that would clash with their family responsibilities. High-paying jobs in the manufacturing sector, for example, provide few opportunities for part-time or flexible schedules. In fact, many require overtime that essentially excludes most working mothers.

Instead, three-quarters of working-class women must take traditional female jobs that offer more flexible schedules. Yet in doing so they sacrifice pay and benefits and must work more nonstandard hours. One-half of young mothers with less education work evenings or night shifts or on weekends. In a cruel irony, this makes it more difficult to care for their children.

The limited choices mothers face results in what Columbia professor Jane Waldfogel aptly labels the "family gap." While young women without children earn 90 percent of men's wages, mothers earn only 60 percent. The United States has the largest "family gap" among industrialized countries.

Despite these barriers to working mothers, little attention has been focused on the need for change. The long-held assumption that men are the principal breadwinners of families and that spouses are merely providing "pin money" and are somehow less reliant on their wages and benefits still curbs the urgency for reform. This assumption, however, is inconsistent with the facts. Women's incomes are essential to the well-being of low-income families. Women in many married couples are the sole support of the family. In 1993, one out of every five married couples was supported solely by the wife's income, an increase of 14 percent from 1980. Among married couples, women contribute on average one-third of the family income. And women are the sole earners in nearly two-thirds of families maintained by a single person.

Minorities face other obstacles to better-paying jobs. While lower levels of formal education among African Americans and Latinos hamper their prospects, discrimination still plays a large role. Nonwhites with comparable levels of education earn less and are less likely to be working than whites. Within occupational groups, race plays a role in determining job levels and thus factors such as pay, benefits, and the degree of autonomy on the job.

And minorities hold a disproportionate share of the low-wage temporary-help industry jobs with black workers twice as likely to hold these jobs as whites. More than 20 percent of the agency temp workers are black, yet they represent only 12 percent of standard full-time workers and Latinos are twice as likely to be on-call workers than whites.

Hiring discrimination continues to plague inner-city African-American males. Many employers prefer whites, black women, and Latino immigrants to black males. This discrimination excludes them from the "better" jobs frequently found in manufacturing and from suburban jobs where employers serve predominately white clientele. But according to Harry J. Holzer, Georgetown professor of public policy and a leading expert on minority labor market issues, "not all types of employers discriminate equally." Small establishments, a large proportion of the American workplaces, are some of the worse offenders.

Yet it is immigrants who generally work in the lowest rungs of the low-wage workforce. Amendments to the immigration laws in 1965 began a new wave of immigration to the United States, principally from Latin America, the West Indies, and Asia. Between 1970 and 1996, the number of foreign-born increased by fifteen million, rising from 4.8 percent to 9.3 percent of the U.S. population. By the mid-eighties, 600,000 new immigrants were coming into this country each year. And today, one out of every five children in the United States lives in an immigrant family.

This increase in the immigrant population had a significant effect on the workforce. Between 1996 and 1999 alone, the number of foreign-born workers employed in the labor force increased 17 percent from 13.4 million to more than 15.7 million. Three-quarters of these immigrants live in six states: California, New York, Texas, Florida, New Jersey, and Illinois. In California, over 30 percent of the working-age population is foreign-born. And these figures do not include the eight to nine million undocumented workers that the 2000 census suggests are currently in the United States.

These new immigrants work in a wide array of jobs, but they are more likely than natives to work in the harshest jobs in the low-wage workforce. Forty-three percent of foreign-born workers were employed in low-wage jobs in 1997. The economic gap between today's immigrants and native-born workers is three times larger than it was during the last major wave of immigration at the turn of the century. Male immigrants today typically earn only 77 percent of what natives earn, with Mexican-born men earning less than half.

Immigrants are more likely than natives to be food-preparation workers, sewing machine operators, parking lot attendants, housekeepers, waiters, private-household cleaners, food processing workers, agricultural workers, elevator operators and janitors, operators, fabricators, and laborers. Almost half of all housekeepers are immigrants. In states where there are large immigrant populations, such as California and New York, three out of four textile workers are immigrants. These occupations have the greatest number of jobs that pay below $8.50 per hour. Few of their employers provide health insurance, pension plans, sick leave or family leave, and these jobs have the least advancement possibilities. One in three Latinos, for example, are not insured through their employers.

Immigrants are funneled into some of the most hazardous and unhealthy jobs, such as roofing, trench digging, and carrying heavy materials. Latino immigrants, for example, die from workplace injuries at a 20 percent higher rate than either blacks or whites. And the lack of training and instruction in their native language on safety and health in these hazardous workplaces aggravates this situation.

Certainly, English-language proficiency and educational barriers play a part in limiting immigrant job options, especially for a notable proportion of Latino immigrants. Only half the Mexican immigrants have attended secondary school, and only one-third have graduated. This minimal education prevents many immigrant workers from gaining certain higher-paying positions. And the lack of English proficiency disqualifies them from jobs that require reading or communication skills.

But there is a more pernicious reason why immigrants face the most abysmal conditions—their vulnerability. Immigrants are less likely to know their rights, and undocumented workers fear deportation if they complain about workforce abuse. Some employers, in fact, illegally recruit undocumented workers. As University of Missouri sociologist William Heffernan, who studies the meat processing industry, notes, "This has been around for a long time in the meat processing industry. Employers can take advantage of these people because they can threaten to send them back."

This same exploitive strategy occurs in other industries. A 1998 Department of Labor study determined that two-thirds of Los Angeles and three-quarters of New York garment factories that employ a large proportion of immigrants violated wage laws. Many undocumented workers were working forty-eight hours and making $180 per week. These conditions have been largely ignored, leaving immigrants in the worst and most abusive jobs.

* * *

Workers with less education find it difficult to find quality jobs in the United States. Yet, in spite of an increase in white males into the lower end of the labor market, there still exists a caste-like system with women, minorities, and immigrants at the bottom of this labor force. They face this situation with little ability to provide for their families and with little hope of movement in a society that practically worships the concept of social mobility. Who does this hurt? Certainly the workers. But there are other consequences to these workers' children, our society, and to all of us standing by.

Chapter 6
Health Care

The health care system in the United States is one of the most technologically advanced in the world. People come to the United States from other countries because the level of care available here is state-of-the-art—if they have the means to afford it. Indeed, health care in this country is rationed by ability to pay. For people in the upper class, access to health care is virtually unlimited; however, about 46 million people are uninsured and thus left with little or no health care. Access is not the only important factor when it comes to health care. Patients must also have the means and education to institute the changes recommended by medical professionals, and they must be able to afford the medications, therapy, and diet changes that frequently accompany a medical diagnosis. The ability to make changes, to buy medications, and to make healthy choices is fundamentally determined by one's location in the class system.

In "Life at the Top in America Isn't Just Better, It's Longer," Janny Scott (2005) of the *New York Times* followed three individuals through their experiences with heart attacks. At the two extremes were an upper-class male patient, Jean Miele, and a lower-class female patient, Ewa Gora. The differences in their experiences were apparent from the very start. As soon as Miele began experiencing symptoms, his friends insisted that they call an ambulance. Gora, on the other hand, waited for hours thinking the pain would go away. Miele got immediate attention, including angioplasty within minutes of his heart attack, whereas Gora was given drugs and told to schedule an angiogram that she later cancelled.

Miele had a social network that supported healthy lifestyle changes, had access to a nearby facility for exercising and the time to use it, and was financially able to decrease his work load; he could also avail himself of the healthy meals cooked by his wife, who adopted changes into her own life. In addition, Miele was on an equal social footing with the medical professionals caring for him and could engage in decisions about his health more as a peer than as a subordinate. Gora, by contrast, could give up work only temporarily and lacked a social network that supported dietary changes. Moreover, her social status affected her interactions with medical care personnel, and her limited educational background affected her ability to comprehend her medical situation.

The complexities involved in health and in people's access to health care are epitomized in these two experiences. Lifestyle variations between the classes, largely a function of education and opportunity, play a part in both health and health care. Clearly, access to medical care, the ability to communicate effectively with health care providers, and the opportunity to institute lifestyle changes are affected by social class. This is true even of a physician's willingness to recommend procedures, medicines, and lifestyle changes, as this is motivated largely by the doctor's perception that patients will (1) understand and (2) follow through on his or her recommendations.

Previous discussions in this book addressed the growing inequality gap—a gap that is equally important in health care. Indeed, to an increasing extent upper-class individuals are living longer and better lives than lower-class individuals (Scott, 2005). The readings in this section note the manifest ways in which social class affects health care.

REFERENCES

Scott, Janny. 2005. "Class Matters: Life at the Top in America Isn't Just Better, It's Longer," *New York Times*. Available online at http://www.nytimes.com/2005/05/16/national/class/HEALTH-INAL.html?ex=1144900800&en=9b8e4e9a1f850910&ei=5070.

13. As the Rich Get Richer, Do People Get Sicker?
Researchers Debate Whether Income Inequality Impairs Public Health

Lila Guterman

Robin Hood is alive and well in academe, in the form of an epidemiologist who works on the outskirts of Sherwood Forest.

Richard G. Wilkinson, a professor at the University of Nottingham, in England, took up the brigand's cloak 11 years ago when he reported that public health suffers where large gaps exist between rich and poor. In a study of nine developed countries—Australia, Canada, the United States, and six nations in Western Europe—Mr. Wilkinson found that on average, people in nations with great economic disparities, such as Britain, died younger than did those in more uniform societies, like Sweden. To improve overall health, he suggested, take money from the rich and give it to the poor.

That result sparked a flurry of research on the link between income inequality and health. Studies in the United States by other health specialists added ammunition to Mr. Wilkinson's theory by showing that among the states, the larger the gap between rich and poor, the higher the mortality rate.

But a volley of opposing fire has rained down of late on the band of researchers who link income gaps with poor health. Critics in economics as well as epidemiology argue that many of the initial health studies were flawed, and that their originators identify trends that don't exist so that they can advocate gallantly for income redistribution. The academic Robin Hoods fight back, charging that their critics are motivated by conservative politics favoring the wealthy.

"People can always explain why they think that somebody else's results are anomalous," says Mr. Wilkinson.

Neither Well Nor Well Off

Researchers have known for decades that health depends in no small part on wealth—in general, the richer people are, the longer they will live. The reasons are intuitive: Money can buy adequate food, clean water, and good health care.

But the advantages of wealth level off among the richest countries. The citizens of the United States have some of the highest incomes in the world, but in 1999, they ranked 18th in life expectancy of the 28 countries in the Organization for Economic Cooperation and Development, or OECD.

Mr. Wilkinson and others have argued that once countries reach a threshold above dire poverty, economic growth may stop fueling improvements in health. In a 1992 study published in the *British Medical Journal*, Mr. Wilkinson reported that the gap between rich and poor in many countries affected life expectancy even more than did absolute income.

"The implications of Wilkinson's theory for economic goals could hardly be more radical," wrote Ichiro Kawachi and Bruce P. Kennedy in *The Health of Nations: Why Inequality Is Harmful to Your Health* (The New Press, 2002). "If people wish to lead longer and healthier lives, then their governments had better start paying attention to a fairer distribution of the national product."

These two faculty members at the Harvard School of Public Health have joined the researchers following Mr. Wilkinson's lead. Along with their colleague Deborah Prothrow-Stith, Dr. Kawachi and Mr. Kennedy compared mortality rates across the United States and linked them to a characteristic that economists use called the Robin Hood index (see figure 6.1). The index approximates the proportion of income that would have to be taken from the richer half of the population and given to the poorer half to balance the distribution of wealth. In

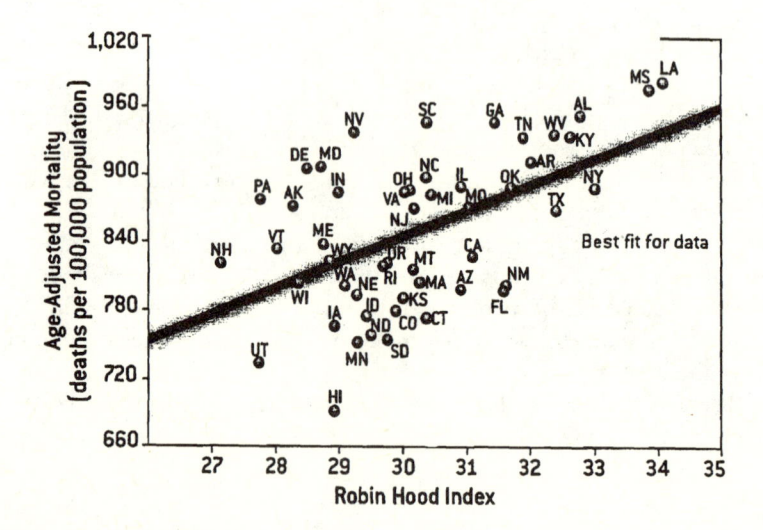

Figure 6.1

Robin Hood Index is a measure of income inequality; it is the percentage of total community income that must be taken from the rich (those with above-average incomes) and given to the poor (those below the average) to achieve an equal distribution. U.S. states with a high Robin Hood index also tend to have high mortality rates.

data from the U.S. census of 1990, the index varied from 27.13 percent in New Hampshire, the most equitable state, to 34.05 percent in Louisiana.

The researchers reported in the *British Medical Journal* in 1996 a strong correlation between the Robin Hood index and mortality—the more unequal a state's wealth distribution, the more likely its citizens were to die early. A larger Robin Hood index tracked with higher rates of coronary heart disease, cancer, and homicide.

The researchers did not determine whether income disparity, like pollution, harms people's health whatever their status, or simply takes such a toll on poor people's health that the overall average falls.

In the same issue of the journal, another group of researchers reported similar results. George A. Kaplan and John Lynch, both now in the epidemiology department at the University of Michigan at Ann Arbor, led a group that measured the wealth gap by calculating the percentage of total income earned by the poorer half of the population in each of the 50 states.

Like the Harvard team, they found that income inequality closely paralleled mortality rates as well as rates of low birth weight, homicide, violent crime, and smoking. They also found that as income inequality increased, so did rates of unemployment, imprisonment, lack of medical insurance, and low educational status.

"We showed that the states that had the highest levels of income inequality had the smallest proportion of their budget spent on education and had the fewest number of books per capita in public libraries," says Mr. Kaplan.

Library books may partly explain why Robin Hood's methods could improve public health. Countries and states vary greatly in how much they invest in social services, Mr. Kaplan says, and the differences reflect a gap in wages. Both states and countries with big disparities, he says, are unlikely to invest in services like public transportation, education, environmental protection, and publicly financed health care. To Mr. Kaplan, inequality serves as a marker for a cluster of conditions that affect health.

But some researchers, including Mr. Wilkinson, think that inequality harms people's health directly, through psychosocial processes. "Wide income distributions create social prejudices and ideas of superiority and inferiority, dominance and subordination," he says. As a result, he argues, inequality weakens social trust and increases stress and violence.

Clyde Hertzman, a professor of health care and epidemiology at the University of British Columbia, agrees that psychosocial processes play a major role in a link between inequality and mortality. "Life experience influences the way in which the human body defends itself against disease," he says.

CRUNCHING THE NUMBERS

The vagueness of those kinds of statements, however, makes researchers like Jennifer M. Mellor cringe.

"One might observe an influence of income inequality on mortality rates," says Ms. Mellor, an assistant professor of economics at the College of William and Mary, "but that could be due to something else."

The true cause could have been obscured by the way the studies were done, say Ms. Mellor and Jeffrey Milyo, an assistant professor at the University of Chicago's Harris School of Public Policy. Many of the studies that reported links between income inequality and mortality failed to control for individual characteristics like income, education, and race, they say. Without controlling for individual income, for instance, studies may simply reflect a connection between an area's having large numbers of poor people and its high mortality rates. When individual characteristics are taken into account, the link to the earnings gap often disappears, Ms. Mellor and Mr. Milyo say.

"Income inequality does not have its own independent effect on health," says Ms. Mellor.

Mr. Milyo makes an even sharper attack on the Robin Hood research: "Being able to argue there's a connection between inequality and public health is pleasing for ideological reasons, and therefore [some researchers] lower the standard of evidence that they require to support that hypothesis."

The two researchers decided to test the hypothesis themselves. If the wealth gap harms health, they reckoned, then mortality records should reflect changes in that gap over time. But they found no such changes in mortality rates in American data over 10- and 20-year periods from 1950 to 1990, a time of growing distance between rich and poor.

Dr. Kawachi shrugs off their study and many of their criticisms. "We don't fully understand the lag period between inequality and subsequent health," he says. Other variables, such as changes in medical technology, affect life expectancy and could hide the effects of changing income inequality over time, he says.

He shoots back at Mr. Milyo and Ms. Mellor, saying that many studies have, indeed, controlled for individual characteristics and still found a link between inequality and health, particularly in the United States. "The only ones that haven't are Milyo and Mellor's," he says. "They overcontrol."

For instance, controlling for education makes little sense, he says, because that variable could lie on the pathway linking inequality to health: States with high inequality could invest less in education, which then might result in citizens' not going to college, making less money, and consequently suffering more disease while having less access to health care.

Dr. Kawachi says of Mr. Milyo, "He's doing a form of analysis that's almost guaranteed to produce a null result. He's got some kind of mission to find that there's nothing going on."

Dr. Hertzman, of British Columbia, charges that the critics' mission is political, not scientific: "People simply don't want to see these kinds of ideas gain currency, because they drive society in a direction that people don't want to see it go."

SHOOTING THE GAP

But even the staunchest believers in the Robin Hood hypothesis admit that some criticisms have hit the target. Mr. Wilkinson's original study, for instance, has come under attack. Other studies, which controlled for individual income, included additional European countries, or looked at the same countries' data 10 years later, found no significant link between wealth inequality and life expectancy. And the results of studies that control for individual income have been mixed, with no link found in many countries.

Researchers take very different views of those results and have even come to opposite conclusions based on analyses of the same data. Dr. Kawachi says some studies failed because they looked for the trend in areas within countries like Japan, Denmark, and New Zealand, which are more equitable over all than the United States. He posits that there may be some threshold level of inequality below which a country's social systems may blunt the income gap's effects. He proposes that more studies should be done on highly unequal countries, such as Chile, where he has recently found that greater inequality correlates with poor health across 285 geographical communities.

But Mr. Lynch, of Michigan, says he has had a change of heart since conducting some of the studies that link income inequality to mortality in the United States. "I suppose you'd say I was a believer," he says, but now "I don't think the evidence is very solid."

Part of the problem, he says, is that—with the exception of the studies of the 50 states, which he considers strong—many studies make comparisons among only a few regions. "Tiny shifts in one or two [data points] can generate, or not generate, correlations," he says. "That's not the kind of robust finding we'd like to be building health policy on." Income inequality, he acknowledges, may affect public health in some circumstances, but he doubts that such a trend will prove general.

His colleague, Mr. Kaplan, takes a more favorable view of the Robin Hood hypothesis but also believes that inequality takes on more importance in some places and times than in others. "This isn't a relationship that is cast in stone," he says. "I think there's still evidence to believe there's a relationship in the U.S. It hasn't been looked at as extensively in other countries."

"Whether or not the notion ends up being a viable one," he adds, "the take-home message to me has always been that ... as you change the economic conditions under which people live, as you change the social arrangements that make life easier or harder, you also see changes in the health of the overall population."

Whatever their point of view, researchers can test their theories on natural socioeconomic experiments taking place in countries where the income disparity is changing.

In the United States, for instance, the gap grew between 1970 and 2001 as the richest 5 percent of households increased their average income from around $33,300 to $260,500, at the same time that the average income earned by the poorest 20 percent of households increased from $2,000 to $10,100.

If continuing research proves the Robin Hood theory to be true, its proponents may still enjoy only a hollow victory—the findings seem to have had little effect on public policy in the United States. "I'm afraid my research has the perfect negative correlation with policy outcomes," says Dr. Kawachi. "We publish something, and the direction of the country goes exactly the other way."

14. Sick of Poverty
Robert Sapolsky

Rudolph Virchow, the 19th-century German neuroscientist, physician and political activist, came of age with two dramatic events—a typhoid outbreak in 1847 and the failed revolutions of 1848. Out of those experiences came two insights for him: first, that the spread of disease has much to do with appalling living conditions, and second, that those in power have enormous means to subjugate the powerless. As Virchow summarized in his famous epigram, "Physicians are the natural attorneys of the poor."

Physicians (and biomedical scientists) are advocates of the underprivileged because poverty and poor health tend to go hand in hand. Poverty means bad or insufficient food, unhealthy living conditions and endless other factors that lead to illness. Yet it is not merely that poor people tend to be unhealthy while everyone else is well. When you examine socioeconomic status (SES), a composite measure that includes income, occupation, education and housing conditions, it becomes clear that, starting with the wealthiest stratum of society, every step downward in SES correlates with poorer health.

This "SES gradient" has been documented throughout Westernized societies for problems that include respiratory and cardiovascular diseases, ulcers, rheumatoid disorders, psychiatric diseases and a number of cancers. It is not a subtle statistical phenomenon. When you compare the highest versus the lowest rungs of the SES ladder, the risk of some diseases varies 10–fold. Some countries exhibit a five- to 10-year difference in life expectancy across the SES spectrum. Of the Western nations, the U.S. has the steepest gradient; for example, one study showed that the poorest white males in America die about a decade earlier than the richest.

So what causes this correlation between SES and health? Lower SES may give rise to poorer health, but conversely, poorer health could also give rise to lower SES. After all, chronic illness can compromise one's education and work productivity, in addition to generating enormous expenses.

Nevertheless, the bulk of the facts suggests that the arrow goes from economic status to health—that SES at some point in life predicts health measures later on. Among the many demonstrations of this point is a remarkable study of elderly American nuns. All had taken their vows as young adults and had spent many years thereafter sharing diet, health care and housing, thereby controlling for those lifestyle factors. Yet in their old age, patterns of disease, incidence of dementia and longevity were still significantly predicted by their SES status from when they became nuns, at least half a century before.

INADEQUATE EXPLANATIONS

So, to use a marvelous phrase common to this field, how does SES get "under the skin" and influence health? The answers that seem most obvious, it turns out, do not hold much water. One such explanation, for instance, posits that for the poor, health care may be less easily accessible and of lower quality. This possibility is plausible when one considers that for many of the poor in America, the family physician does not exist, and medical care consists solely of trips to the emergency room.

But that explanation soon falls by the wayside, for reasons made clearest in the famed Whitehall studies by Michael G. Marmot of University College London over the past three decades. Marmot and his colleagues have documented an array of dramatic SES gradients in a conveniently stratified population, namely, the members of the British civil service (ranging from blue-collar workers to high-powered executives). Office messengers and porters, for example, have far higher mortality rates from chronic heart disease than administrators and professionals do. Lack of access to medical attention cannot explain the phenomenon, because the U.K., unlike the U.S., has universal health care. Similar SES gradients also occur in other countries with socialized medicine, including the health care Edens of Scandinavia, and the differences remain significant even after researchers factor in how much the subjects actually use the medical services.

Another telling finding is that SES gradients exist for diseases for which health care access is irrelevant. No amount of medical checkups, blood tests and scans will change the likelihood of someone getting type 1 (juvenile-onset) diabetes or rheumatoid arthritis, yet both conditions are more common among the poor.

The next "obvious" explanation centers on unhealthy lifestyles. As you descend the SES ladder in Westernized societies, people are more likely to smoke, to drink excessively, to be obese, and to live in a violent or polluted or densely populated neighborhood. Poor people are also less likely to have access to clean water, healthy food and health clubs, not to mention adequate heat in the winter and air conditioning in the summer. Thus, it seems self-evident that lower SES gets under the skin by increasing risks and decreasing protective factors. As mordantly stated by Robert G. Evans of the University of British Columbia, "Drinking sewage is probably unwise, even for Bill Gates."

What is surprising, though, is how little of the SES gradient these risk and protective factors explain. In the Whitehall studies, controlling for factors such as smoking and level of exercise accounted for only about a third of the gradient. This same point is made by studies comparing health and wealth among, rather than within, nations. It is reasonable to assume that the wealthier a country, the more financial resources its citizens have to buy protection and avoid risk. If so, health should improve incrementally as one moves up the wealth gradient among nations, as well as among the citizens within individual nations. But it does not. Instead, among the wealthiest quarter of countries on earth, there is no relation between a country's wealth and the health of its people.

Thus, health care access, health care utilization, and exposure to risk and protective factors explain the SES/health gradient far less well than one might have guessed. One must therefore consider whether most of the gradient arises from a different set of considerations: the psychosocial consequences of SES.

Psychosocial Stress

Ideally, the body is in homeostatic balance, a state in which the vital measures of human function—heart rate, blood pressure, blood sugar levels and so on—are in their optimal ranges. A stressor is anything that threatens to disrupt homeostasis. For most organisms, a stressor is an acute physical challenge—for example, the need for an injured gazelle to sprint for its life or for a hungry predator to chase down a meal. The body is superbly adapted to dealing with short-term physical challenges to homeostasis. Stores of energy, including the sugar glucose, are released, and cardiovascular tone increases to facilitate the delivery of fuel to exercising muscle throughout the body. Digestion, growth, tissue repair, reproduction and other physiological processes not needed to survive the crisis are suppressed. The immune system steps up to thwart opportunistic pathogens. Memory and the senses transiently sharpen.

But cognitively and socially sophisticated species, such as we primates, routinely inhabit a different realm of stress. For us, most stressors concern interactions with our own species, and few physically disrupt homeostasis. Instead these psychosocial stressors involve the anticipation (accurate or otherwise) of an impending challenge. And the striking characteristic of such psychological and social stress is its chronicity. For most mammals, a stressor lasts only a few minutes. In contrast, we humans can worry chronically over a 30-year mortgage.

Unfortunately, our body's response, though adaptive for an acute physical stressor, is pathogenic for prolonged psychosocial stress. Chronic increase in cardiovascular tone brings stress-induced hypertension. The constant mobilization of energy increases the risk or severity of diseases such as type 2 (adult-onset) diabetes. The prolonged inhibition of digestion, growth, tissue repair and reproduction increases the risks of various gastrointestinal disorders, impaired growth in children, failure to ovulate in females and erectile dysfunction in males. A too-extended immune stress response ultimately suppresses immunity and impairs disease defenses. And chronic activation of the stress response impairs cognition, as well as the health, functioning and even survival of some types of neurons.

An extensive biomedical literature has established that individuals are more likely to activate a stress response and are more at risk for a stress-sensitive disease if they (a) feel as if they have minimal *control* over stressors, (b) feel as if they have no *predictive information* about the duration and intensity of the stressor, (c) have few *outlets* for the frustration caused by the stressor, (d) interpret the stressor as evidence of circumstances *worsening,* and (e) lack *social support* for the duress caused by the stressors.

Psychosocial stressors are not evenly distributed across society. Just as the poor have a disproportionate share of physical stressors (hunger, manual labor, chronic sleep deprivation with a second job, the bad mattress that can't be replaced), they have a disproportionate share of psychosocial ones. Numbing assembly line work and an occupational lifetime spent taking orders erode workers' sense of control. Unreliable cars that may not start in the morning and paychecks that may not last the month inflict unpredictability. Poverty rarely allows stress-relieving options such as health club memberships, costly but relaxing hobbies, or sabbaticals for rethinking one's priorities. And despite the heartwarming stereotype of the "poor but loving community," the working poor typically have less social support than the middle and upper classes, thanks to the extra jobs, the long commutes on public transit, and other burdens.

Marmot has shown that regardless of SES, the less autonomy one has at work, the worse one's cardiovascular health. Furthermore, low control in the workplace accounts for about half the SES gradient in cardiovascular disease in his Whitehall population.

Feeling Poor

Three lines of research provide more support for the influence of psychological stress on SES-related health gradients. Over the past decade Nancy E. Adler of the University of California, San Francisco, has explored the difference between objective and subjective SES and the relation of each to health. Test subjects were shown a simple diagram of a ladder with 10 rungs and then asked, "In society, where on this ladder would you rank yourself in terms of how well you're doing?" The very openness of the question allowed the person to define the comparison group that felt most emotionally salient.

As Adler has shown, a person's subjective assessment of his or her SES takes into account the usual objective measures (education, income, occupation and residence) as well as measures of life satisfaction and of anxiety about the future. Adler's provocative finding is that subjective SES is at least as good as objective SES at predicting patterns of cardiovascular function, measures of metabolism, incidences of obesity and levels of stress hormones—suggesting that the subjective feelings may help explain the objective results.

This same point emerges from comparisons of the SES/health gradient among nations. A relatively poor person in the U.S. may objectively have more financial resources to purchase health care and protective factors than a relatively wealthy person in a less developed country yet, on average, will still have a shorter life expectancy. For example, as Stephen Bezruchka of the University of Washington emphasizes, people in Greece on average earn half the income of Americans yet have a longer life expectancy. Once the minimal resources are available to sustain a basic level of health through adequate food and housing, absolute levels of income are of remarkably little importance to health. Although Adler's work suggests that the objective state of *being* poor adversely affects health, at the core of that result is the subjective state of *feeling* poor.

Being Made to Feel Poor

Another body of research arguing that psychosocial factors mediate most of the SES/health gradient comes from Richard Wilkinson of the University of Nottingham in England. Over the past 15 years he and his colleagues have reported that the extent of income inequality in a community is even more predictive than SES for an array of health measures. In other words, absolute levels of income aside, greater disparities in income between the poorest and the wealthiest in a community predict worse average health. (David H. Abbott of the Wisconsin National Primate Research Center and I, along with our colleagues, found a roughly equivalent phenomenon in animals: among many nonhuman primate species, less egalitarian social structures correlate with higher resting levels of a key stress hormone—an index for worse health—among socially subordinate animals.)

Wilkinson's subtle and critical finding has generated considerable controversy. One dispute concerns its generality. His original work suggested that income inequality was relevant to health in many European and North American countries and communities. It has become clear, however, that this relation holds only in the developed country with the greatest of income inequalities, namely, the U.S.

Whether considered at the level of cities or states, income inequality predicts mortality rates across nearly all ages in the U.S. Why, though, is this relation not observed in, say, Canada or Denmark? One possibility is that these countries have too little income variability to tease out the correlation.

Some critics have questioned whether the linkage between income inequality and worse health is merely a mathematical quirk. The relation between SES and health follows an asymptotic curve: dropping from the uppermost rung of society's ladder to the next-to-top step reduces life expectancy and other measures much less drastically than plunging from the next-to-bottom rung to the lowest level. Because a community with high levels of income inequality will have a relatively high number of individuals at the very bottom, where health prospects are so dismal, the community's average life expectancy will inevitably be lower than that of an egalitarian community, for reasons that have nothing to do with psychosocial factors. Wilkinson has shown, however, that decreased income inequality predicts better health for both the poor and the wealthy. This result strongly indicates that the association between illness and inequality is more than just a mathematical artifact.

Wilkinson and others in the field have long argued that the more unequal income in a community is, the more psychosocial stress there will be for the poor. Higher income inequality intensifies a community's hierarchy and makes social support less available: truly symmetrical, reciprocal, affiliative support exists only among equals. Moreover, having your nose rubbed in your poverty is likely to lessen your sense of control in life, to aggravate the frustrations of poverty and to intensify the sense of life worsening.

If Adler's work demonstrates the adverse health effects of feeling poor, Wilkinson's income inequality work suggests that the surest way to feel poor is to be *made* to feel poor—to be endlessly made aware of the haves when you are a have-not. And in our global village, we are constantly made aware of the moguls and celebrities whose resources dwarf ours.

John W. Lynch and George A. Kaplan of the University of Michigan at Ann Arbor have recently proposed another way that people are made to feel poor. Their "neomaterialist" interpretation of the income inequality phenomenon—which is subtle, reasonable and, ultimately, deeply depressing—runs as follows: Spending money on public goods (better public transit, universal health care and so on) is a way to improve the quality of life for the average person. But by definition, the bigger the income inequality in a society, the greater the financial distance between the average and the wealthy. The bigger this distance, the less the wealthy have to gain from expenditures on the public good. Instead they would benefit more from keeping their tax money to spend on their private good—a better chauffeur, a gated community, bottled water, private schools, private health insurance. So the more unequal the income is in a community, the more incentive the wealthy will have to oppose public expenditures benefiting the health of the community. And within the U.S., the more income inequality there is, the more power will be disproportionately in the hands of the wealthy to oppose such public expenditures. According to health economist Evans, this scenario ultimately leads to "private affluence and public squalor."

This "secession of the wealthy" can worsen the SES/health gradient in two ways: by aggravating the conditions in low-income communities (which account for at least part of the increased health risks for the poor) and by adding to the psychosocial stressors. If social and psychological stressors are entwined with feeling poor, and even more so with feeling poor while being confronted with the wealthy, they will be even more stressful when the wealthy are striving to decrease the goods and services available to the poor.

SOCIAL CAPITAL

A third branch of support for psychosocial explanations for the relation between income inequality and health comes from the work of Ichiro Kawachi of Harvard University, based on the concept of "social capital." Although it is still being refined as a measure, social capital refers to the broad levels of trust and efficacy in a community. Do people generally trust one another and help one another out? Do people feel an incentive to take care of commonly held resources (for example, to clean up graffiti in public parks)? And do people feel that their organizations—such as unions or tenant associations—actually have an impact? Most studies of social capital employ two simple measures, namely, how many organizations people belong to and how people answer a question such as, "Do you think most people would try to take advantage of you if they got a chance?"

What Kawachi and others have shown is that at the levels of states, provinces, cities and neighborhoods, low social capital predicts bad health, bad self-reported health and high mortality rates. Using a complex statistical technique called path analysis, Kawachi has demonstrated that (once one controls for the effects of absolute income) the strongest route from income inequality to poor health is through the social capital measures—to wit, high degrees of income inequality come with low levels of trust and support, which increases stress and harms health.

None of this is surprising. As a culture, America has neglected its social safety nets while making it easier for the most successful to sit atop the pyramids of inequality. Moreover, we have chosen to forgo the social capital that comes from small, stable communities in exchange for unprecedented opportunities for mobility and anonymity. As a result, all measures of social epidemiology are worsening in the U.S. Of Westernized nations, America has the greatest income inequality (40 percent of the wealth is controlled by 1 percent of the population) and the greatest discrepancy between expenditures on health care (number one in the world) and life expectancy (as of 2003, number 29).

The importance of psychosocial factors in explaining the SES/health gradient generates a critical conclusion: when it comes to health, there is far more to poverty than simply not having enough money. (As Evans once stated, "Most graduate students have had the experience of having very little money, but not of poverty. They are very different things.") The psychosocial school has occasionally been accused of promulgating an antiprogressive message: don't bother with universal health care, affordable medicines and other salutary measures because there will still be a robust SES/health gradient after all the reforms. But the lesson of this research is not to abandon such societal change. It is that so much more is needed.

Note

Robert Sapolsky is professor of biological sciences, neurology and neurological sciences at Stanford University and a research associate at the National Museums of Kenya. In his laboratory work, he focuses on how stress can damage the brain and on gene therapy for the nervous system. In addition, he studies populations of wild baboons in East Africa, trying to determine the relation between the social rank of a baboon and its health. His latest book is *Monkeyluv and Other Essays on Our Lives as Animals* (Scribner, 2005).

Chapter 7
Education

Education is one of the most important aspects of social mobility, and it affects children from a very early age. Evidence suggests that children who are read to in early childhood tend to be more successful as they move through the educational system. It has therefore been recommended that parents read to children, buy children's books, and provide an atmosphere that supports learning. Many factors, however, can affect a parent's ability to provide that atmosphere. For example, parents' educational background, working more than one job, doing shift work, and being a single parent can affect whether, or how much, a child is exposed to books. Attending preschool is another alternative that gives advantages to children, but preschools are expensive and only 60 percent of those eligible for Head Start receive the benefits of this program for the poor. A good start on education, however, is only one issue affecting education.

Differences in educational attainment arise as a consequence of the social class of the neighborhood where the school is located. Schools in poor districts are more likely to be in unsafe neighborhoods and may fall prey to a bevy of environmental factors that affect student learning. Evidence from Louisiana (Mielke, Berry, Mielke, Powell, and Gonzales, 2005) suggests that school performance on standardized examinations mandated by the "No Child Left Behind" policy varies as a function of environmental factors. Specifically, researchers found a strong positive association between heavy-metal contamination in soils surrounding neighborhood schools and performance on standardized exams. Not surprisingly, the areas with the most contaminated soils were the low-income neighborhoods. This research focuses on factors affecting low-income neighborhoods that usually do not enter into policy considerations and are often off the radar screen when it comes to discussing issues of class.

Schools in poor neighborhoods, when compared to those in more affluent neighborhoods, tend to have less competent teachers, more crowded classrooms, and fewer teaching resources. In many cases, by the time poor students reach high school, they are years behind their affluent counterparts; in addition, they are less likely to complete high school. Yet high school graduation is one of the most important predictors for one's future success—and social class is a factor affecting whether a student will graduate. Data collected by the U.S. Department of Education (2000) reveal that 28.9 percent of students in the bottom quintile drop out of school before high school graduation, compared to only 9.9 percent of students from the top quintile. The lack of a high school diploma profoundly affects life chances later. For instance, yearly median income for twenty-five-year-olds without a high school degree is $15,334—a figure that, for high school graduates, is nearly doubled at $29,294 a year (Greene, 2002).

For those who do complete high school, social networks coupled with educational background affect their chances of going on to college. In affluent high schools, students are more likely to talk about *where* they will go to college, not *if* they will go to college. Indeed, among students in poor neighborhoods, the discussion is more likely to focus on the necessity of getting a job than on attending college. Such students may choose work over college because their families need financial help, because they see a job as a means of escaping a depressing situation, or because they cannot afford college without earning money for tuition. In the latter case, the students may talk about going to college when they can afford it but then become trapped in the low-wage game of living paycheck to paycheck.

In addition, college is expensive. There was a period in the United States when low-income individuals had access to grants to provide for college tuition payments, but budget cuts and changes in policies have affected the number and types of grants available. A study reported in *USA Today* (2004) found that 66 percent of students in the highest-income quartile enroll in college within two years of high school graduation, compared to only 20 percent of students in the bottom quartile. Moreover, high-income students are six times likelier than low-income students to earn a bachelor's degree within five years. The study attributes these differences to the fact that members of the lower classes lack financial help and receive poor academic preparation in the K–12 system.

Schools of higher education are stratified according to cost, prestige, and resources. For the most part, students from the lower classes who do go to college attend community colleges, those from the middle class attend state colleges and universities, and those from the upper class attend elite private universities. Among students attending the most prestigious 146 colleges, 75 percent are from affluent families while only 3 percent are from the poorest segment (reported in *USA Today,* 2004). The specific college one attends further affects work opportunities and networking possibilities. The higher the status of the college, the more prospects are afforded its graduates. The first reading in this section argues that schools seeking to close the achievement gap between black and white students must take into account the social class characteristics that influence student learning. The second reading demonstrates how college admission requirements are skewed in favor of affluent children.

References

Greene, Jay P. 2002. "High School Graduation Rates in the United States," Manhattan Institute for Policy Research. Available online at http://www.manhattan-institute.org/html/cr_baeo.htm.

Mielke, Howard W., Kenneth J. Berry, Paul W. Mielke, Eric T. Powell, and Christopher R. Gonzales. 2005. "Multiple Metal Accumulation as a Factor in Learning Achievement Within Various New Orleans Elementary School Communities," *Environmental Research* 97: 67–75.

USA Today. 2004. "Low-Income College Students Are Increasingly Left Behind" (January 14). Available online at http://www.usatoday.com/news/education/2004-01-14-low-income-students_x.htm.

U.S. Department of Education. 2000. "Event Dropout Rates and Number and Distribution of 15- Through 24-Year-Olds Who Dropped Out of Grades 10–12, by Background Characteristics: October 2000." Available online at http://nces.ed.gov/pubs2002/droppub_2001/tables/table1.asp.

15. A Wider Lens on the Black-White Achievement Gap

Richard Rothstein

The fiftieth anniversary of the Supreme Court's school desegregation order in *Brown v. Board of Education* has intensified public awareness of the persistent gap in academic achievement between black students and white students. The black-white gap is made up partly of the difference between the achievement of all lower-class students and that of middle-class students, but there is an additional gap between black students and white students—even when the blacks and whites come from families with similar incomes.

The American public and its political leaders, along with professional educators, have frequently vowed to close these gaps. Americans believe in the ideal of equal opportunity, and they also believe that the best way to ensure that opportunity is to enable all children, regardless of their parents' stations, to leave school with skills that position them to compete fairly and productively in the nation's democratic governance and occupational structure. The fact that children's skills can so clearly be predicted by their race and family economic status is a direct challenge to our democratic ideals.

Policy makers almost universally conclude that these existing and persistent achievement gaps must be the result of wrongly designed school policies—either expectations that are too low, teachers who are insufficiently qualified, curricula that are badly designed, classes that are too large, school climates that are too undisciplined, leadership that is too unfocused, or a combination of these factors.

Americans have come to the conclusion that the achievement gap is the fault of "failing schools" because common sense seems to dictate that it could not be otherwise. After all, how much money a family has or the color of a child's skin should not influence how well that child learns to read. If teachers know how to teach reading—or math or any other subject—and if schools emphasize the importance of these tasks and permit no distractions, children should be able to learn these subjects, whatever their family income or skin color.

This commonsense perspective, however, is misleading and dangerous. It ignores how social-class characteristics in a stratified society such as ours may actually influence learning in school. It confuses social class, a concept that Americans have historically been loath to consider, with two of its characteristics: income and, in the U.S., race. For it is true that low income and skin color themselves don't influence academic achievement, but the collection of characteristics that define social-class differences inevitably influences that achievement.

SOCIAL CLASS AND ITS IMPACT ON LEARNING

Distinctly different child-rearing patterns are one mechanism through which class differences affect the academic performance of children. For example, parents of different social classes often have different ways of disciplining their children, different ways of communicating expectations, and even different ways of reading to their children. These differences do not express themselves consistently or in the case of every family; rather, they influence the average tendencies of families from different social classes.

That there would be personality and child-rearing differences, on average, between families in different social classes makes sense when you think about it. If upper-middle-class parents have jobs in which they are expected to collaborate with fellow employees, create new solutions to problems, or wonder how to improve their contributions, they are more likely to talk to their children in ways that differ from those of lower-class parents whose own jobs simply require them to follow instructions without question. Children who are reared by parents who are professionals will, on average, have more inquisitive attitudes toward the material presented by their teachers than will children who are reared by working-class parents. As a result, no matter how competent the teacher, the academic achievement of lower-class children will, on average, almost inevitably be less than that of middle-class children. The probability of such reduced achievement increases as the characteristics of lower-social-class families accumulate.

Many social and economic manifestations of social class also have important implications for learning. Health differences are among them. On average, lower-class children have poorer vision than middle-class children, partly because of prenatal conditions and partly because of how their eyes are trained as infants. They have poorer oral hygiene, more lead poisoning, more asthma, poorer nutrition, less adequate pediatric care, more exposure to smoke, and a host of other problems. Each of these well-documented social-class differences is likely to have a palpable effect on academic achievement, and the combined influence of all of these differences is probably huge.

The growing unaffordability of adequate housing for low-income families is another social-class characteristic that has a demonstrable effect on average achievement. Children whose families have difficulty finding stable housing are more likely to be mobile, and student mobility is an important cause of low student achievement. Urban rents have risen faster than working-class incomes. Even families in which parents' employment is stable are more likely to move when they fall behind in rent payments. In some schools in minority neighborhoods, this need to move has boosted mobility rates to more than 100%: for every seat in the school, more than two children were enrolled at some time during the year.[1] It is hard to imagine how teachers, no matter how well trained, could be as effective for children who move in and out of their classrooms as they can be for children whose attendance is regular.

Differences in wealth between parents of different social classes are also likely to be important determinants of student achievement, but these differences are usually overlooked because most analysts focus only on annual income to indicate disadvantage. This practice makes it hard to understand, for example, why black students, on average, score lower than white students whose family incomes are the same. It is easier to understand this pattern when we recognize that children can have similar family *incomes* but be ranked differently in the social-class structure, even in economic terms. Black families with low income in any particular year are likely to have been poor for longer than white families with similar income in that year. White families are also likely to own far more assets that support their children's achievement than are black families at the same level of current income.

I use the term "lower class" here to describe the families of children whose achievement will, on average, be predictably lower than the achievement of middle-class children. American sociologists were once comfortable with this term, but it has fallen out of fashion. Instead, we tend to use such euphemisms as "disadvantaged" students, "at-risk" students, "inner-city" students, or students of "low socioeconomic status." None of these terms, however, can capture the central characteristic of lower-class families: a collection of occupational, psychological, personality, health, and economic traits that interact, predicting performance—not only in schools but in other institutions as well—that, on average, differs from the performance of families from higher social classes.

Much of the difference between the average performance of black children and that of white children can probably be traced to differences in their social-class characteristics. But there are also cultural characteristics that are likely to contribute a bit to the black-white achievement gap. These cultural characteristics may have identifiable origins in social and economic conditions—for example, black students may value education less than white students because a discriminatory labor market has not historically rewarded black workers for their education—but values can persist independently and outlast the economic circumstances that gave rise to them.

Some lower-class children do achieve at high levels, and many observers have falsely concluded from this that therefore all lower-class children should be able to succeed with appropriate instruction. One of the bars to our understanding of the achievement gap is that most Americans, even well-educated ones, are not expert in discussions of statistical distributions. The achievement gap is a phenomenon of averages, a difference between the average achievement level of lower-class children and the average achievement level of middle-class children. In human affairs, every average characteristic is a composite of many widely disparate characteristics.

For example, we know that lead poisoning has a demonstrable impact on young children's I.Q. scores. Children with high exposure to lead—from fumes or from ingesting paint or dust—have I.Q. scores that, on average, are several points lower than those of children who are not so exposed. But this does not mean that every child with lead poisoning has a lower I.Q. Some children with high lead levels in their blood have higher I.Q. scores than typical children with no lead exposure. When researchers say that lead poisoning seems to affect academic performance, they do not mean that every lead-exposed child performs less well. But the high performance of a few lead-exposed children does not disprove the conclusion that lead exposure is likely to harm academic achievement.

This kind of reasoning applies to each of the social-class characteristics that I discuss here, as well as to the many others that, for lack of space or my own ignorance, I do not discuss. In each case, class differences in social or economic circumstances probably cause differences in the average academic performance of children from different social classes, but, in each case, some children with lower-class characteristics perform better than typical middle-class children.

SCHOOL REFORMS ALONE ARE NOT ENOUGH

The influence of social-class characteristics is probably so powerful that schools cannot overcome it, no matter how well trained their teachers and no matter how well designed their instructional programs and climates. But saying that a social-class achievement gap should be expected is not to make a logical statement. The fact that social-class differences are associated with, and probably cause, a big gap in academic performance does not mean that, in theory, excellent schools could not offset these differences. Indeed, today's policy makers and educators make many claims that higher standards, better teachers, more accountability, better discipline, or other effective practices can close the achievement gap.

The most prominent of these claims has been made by the Heritage Foundation (conservative) and the Education Trust (more liberal), by economists and statisticians who claim to have shown that better teachers do in fact close the gap, by prominent educators, and by social critics. Many (though not all) of the instructional practices promoted by these commentators are well designed, and these practices probably do succeed in delivering a better education to some lower-class children. But a careful examination of each claim that a particular school or practice has closed the race or social-class achievement gap shows that the claim is unfounded.

In some cases, a claim may fail because it reflects a statistical fluke—a school successful for only one year, in only one subject, or in only one grade—or because it reports success only on tests of the most basic skills. In other cases, a claim may fail because the successful schools identified have selective student bodies. Remember that the achievement gap is a phenomenon of averages—it compares the average achievement of lower and middle-class students. In both social classes, some students perform well above or below the average performance of their social-class peers. If schools can select (or attract) a disproportionate share of lower-class students whose performance is above average for their social class, those schools can appear to be quite successful. Many such schools are excellent and should be commended. But their successes provide no evidence that their instructional approaches would close the achievement gap for students who are average for their social-class groups.

LIMITATIONS OF THE CURRENT TESTING REGIME

Whether efforts to close the social-class achievement gap involve in-school reforms or socioeconomic reforms, it is difficult to know precisely how much any intervention will narrow the gap. We can't estimate the effect of various policies partly because we don't really know how big the achievement gap is overall or how big it is in particular schools or school systems.

This lack of knowledge about the size of the gap or the merits of any particular intervention might surprise many readers because so much attention is devoted these days to standardized test scores. It has been widely reported that, on average, if white students score at around the 50th percentile on a standardized math or reading test, black students typically score around the 23rd percentile. (In more technical statistical terms, black students score, on average, between 0.5 and 1.0 standard deviations below white students.)

But contrary to conventional belief, this may not be a good measure of the gap. Because of the high stakes attached to standardized tests in recent years, schools and teachers are under enormous pressure to raise students' test scores. The more pressure there has been, the less reliable these scores have become. In part, the tests themselves don't really measure the gap in the achievement of high standards because high standards (such as the production of good writing and the development of research skills and analysis) are expensive to test, and public officials are reluctant to spend the money. Instead, schools have tended to use inexpensive standardized tests that mostly, though not entirely, assess more basic skills. Gaps that show up on tests of basic skills may be quite different from the gaps that would show up on tests of higher standards of learning. And it is not the case that students acquire a hierarchy of skills sequentially. Thus truly narrowing the achievement gap would not require children to learn "the basics" first. Lower-class children cannot produce typical middle-class academic achievement unless they learn basic and more advanced skills simultaneously, with each reinforcing the other. This is, in fact, how middle-class children who come to school ready to learn acquire both basic and advanced skills.

The high stakes recently attached to standardized tests have given teachers incentives to revise the priorities of their instruction, especially for lower-class children, so that they devote greater time to drill on basic skills and less time to other, equally important (but untested) learning areas in which achievement gaps also appear. In a drive to raise test scores in math and reading, the curriculum has moved away not only from more advanced mathematical and literary skills, but also from social studies, literature, art, music, physical education, and other important subjects that are not tested for the purpose of judging school quality. We don't know how large the race or social-class achievement gaps are in these subjects, but there is no reason to believe that gaps in one domain are the same as the gaps in others or that the relationships between gaps in different domains will remain consistent at different ages and on different tests.

For example, educational researchers normally expect that gaps in reading will be greater than gaps in math, probably because social-class differences in parental support play a bigger role for reading than for math. Parents typically read to their very young children, and middle-class parents do so more and in more intellectually stimulating ways, but few parents do math problems with their young children. Yet, on at least one test of entering kindergartners, race and social-class gaps in math exceed those in reading.

THE IMPORTANCE OF NONCOGNITIVE SKILLS

We also don't know the extent of the social-class gaps in noncognitive skills—such character traits as perseverance, self-confidence, self-discipline, punctuality, the ability to communicate, social responsibility, and the ability to work with others and resolve conflicts. These are important goals of public education. In some respects, they may be more important than academic outcomes.

Employers, for example, consistently report that workers have more serious shortcomings in these noncognitive areas than in academic areas. Econometric studies show that noncognitive skills are a stronger predictor of future earnings than are test scores. In public opinion surveys, Americans consistently say they want schools to produce good citizens and socially responsible adults first and high academic proficiency second. Yet we do a poor job—actually, no job at all—of assessing whether schools are generating such noncognitive outcomes. And so we also do a poor job of assessing whether schools are successfully narrowing the social-class gap in these traits or whether social and economic reform here, too, would be necessary to narrow these gaps.

There is some evidence that the noncognitive social-class gaps should be a cause for concern. For very young children, measures of antisocial behavior mirror the gaps in academic test scores. Children of lower social classes exhibit more antisocial behavior than children of higher social classes, both in early childhood and in adolescence. It would be reasonable to expect that the same social and economic inequalities that seem likely to produce gaps in academic test scores also produce differences in noncognitive traits.

In some areas, however, it seems that noncognitive gaps may be smaller than cognitive ones. In particular, analyses of some affirmative action programs in higher education find that, when minority students with lower test scores than white students are admitted to colleges, the lower-scoring minority students may exhibit more leadership, devote more serious attention to their studies, and go on to make greater community contributions. This evidence reinforces the importance of measuring noncognitive student characteristics, something that few elementary or secondary schools attempt. Until we begin to measure these traits, we will have no insight into the extent of the noncognitive gaps between lower and middle-class children.

Moving Forward

Three tracks should be pursued vigorously and simultaneously if we are to make significant progress in narrowing the achievement gap. The first track is school improvement efforts that raise the quality of instruction in elementary and secondary schools. The second track is expanding the definition of schooling to include crucial out-of-school hours in which families and communities now are the sole influences. This means implementing comprehensive early childhood, after-school, and summer programs. And the third track is social and economic policies that will enable children to attend school more equally ready to learn. These policies include health services for lower-class children and their families, stable housing for working families with children, and the narrowing of growing income inequalities in American society.

Many of the reforms in curriculum and school organization that are promoted by critics of education have merit and should be intensified. Repairing and upgrading the scandalously decrepit school facilities that serve some lower-class children, raising salaries to permit the recruitment of more qualified teachers for lower-class children, reducing class sizes for lower-class children (particularly in the early grades), insisting on higher academic standards that emphasize creativity and reasoning as well as basic skills, holding schools accountable for fairly measured performance, having a well-focused and disciplined school climate, doing more to encourage lower-class children to intensify their own ambitions—all of these policies and others can play a role in narrowing the achievement gap. These reforms are extensively covered in a wide range of books, articles, and public discussions of education, so I do not dwell on them here. Instead, my focus is the greater importance of reforming social and economic institutions if we truly want children to emerge from school with equal preparation.

Readers should not misinterpret this emphasis as implying that better schools are not important or that school improvement will not make a contribution to narrowing the achievement gap. Better school practices can no doubt narrow the gap. However, school reform is not enough.

In seeking to close the achievement gap for low-income and minority students, policy makers focus inordinate attention on the improvement of instruction because they apparently believe that social-class differences are immutable and that only schools can improve the destinies of lower-class children. This is a peculiarly American belief—that schools can be virtually the only instrument of social reform—but it is not based on evidence about the relative effectiveness of economic, social, and educational improvement efforts.

While many social-class characteristics are impervious to short-term change, many can easily be affected by public policies that narrow the social and economic gaps between lower- and middle-class children. These policies can probably have a more powerful impact on student achievement (and, in some cases, at less cost) than an exclusive focus on school reform. But we cannot say so for sure, because social scientists and educators have devoted no effort to studying the relative costs and benefits of nonschool and school reforms. For example, establishing an optometric clinic in a school to improve the vision of low-income children could have a bigger impact on their test scores than spending the same money on instructional improvement.[2] Greater proportions of low-income than middle-class children are distracted by the discomfort of untreated dental cavities, and dental clinics can likewise be provided at costs comparable to what schools typically spend on less effective reforms. We can't be certain if this is the case, however, because there have been no experiments to test the relative benefits of these alternative strategies. Of course, proposals to improve all facets of the health of lower-class children, not just their vision and oral health, should be evaluated for their academic impacts.

A full array of health services will be costly, but that cost cannot be avoided if we are truly to embrace the goal of raising the achievement of lower-class children. Some of these costs are not new, of course, and some can be recouped by school clinics by means of reimbursements from other underutilized government programs, such as Medicaid.

Other social reforms—for example, an increase in the number of Section 8 housing vouchers to increase the access of lower-class families to stable housing—also could have a significant educational impact.

Incomes have become more unequally distributed in the United States in the last generation, and this inequality contributes to the academic achievement gap. Proposals for a higher minimum wage or increases in earned income tax credits, which are designed to help offset some of this inequality, should be considered education policies as well as economic ones, for they would be likely to result in higher academic performance from children whose families are more secure.

Although conventional opinion is that "failing" schools contribute mightily to the achievement gap, the evidence indicates that schools already do a great deal to combat it. Most of the social-class difference in average academic potential exists by the time children are 3 years old. This difference is exacerbated over the years that children spend in school, but during these years, the growth in the gap occurs mostly in the after-school hours and during the summertime, when children are not actually in classrooms.[3]

So in addition to school improvement and broader reforms to narrow the social and economic inequalities that produce gaps in student achievement, investments should be made to expand the definition of schooling to cover those crucial out-of-school hours. Because the gap is already huge at 3 years old, the most important focus of this investment should probably be early childhood programs. The quality of these programs is as important as the existence of the programs themselves. To narrow the gap, early childhood care, beginning with infants and toddlers, should be provided by adults who can offer the kind of intellectual environment that is typically experienced by middle-class infants and toddlers. This goal probably requires professional care givers and low child/adult ratios.

Providing after-school and summer experiences to lower-class children that are similar to those middle-class children take for granted would be likely to play an essential part in narrowing the achievement gap. But these experiences should not be restricted only to remedial programs in which lower-class children get added drill in math and reading. Certainly, remedial instruction should be part of an adequate after-school and summer program—but only a part. The advantage that middle-class children gain after school and in the summer probably comes mostly from the self-confidence they acquire and the awareness they develop of the world outside their homes and immediate communities and from organized athletics, dance, drama, museum visits, recreational reading, and other activities that develop their inquisitiveness, creativity, self-discipline, and organizational skills. After-school and summer programs can be expected to have a chance of narrowing the achievement gap only by attempting to duplicate such experiences.

For nearly half a century, the association of social and economic disadvantage with a student achievement gap has been well known to economists, sociologists, and educators. However, most have avoided the obvious implications of this understanding: raising the achievement of lower-class children requires the amelioration of the social and economic conditions of their lives, not just school reform. Perhaps we are now ready to reconsider this needlessly neglected opportunity.

NOTES

Richard Rothstein is a research associate with the Economic Policy Institute, Washington, D.C., and a visiting lecturer at Teachers College, Columbia University, New York City. This reading is adapted from the introduction to his new book, *Class and Schools: Using Social, Economic, and Educational Reform to Close the Black-White Achievement Gap* (Economic Policy Institute/Teachers College, 2004). © 2004, Economic Policy Institute/Teachers College. Copies may be ordered at www.epinet.org.

1. David Kerbow, "Patterns of Urban Student Mobility and Local School Reform," *Journal of Education for Students Placed at Risk*, vol. 12, 1996, pp. 147–69; and James Bruno and Jo Ann Isken, "Inter- and Intraschool Site Student Transiency: Practical and Theoretical Implications for Instructional Continuity at Inner-City Schools," *Journal of Research and Development in Education*, vol. 29, 1996, pp. 239–52.

2. Paul Harris, "Learning-Related Visual Problems in Baltimore City: A Long-Term Program," *Journal of Optometric Vision Development*, vol. 33, 2002, pp. 75–115; and Marge Christensen Gould and Herman Gould, O.D., "A Clear Vision for Equity and Opportunity," *Phi Delta Kappan*, December 2003, pp. 324–29.

3. See Meredith Phillips, "Understanding Ethnic Differences in Academic Achievement: Empirical Lessons from National Data," in David W. Grissmer and J. Michael Ross, eds., *Analytic Issues in the Assessment of Student Achievement* (Washington, D.C.: U.S. Department of Education, NCES 2000-050, 2000), pp. 103–32, available at http://nces.ed.gov pubs2000/2000osoa.pdf; Richard L. Allington and Anne McGill-Franzen, "The Impact of Summer Setback on the Reading Achievement Gap," *Phi Delta Kappan*, September 2003, pp. 68–75; and Doris Entwisle and Karl L. Alexander, "Summer Setback: Race, Poverty, School Composition, and Mathematics Achievement in the First Two Years of School," *American Sociological Review*, February 1992, pp. 72–84.

16. Does Meritocracy Work?
Ross Douthat

For a parent drowning in glossy college mailings, a college admissions officer deluged with applications, or a student padding a resume with extracurricular activities, it's easy to see applying to college as a universal American rite of passage—a brutal and ecumenical process that ushers each generation of stressed-out applicants into the anteroom of adulthood. But for many American teenagers the admissions process is something else entirely—a game that is dramatically rigged against them, if they even play it. In a country where a college degree is a prerequisite for economic and social advancement, rich and upper-middle-class students can feel secure about their chances. They may not have the grades or the good fortune to attend their first-choice schools, but they're still likely to be admitted to a college that matches their interests and ambitions reasonably well. For those further down the socioeconomic ladder, though, getting in is hard, and getting through can be even harder.

Native intelligence and academic achievement do lift many poor students into college. But especially where elite colleges are concerned, students from well-off families have a big advantage. The figures are stark. If you hope to obtain a bachelor's degree by age twenty-four, your chances are roughly one in two if you come from a family with an annual income over $90,000; roughly one in four if your family's income falls between $61,000 and $90,000; and slightly better than one in ten if it is between $35,000 and $61,000. For high schoolers whose families make less than $35,000 a year the chances are around one in seventeen.

This is not how the modern meritocracy was supposed to work. American higher education was overhauled in the middle years of the twentieth century to be a force for near universal opportunity—or so the overhaulers intended. The widespread use of the SAT would identify working-class kids with high "scholastic aptitude," as the initialism then had it (since 1994 the SAT has been for "scholastic assessment"), and give them the academic chances they deserved. Need-based financial aid and government grants would ensure that everyone who wanted a college education could afford one. Affirmative action would diversify campuses and buoy disadvantaged minorities.

Part of this vision has come to pass. Minority participation in higher education has risen since the 1960s, and college campuses are far more racially and ethnically diverse today than they were back a century ago. But the socioeconomic diversity that administrators assumed would follow has failed to materialize. It's true that more low-income students *enroll* in college now than in the 1970s—but they are less likely to graduate than their wealthier peers. Through boom and recession, war and peace, the proportion of the poorest Americans obtaining college degrees by age twenty-four has remained around six percent.

This is not something that most colleges like to discuss—particularly elite schools, which have long taken pride in their supposed diversity. But the idea that the meritocracy isn't working is gaining currency among observers of higher education. It's visible in recent high-profile changes in the financial-aid policies of such schools as Harvard, Princeton, and the University of Virginia; as a thread of disquiet running through the interviews this magazine has conducted with admissions officers over the past two years; and as the unpleasant but undeniable conclusion of a number of new studies.

The most prominent of these studies was headed by William Bowen, a former president of Princeton, who since leaving that office, in 1988, has produced a series of weighty analyses of college admissions—on the consequences of racial preferences, the role of athletics, and, most recently, the question of socioeconomic diversity. In the recently published book *Equity and Excellence in American Higher Education,* Bowen and his coauthors use detailed data from the 1995 entering class at nineteen selective schools—five Ivies, ten small liberal arts colleges, and four flagship state universities—to argue that elite universities today are as much "bastions of privilege" as they are "engines of opportunity." Only six percent of the students at these schools are first-generation collegians; only 11 percent of the graduates come from families in the country's bottom economic quartile. The picture is even worse in another recent study. The education expert Anthony Carnevale and the economist Stephen Rose surveyed 146 top colleges and found that only three percent of their students came from the bottom economic quartile of the U.S. population—whereas 74 percent came from the top one.

At the very least, the persistence of this higher-education gap suggests that the causes of the decades-old growth in economic inequality are deeper than, say, tax cuts or the ebb and flow of the stock market. Inequality of income breeds inequality of education, and the reverse is also true: as long as the financial returns on a college degree continue to rise, the upper and upper-middle classes are likely to pull further away from the working and lower classes.

The United States still leads most countries by a considerable margin in proportion of the population with a college degree (27 percent). But when the sample is narrowed to those between the ages of twenty-five and thirty-four, we slip into the pack of industrialized nations, behind Canada, Japan, and five others. Further, the U.S. college-age population is swelling (it will increase by about 3.9 million during this decade, according to one estimate), with much of the growth occurring among low-income Hispanics, one of the groups least likely to attend college. Educating this population is an enormous challenge—one that we are unprepared to meet.

The obvious culprits are the universities, which have trumpeted their commitment to diversity and equal access while pursuing policies that favor better-off students. Not only is admitting too many low-income students expensive, but it can be bad for a school's rankings and prestige—and in the long run prestige builds endowments.

The current arms race for higher rankings began in earnest in the early 1980s, when the post–Baby Boom dearth of applicants sent colleges, both public and private, scrambling to keep tuition revenue coming in. It has been sustained by anxious Boomer parents, by the increasing financial advantages of a college degree, by cutbacks in government aid, and by magazines eager to make money from ranking America's top schools. The rankings rely on statistics such as average SAT scores, alumni giving, financial resources, and graduation rates. Attracting students with high scores *and* high family incomes offers the biggest gains of all.

Meanwhile, the admissions process is strewn with practical obstacles for low-income students. Early-admissions programs, for instance, which James Fallows has discussed in these pages (see "The Early-Decision Racket," September 2001 *Atlantic),* offer many benefits to applicants, but they almost exclusively help wealthy students, whose parents and guidance counselors are more likely to have the resources to take advantage of them. Poorer students are also less likely to know about the availability of financial aid, and thus more likely to let "sticker shock" keep them from applying in the first place. And a poor student put on a waiting list at a selective school is less likely than a well-to-do student to be accepted, because often a school has exhausted its financial-aid budget before it turns to the list.

In this scramble selectivity is "the coin of the realm," as one admissions officer put it to *The Atlantic* last year. More and more schools define themselves as "selective" in an effort to boost their position and prestige, and fewer and fewer offer the kind of admissions process that provides real opportunities for poorer students. As a result, those disadvantaged students who do attend college are less and less likely to find themselves at four-year schools. Among students who receive Pell Grants—the chief need-based form of federal assistance—the share attending four-year colleges fell from 62 percent in 1974 to 45 percent in 2002: the share attending two-year schools rose from 38 percent to 55 percent.

The advantage to well-off students is particularly pronounced at private colleges and universities. Over the course of the 1990s, for instance, the average private-school grant to students from the top income quartile grew from $1,920 to $3,510, whereas the average grant to students from the lowest income quartile grew from $2,890 to $3,460. And for all the worry of the middle class over rising tuition, increases in grant dollars often outstrip increases in tuition costs for middle- and upper-income students—but not for their poorer peers. In the second half of the 1990s, a study by the Lumina Foundation (a higher-education nonprofit) found, families with incomes below $40,000 received less than seventy cents in grants for every dollar increase in private-college tuition. All other families, including the richest, received more than a dollar in aid for every dollar increase in tuition.

It isn't just schools that have moved their aid dollars up the income ladder. State and federal governments have done the same. Since the 1980s public funds have covered a shrinking share of college costs, and with entitlements claiming an ever growing chunk of state and federal budgets, the chance of a return to the free-spending 1970s seems remote. But even when higher-education outlays have increased—they did during the 1990s boom years, for instance—government dollars have been funneled to programs that disproportionately benefit middle- and upper-income college students.

Both colleges and states have increasingly invested in "merit-based" scholarships, which offer extra cash to high-performing students regardless of need; these programs are often modeled on Georgia's HOPE scholarship, established in 1993 and funded by a state lottery, and thus amount to a form of regressive taxation. The federal government, meanwhile, has used tax credits to help parents defray the cost of college—a benefit that offers little to low-income families. Pell Grants have been expanded, but the purchasing power of individual grants hasn't kept pace with rising tuition.

Overall, American financial aid has gradually moved from a grant-based to a loan-based system. In 1980, 41 percent of all financial-aid dollars were in the form of loans; today 59 percent are. In the early 1990s Congress created a now enormous "no-need" loan program; it has been a boon for upper-income students, who can more easily afford to repay debts accrued during college. At the same time, the federal government allowed families to discount home equity when assessing their financial circumstances, making many more students eligible for loans that had previously been reserved for the poorest applicants. The burdens associated with loans may be part of the reason why only 41 percent of low-income students who enter four-year colleges graduate within five years, compared with 66 percent of high-income students.

All these policy changes have been politically popular, supported by Democratic and Republican politicians alike. After all, the current financial-aid system is good for those voters—middle-class and above—who already expect to send their kids to college, and who are more likely to take the cost of college into consideration when they vote. And though Americans support the ideal of universal educational opportunity, they also support the somewhat nebulous notion of merit and the idea that a high SAT score or good grades should be rewarded with tuition discounts—especially when it's their children's grades and SAT scores that are being rewarded.

But it's not enough to blame the self-interest of many universities or the pandering of politicians for the lack of socioeconomic diversity in higher education. There's also the uncomfortable fact that a society in which education is so unevenly distributed may represent less a failure of meritocracy than its logical endpoint.

That the meritocracy would become hereditary was the fear of Michael Young, the British civil servant who coined the term. His novel *The Rise of the Meritocracy* (1958)—written in the form of a dry Ph.D. thesis that analyzed society from the vantage point of 2034—envisions a future of ever more perfect intelligence tests and educational segregation, in which a cognitive elite holds sway until the less intelligent masses rise to overthrow their brainy masters. A scenario of stratification by intelligence was raised again in 1971, in these pages, by the Harvard psychologist Richard Herrnstein, and in 1994 by Herrnstein and Charles Murray, in their controversial best seller *The Bell Curve*. That book is now remembered for suggesting the existence of ineradicable racial differences in IQ, but its larger argument was that America is segregated according to cognitive ability—and there's nothing we can do about it.

Today Young's dystopian fears and *The Bell Curve*'s self-consciously hardheaded realism seem simplistic; both reduce the complex questions of merit and success to a matter of IQ, easily tested and easily graphed. The role that inherited intelligence plays in personal success remains muddy and controversial, but most scholars reject the "Herrnstein Nightmare" (as the journalist Mickey Kaus dubbed it) of class division by IQ.

It doesn't really matter, though, whether our meritocracy passes on success genetically, given how completely it is passed on through wealth and culture. The higher one goes up the income ladder, the greater the emphasis on education and the pressure from parents and peers to excel at extracurricular achievement—and the greater the likelihood of success. (Even the admissions advantage that many schools give to recruited athletes—often presumed to help low-income students—actually tends to disproportionately benefit the children of upper-income families, perhaps because they are sent to high schools that encourage students to participate in a variety of sports.) In this inherited meritocracy the high-achieving kid will not only attend school with other high achievers but will also marry a high achiever and settle in a high-achieving area—the better to ensure that his children will have all the cultural advantages he enjoyed growing up.

Powerful though these cultural factors are, change is possible. The same studies that reveal just how class-defined American higher education remains also offer comfort for would-be reformers. Certainly, policies that strengthen families or improve elementary education undercut social stratification more effectively than anything colleges do. For now, however, numerous reasonably prepared students—300,000 a year, by one estimate—who aren't going to college could be. And many students who are less likely than their higher-income peers to attend the most selective schools would thrive if admitted.

The obvious way to reach these students is to institute some sort of class-based affirmative action—a "thumb on the scale" for low-income students that is championed by Bowen and by Carnevale and Rose in their analyses of educational inequality. Many elite universities claim to pursue such policies already, but Bowen's study finds *no* admissions advantage for poor applicants to the selective schools in the sample simply for being poor. In contrast, a recruited athlete is 30 percent more likely to be admitted than an otherwise identical applicant; a member of an underrepresented minority is 28 percent more likely; and a "legacy" (alumni child) or a student who applies early is 20 percent more likely.

As an alternative Bowen and his coauthors propose that selective schools begin offering a 20 percent advantage to low-income students—a policy with "a nice kind of symbolic symmetry" to the advantage for legacies, they point out. By their calculations, this would raise the proportion of low-income students at the nineteen elite schools in their sample from 11 to 17 percent, without much impact on the schools' academic profiles.

Class-based affirmative action has an obvious political advantage: it's more popular with the public than race-based affirmative action. (Bowen envisions socioeconomic diversity as a supplement to racial diversity, not a replacement.)

Increasing socioeconomic diversity might offer something to both sides of the red-blue divide—to a Democratic Party rhetorically committed to equalizing opportunity, and to a Republican Party that increasingly represents the white working class, one of the groups most likely to benefit from having the scales weighted at elite universities.

But however happy this may sound in theory, one wonders how likely schools are to adopt class-based preferences. As Carnevale and Rose put it, doing so "would alienate politically powerful groups and help less powerful constituencies"; Bowen notes that it would reduce income from tuition and alumni giving. A selective school might court backlash every time it admitted a poor kid with, say, a middle-range SAT over an upper-middle-class kid with a perfect score. It's doubtful that many colleges would be willing to accept the losses—and, for the more selective among them, the possible drop in *U.S. News* rankings.

Even the elite of the elite—schools like the nineteen examined in Bowen's book, which are best able to afford the costs associated with class-based affirmative action—seem more inclined to increase financial aid than to revamp their admissions policies with an eye toward economic diversity. In the past several years schools like Harvard, Princeton, and Brown have shifted financial-aid dollars from loans to grants, helping to ensure a free ride for the neediest students once they get in. Such gestures make for good public relations, and they do help a few students—but they don't make it easier for low-income students to gain admission.

The benefits and the limitations of moving from loans to grants can be observed in the "AccessUVa" program at the University of Virginia, one of the schools in Bowen's sample. In 2003 it had a typical entering class for an elite school—58 percent of the students came from families with annual incomes above $100,000—and in 2004 fewer than six percent of students came from families with incomes below $40,000. In 2004 Virginia announced that for students with family incomes below 150 percent of the poverty line it would eliminate need-based loans and would instead offer grants exclusively (the school has since raised the threshold to include families of four making less than 200 percent of the poverty line, or about $40,000). It would also cap the amount of debt any student could accrue, funding the rest of his or her tuition through grants. The school publicized its increased affordability, with large-scale outreach to poorer parts of the state. It's too early to judge the program's success, but the first year's results are instructive: the number of low-income freshmen increased nearly half, or sixty-six out of a class of about 3,100. This is a praiseworthy if small step: those sixty-six brought the low-income total to 199, or about six percent of the class. But it does not solve the problem of unequal access to higher education.

Significant improvements in access, if and when they come, will probably have little to do with the policies at the most elite schools. In America access ultimately rests on what happens in the vast middle rank of colleges and universities, where most undergraduates are educated—in particular, in state schools.

One thing that's unlikely to happen is a sudden increase in funding for higher education, along the lines of the post–World War II surge that made college possible for so many young people. The budgetary demands of swelling entitlements and military spending, the wariness of voters who perceive schools (sometimes rightly, usually wrongly) to be growing fat off their high tuition, and the cultural chasm between a Republican-controlled government and a lefter-than-thou academy—all this and more ensures that spending on higher education will not leap to the top of the nation's political agenda. Instead, schools and legislators must be willing to experiment.

The good news is that there's no shortage of ideas. Bowen, for instance, points out that state schools might consider rethinking their relatively low tuition, which amounts to a subsidy for wealthy in-state parents. (Indeed, upper-income parents are increasingly choosing to send their children to state schools, presumably with just this advantage in mind.) These schools could keep their official tuition low while charging premiums for better-off applicants. Or they could follow the lead of Miami University, in Ohio, which recently raised in-state tuition to the same level as out-of-state tuition (from $9,150 to $19,730).

What should be done with the extra money? State governments might consider tying funding for schools more tightly to access—either directly, by rewarding those colleges that graduate larger numbers of low-income students, or indirectly, as Bowen and his coauthors suggest, by shifting funding from flagship universities to regional schools, which are more likely to enroll disadvantaged students.

More radically, states might ask how well they are serving their populations by funding public universities directly and allowing the universities to disburse the funds as they see fit. If the point of a public university is to hire superstar faculty members, build world-class research facilities, and compete with Harvard and Yale, then perhaps this way of funding makes sense. (It's worth noting that since the 1970s public schools have spent an increasing share of their funds on research and administration rather than on instruction.) But if the point is to make higher education more accessible, it doesn't.

The Ohio University economist Richard Vedder has suggested that states might consider offering less money to schools and more money to students, in the form of tuition vouchers redeemable at any public institution in their home state. These could be distributed according to financial need: if the average tuition in a state university system were $15,000, a poor student might receive a voucher for $15,000 and a wealthy student one for $3,000. Schools would have less of a financial incentive to admit mostly rich students. Vouchers might also simplify filing for financial aid; the economist Thomas Kane has argued that the sheer complexity of this process deters many low-income students.

Like class-based affirmative action, a voucher program might be able to command support from both sides of the political aisle. The system's market-based efficiency would delight free marketeers (Vedder is affiliated with the conservative American Enterprise Institute), and its potential for increasing access might win the support of egalitarian liberals. And a voucher approach to funding state schools would mean less direct state involvement in higher education, which would please academics and administrators tired of having cost-conscious legislators looking over their shoulders.

Governments and public universities may also have lessons to learn from for-profit schools, which increasingly attract the students shut out of American higher education. Driven by bottom-line concerns, some of these schools enroll students who can't do the work, or promise job opportunities that never materialize. But many are oriented toward the needs of low-income populations. In New York State, for instance, some commercial schools set tuition at around $9,000—exactly the amount that a needy student can expect to receive from a Pell Grant combined with the state's tuition-assistance program. And they tend to serve the kind of students that traditional universities are failing—working adults, for instance, looking for the economic advantages that come with a college degree.

What gives the for-profit schools a leg up is their ability to "unbundle" a college education from its traditional (and costly) campus environment—something made possible in large part by the spread of the Internet. Some for-profit schools are entirely Web-based. Many others have put their reading lists, class registration, and even advising online. This is obviously not a model that a flagship state university is likely to emulate. But it may no longer make sense to spend a vast amount to sustain a traditional campus experience for the few when the same amount can provide an education for the many.

All these experiments—and that's what they are—have drawbacks. Public universities that spend more to improve access and graduation rates could make up for the expense by cutting, say, faculty salaries. Public schools already have a hard time keeping sought-after teachers from jumping to private colleges; if more money were spent enrolling and graduating poorer students, the problem would only worsen.

And the more that market efficiency was brought to bear on higher education, and the more that degree-granting and graduation rates were emphasized over the traditional academic experience, the more the liberal arts would be likely to suffer. Computer classes would crowd out Shakespeare, management courses would replace musical instruction, everyone would learn Spanish and no one Greek. Who would speak up to save liberal education?

The most obvious drawback is that a more egalitarian system, in which a college degree is nearly universal and therefore a less exclusive pathway to later success, would run counter to the interests of upper-middle-class parents—the people who wield the most influence in the politics of higher education. It's elite Americans who would lose out in class-based affirmative action. It's elite Americans who would pay more if state schools raised their tuition and state governments handed out income-adjusted vouchers. And it's elite Americans who would lose some of their standing if educational opportunity were more widely distributed. Why should they give it up? *It's not as if our child doesn't deserve his advantages,* parents might say, after helping that child rack up not only high grades and SAT scores but also a sterling record of community service.

What, really, does an eighteen-year-old high achiever "deserve"? A good college education, certainly—but surely not the kind of advantage that college graduates now enjoy. As Nicholas Lemann put it in *The Big Test,* his history of the American meritocracy, "Let us say you wanted to design a system that would distribute opportunity in the most unfair possible way. A first choice would be one in which all roles were inherited ... A second unfair system might be one that allowed for competition but insisted that it take place as early in life as possible and with school as the arena." Students should be rewarded for academic achievement. But twelve years of parentally subsidized achievement should not hand them an advantage for the next fifty years of their lives.

NOTE

Ross Douthat is g reporter-researcher for *The Atlantic* and the author of *Privilege: Harvard and the Education of the Ruling Class.*

The College Pipeline: Some of the most basic information can also be the hardest to come by—and data about who moves on to what level of education, and when, is a classic case in point. Official education statistics often omit students when they switch schools, or when they drop out and then re-enroll. As a result, there is disagreement over precise numbers. The chart below, derived from a study that followed 12,000 eighth-graders from 1988 through 2000, represents the Department of Education's best available snapshot of what percentage of young people make it through college within twelve years of leaving the eighth grade.

OUT OF EVERY 100 EIGHTH-GRADE STUDENTS ...

78 graduate from high school on time with a standard diploma

Of these, 47 remain in the post-secondary system after their first year

Of these, 60 start college (35 in a four-year college, 25 in a two-year college or trade school) by age 26 or 27

Twelve years after the eighth grade 29 have earned at least a bachelor's degree, five an associate's degree, and three a certificate

Sources: National Center for Education Statistics; National Education Longitudinal Study of 1988/2000 Postsecondary Transcript Files.

CHAPTER 8
JUSTICE AND INJUSTICE

Social class and the justice system interact in a variety of ways. At the most basic level, social class influences the type of crime that is committed, where it is committed, and against whom. Because there is a greater police presence in low-income neighborhoods, people who commit crimes in these neighborhoods stand a better chance of being caught. By contrast, white-collar crimes tend to be committed by members of the middle and upper classes, and because they are often committed with a computer in an office, white-collar criminals have a lower probability of being caught. Moreover, recent statistics indicate that since the war on terror began, attention to white-collar crimes by the Federal Bureau of Investigation has diminished.

When a criminal act is detected, police officers have discretion regarding whether they arrest the perpetrator. Social class, the nature of the offense, and whether the police have had past contact with the perpetrator enter into that decision. In cases where an arrest does occur, the prosecutor has discretion in terms of charging an individual, plea-bargaining the case down to a lesser offense, or dropping the charges. And finally, once charges are filed, judges have discretion in sentencing, including the use of probation or home monitoring as alternatives to jail. At each step in this process, the social class of the individual directly affects the choices that are made: whether an arrest is made, whether the individual is prosecuted, and what punishment is specified.

Members of the upper and lower classes certainly experience the justice system differently. Upper-class individuals have more knowledge of the rights afforded them under the Constitution and are better able to participate in their own defense. They also have more immediate access to quality legal representation.

Under *Miranda v. Arizona* (1966), people who cannot afford legal representation are provided a court-appointed attorney. This decision is an attempt to give members of the lower classes a fairer chance in a judicial system stacked against them, but it is not without problems. First, not all crimes come with the right to representation; and second, not all representation is equal. Many defense attorneys, especially those who offer pro bono (free) legal services, are very overworked. Moreover, there is evidence that some defense attorneys for the poor are ill prepared, even to the point of being incompetent to serve as defense counsel (Radelet and Borg, 2000).

The situation regarding noncriminal legal needs is even bleaker for low-income people because the *Miranda* decision does not extend to civil matters. The Legal Services Corporation (LSC), a nonprofit organization established by Congress to address issues of equal access to the justice system, identified a "justice gap" in the United States and concluded that "at least 80 percent of the civil legal needs of low-income Americans are not being met" (Miller, 2005). The following readings explore the intersection between the justice system and membership in the lower classes in the system of stratification.

References

Miller, Hydi. 2005. "LSC Releases Report on Justice Gap in America," Legal Services Corporation. Available online at http://www.lsc.gov/press/pr_detail_T7_R6.php.

"Miranda Warning." 2006. Wikipedia the Free Encyclopedia. Available online at http://en.wikipedia.org/wiki/Miranda_warning.

Radelet, Michael L., and Marian J. Borg. 2000. "The Changing Nature of Death Penalty Debates," *Annual Review of Sociology* 26: 43–61.

17. The Rich Get Richer and the Poor Get Prison
Jeffrey Reiman

It must be borne in mind that the movement from arrest to sentencing is a funneling process, so that discrimination that occurs at any early stage shapes the population that reaches later stages. Thus, for example, some recent studies find little economic bias in sentence length for people convicted of similar crimes. When reading such studies, however, one should remember that the population that reaches the point of sentencing has already been subject to whatever discrimination exists at earlier stages. If, for example, among people with similar offenses and records, poor people are more likely to be charged and more likely to be convicted, then, even if the sentencing of convicted criminals is even-handed, it will reproduce the discrimination that occurred before.

Arrest and Charging

The problem with most official records of who commits crime is that they are really statistics on who gets arrested and convicted. If, as I will show, the police are more likely to arrest some people than others, these official statistics may tell us more about police than about criminals. In any event, they give us little reliable data about those who commit crimes and do not get caught. Some social scientists, suspicious of the bias built into official records, have tried to devise other methods of determining who has committed a crime. Most often, these methods involve an interview or questionnaire in which the respondent is assured of anonymity and asked to reveal whether he or she has committed any offenses for which he or she could be arrested and convicted. Techniques to check reliability of these self-reports also have been devised; however, if their reliability is still in doubt, common sense dictates that they would understate rather than overstate the number of individuals who have committed crimes and never come to official notice. In light of this, the conclusions of these studies are rather astounding. It seems that crime is the national pastime. The President's Crime Commission conducted a survey of 10,000 households and discovered that "91 percent of all Americans have violated laws that could have subjected them to a term of imprisonment at one time in their lives...."

Any number of reasons can be offered to account for the differences in police treatment of poor versus well-off citizens. Some argue that they reflect that the

---

Note: From Jeffrey Reiman, *The Rich Get Richer and the Poor Get Prison: Ideology, Class and Criminal Justice*, 7/e. Published by Allyn and Bacon, Boston, MA. Copyright © 2004 by Pearson Education. Reprinted by permission of the publisher.

poor have less privacy. What others can do in their living rooms or backyards, the poor do on the street. Others argue that a police officer's decision to book a poor youth and release a middle-class youth reflects either the officer's judgment that the higher-class youngster's family will be more likely and more able to discipline him or her than the lower-class youngster's, or differences in the degree to which poor and middle-class complainants demand arrest. Others argue that police training and police work condition police officers to be suspicious of certain kinds of people, such as lower-class youth, blacks, Mexicans, and so on, and thus more likely to detect their criminality. Still others hold that police mainly arrest those with the least political clout, those who are least able to focus public attention on police practices or bring political influence to bear, and these happen to be the members of the lowest social and economic classes.

Regardless of which view one takes, and probably all have some truth in them, one conclusion is inescapable: One of the reasons the offender "at the end of the road in prison is likely to be a member of the lowest social and economic groups in the country" is that the police officers who guard the access to the road to prison make sure that more poor people make the trip than well-to-do people.

Likewise for prosecutors. A recent study of prosecutors' decisions shows that lower-class individuals are more likely to have charges pressed against them than upper-class individuals. Racial discrimination also characterizes prosecutors' decisions to charge. The *Harvard Law Review* overview of studies on race and the criminal process asserts: "Statistical studies indicate that prosecutors are more likely to pursue full prosecution, file more severe charges, and seek more stringent penalties in cases involving minority defendants than in cases involving nonminority defendants. One study of whites, blacks, and Hispanics arrested in Los Angeles on suspicion of having committed a felony found that, among defendants with equally serious charges and prior records, 59 percent of whites had their charges dropped at the initial screening, compared with 40 percent of blacks and 37 percent of Hispanics.

The *weeding-out of the wealthy* starts at the very entrance to the criminal justice system: The decision about whom to investigate, arrest, or charge is not made simply on the basis of the offense committed or the danger posed. It is a decision distorted by a systematic economic bias that works to the disadvantage of the poor.

This economic bias is a two-edged sword. Not only are the poor arrested and charged out of proportion to their numbers for the kinds of crimes poor people generally commit burglary, robbery, assault, and so forth but when we reach the kinds of crimes poor people almost never have the opportunity to commit, such as antitrust violations, industrial safety violations, embezzlement, and serious tax evasion, the criminal justice system shows an increasingly benign and merciful face. The more likely that a crime is the type committed by middle- and upper-class people, the less likely it is that it will be treated as a criminal offense. When it comes to crime in the streets, where the perpetrator is apt to be poor, he or she is even more likely to be arrested and formally charged. When it comes to crime in the suites, where the offender is apt to be affluent, the system is most likely to deal with the crime non-criminally, that is, by civil litigation or informal settlement. When it does choose to proceed criminally, as we will see in the section on sentencing, it rarely goes beyond a slap on the wrist. Not only is the main entry to the road to prison held wide open to the poor, the access routes for the wealthy are largely sealed off. Once again, we should not be surprised at whom we find in our prisons.

Many writers have commented on the extent and seriousness of "white-collar crime," so I will keep my remarks to a minimum. Nevertheless, for those of us trying to understand how the image of crime is created, four points should be noted.

1. White-collar crime is costly; it takes far more dollars from our pockets than all the FBI Index crimes combined.
2. White-collar crime is widespread, probably much more so than the crimes of the poor.
3. White-collar criminals are rarely arrested or charged; the system has developed kindlier ways of dealing with the more delicate sensibilities of its higher-class clientele.
4. When white-collar criminals are prosecuted and convicted, their sentences are either suspended or lenient when judged by the cost their crimes have imposed on society....

ADJUDICATION AND CONVICTION

Between arrest and imprisonment lies the crucial process that determines guilt or innocence. Studies of individuals accused of similar offenses and with similar prior records show that the poor defendant is more likely to be adjudicated guilty than is the wealthier defendant. In the adjudication process the only thing that *should* count is whether the accused is guilty and whether the prosecution can prove it beyond a reasonable doubt. Unfortunately, at least two other factors that are irrelevant to the question of guilt or innocence significantly affect the outcome: One is the ability of the accused to be free on bail prior to trial, and the second is access to legal counsel able to devote adequate time and energy to the case. Because both bail and high-quality legal counsel cost money, it should come as no surprise that here as elsewhere the poor do poorly....

SENTENCING

On June 28, 1990, the House Subcommittee on Financial Institutions Supervision, Regulation, and Insurance met in the Rayburn House Office Building to hold hearings on the prosecution of savings and loan criminals. The chairman of the subcommittee, Congressman Frank Annunzio, called the meeting to order and said:

The American people are furious with the slow pace of prosecutions involving savings and loan criminals. These crooks are responsible for 1/3, 1/2, or maybe even more, of the savings and loan cost. The American taxpayer will be forced to pay $500 billion or more over the next 40 years, largely because of these crooks. For many Americans, this bill will not be paid until their grandchildren are old enough to retire.

We are here to get an answer to one question: "When are the S&L crooks going to jail?"

The answer from the administration seems to be: "Probably never."

Frankly, I don't think the administration has the interest in pursuing Gucci-clad, white-collar criminals. These are hard and complicated cases, and the defendants often were rich, successful prominent members of their upper-class communities. It is far easier putting away a sneaker-clad high school dropout who tries to rob a bank of a thousand dollars with a stick-up note, than a smooth talking S&L executive who steals a million dollars with a fraudulent note.

Later in the hearing, Chairman Annunzio questioned the administration's representative:

You cited, Mr. Dennis, several examples in your testimony of successful convictions with stiff sentences, but the average sentence so far is actually about 2 years, compared to an average sentence of about 9 years for bank robbery. Why do we throw the book at people who rob a bank in broad daylight but we coddle people who ... rob the bank secretly?

Twelve years later, on July 11, 2002, at a hearing of the Crime and Drugs Subcommittee of the Senate Judiciary Committee on the subject of "Penalties for White Collar Crimes: Are We Really Getting Tough on Crime," Senator Joseph Biden, Jr., said:

Under federal law, if ... you steal a car out of my driveway and you drive it across [the state line] into Pennsylvania, ten years. Ten years, federal guideline. You take a pension by violating ERISA, the federal system to safeguard pensions, misdemeanor, maximum one year. The pension may be worth $1,800,000. My car may be worth $2,000.

The simple fact is that the criminal justice system reserves its harshest penalties for its lower-class clients and puts on kid gloves when confronted with a better class of crook....

We have seen ... that the criminal justice system is triply biased against the poor. First, there is the economic class bias [concerning] *harmful acts* as to which get labeled crimes and which are treated as regulatory matters, as we saw in the previous chapter. Second, there is economic class bias *among crimes* that we have seen in this chapter. The crimes that poor people are likely to commit carry harsher sentences than the "crimes in the suites" committed by well-to-do people. Third, *among defendants convicted of the same crimes,* the poor receive less probation and more years of confinement than well-off defendants, assuring us once again that the vast majority of those put behind bars are from the lowest social and economic classes in the nation. On either side of the law, the rich get richer....

SUMMARY

In this chapter I have mainly tried to document that, *even among those dangerous acts that our criminal justice system labels as crimes,* the system works to make it more likely that those who end up in jail or prison will be from the bottom of society. This works in two broad ways:

1. *For the same crime,* the system is more likely to investigate and detect, arrest and charge, convict and sentence, sentence to prison and for a longer time, a lower-class individual than a middle- or upper-class individual. To support this we reviewed a large number of studies comparing the treatment of high- and low-socioeconomic offenders and of white and nonwhite offenders, from arrest through sentencing for the same crimes.

2. *Between crimes that are characteristically committed by poor people (street crimes) and those characteristically committed by the well-off (white-collar and corporate crimes),* the system treats the former much more harshly than the latter, even when the crimes of the well-off take more money from the public or cause more death and injury than the crimes of the poor. To support this we compared the sentences meted out for robbery with those for embezzlement, for grand theft, and Medicaid-provider fraud, and we looked at the treatment of those responsible for death and destruction in the workplace as well as those responsible for the savings and loan scandal and the recent financial cheating at Enron and other major corporations.

18. POVERTY AND VIOLENT CRIME
Elliott Currie

The depths of social exclusion and deprivation in the United States has ramifications for virtually every aspect of our common life—including our level of violent crime. As we'll see, the relationship is complex and sometimes indirect. But it is critically important in understanding America's affliction with violence. How do we know this?

Studies of the correlates of international differences in violent crime offer one kind of evidence. Countries where there is a wide gap between rich and poor routinely show higher levels of violent crime—which helps explain why the world's *worst* levels of violence have been found in places like Colombia, Venezuela, South Africa, and Mexico, where inequalities are even harsher and more consequential than in the United States. Look closer, and it becomes apparent that violence is worse in neglectful or mean-spirited societies than in more generous ones—even if they are poorer. Societies with weak "safety nets" for the poor and economically insecure are more likely than others at a comparable level of development to be wracked by violence.

That is one conclusion, for example, of a study by Rosemary Gartner of the University of Toronto, who examined homicide rates in eighteen developed countries from 1950 to 1980. Even in the earlier part of the period, the United States already suffered considerably higher rates of homicide than the other countries, and the *composition* of American homicide was different as well: America's homicide victims were more likely to have been murdered by strangers, as opposed to intimates, than were murder victims in other countries. And though homicide increased somewhat for the eighteen countries as a whole over the thirty-year period, the extraordinary dominance of the United States remained unchanged. On average, American men died of homicide at an annual rate of about 14 per 100,000 during these years. The next-highest rate—about 4 per 100,000—was in Finland. No other country among the eighteen had a rate as high as 3 per 100,000, and several—including Denmark, England and Wales, Ireland, Holland, and Switzerland—had rates below 1 per 100,000.

What accounted for these differences? Gartner's study points to several factors. Economic inequality had a powerful effect on the countries' homicide levels. A measure of "social security" expenditure as a proportion of GNP—including cash benefits for social welfare and family allowances, along with unemployment insurance, public health spending, and other ameliorative programs—likewise had a strong effect on the risks of homicide for every age group. High divorce rates, ethnic and cultural heterogeneity, and a cultural leaning toward violence generally (as measured by support for the death penalty and frequent wars) also seemed to promote homicide. But the effects of both inequality and the relative absence of social provision remained powerful even when all else was accounted for.

Other cross-national studies in the past few years have turned up the same general connection between economic inequality and violence. Some have also found that the effect is magnified when wide economic inequality is combined with racial or ethnic discrimination. As a recent study by Steven Messner of the State University of New York at Albany, for example, has shown, countries where a distinctive racial or ethnic group suffers systematic discrimination in economic opportunity tend to have particularly high homicide rates.

Similar findings turn up, over and over again, in studies examining the links between inequality, poverty, and violent crime *within* the United States and other specific countries. In the past, the strength of these connections was often obscured by some of the conventions of social science research. Criminologists often pitted one "variable" against others in explaining patterns of violent crime: poverty *versus* inequality, economic inequality *versus* racial inequality, and so on. Invoking these false dichotomies led to conflicting and sometimes confusing results; some studies concluded that inequality *but not* poverty was associated with violence, or that once race was controlled poverty was unimportant, or vice versa. But in the real world, of course, these "variables" aren't so easily separable. Being poor in America *means* being at the bottom of an exceptionally harsh system of inequality; being black greatly increases the chances of being impoverished and, therefore, trapped at the lower end of the social ladder.

More recent studies that have put these factors together, rather than artificially separating them, have given us powerful evidence of the close connection between violence and social disadvantage. In a seminal analysis of the covariates of homicide in the United States, for example, Kenneth Land, Patricia McCall, and Lawrence Cohen found that a measure of "resource deprivation"—which includes the proportion of families in poverty, the median income, the degree of income inequality, the percentage of the population that is black, and the percentage of children not living with both parents—had "by far the strongest and most invariant effect" on the rate of homicide. That effect held true for cities, metropolitan areas, and states, and prevailed across three different years—1960, 1970, and 1980. "Resource deprivation" was not the *only* explanation for the wide differences in homicide rates among American cities and states—the proportion of the population that was divorced, in particular, also played an important role—but it was the biggest.

Moreover, we also know that the links between disadvantage and violence are strongest for the poorest and most neglected of the poor. If we simply divide the population into broad categories by social class, or what sociologists often call "socioeconomic status" (SES), the group differences in violent crime are less stark. It is when we focus more narrowly on people locked into the most permanent forms of economic marginality in the most impoverished and disrupted communities that we see the highest concentrations of serious violent crime. This pattern appears no matter how we do the study: whether we measure crime by official reports or by "self-reports" from offenders themselves; whether we follow the fate of disadvantaged children and youths over time or compare different neighborhoods in a given city. The 1967 crime commission was right: crime "flourishes where the conditions of life are the worst."

The connection between violent crime and severe deprivation appears clearly, for example, in studies that have followed groups of vulnerable children over time—"longitudinal" studies—like the one done on the island of Kauai, Hawaii, by the psychologist Emmy Werner of the University of California at Davis and her colleagues. Werner followed over five hundred children born in 1955—most of them children of immigrant plantation workers who had not graduated from high school—from birth until age thirty-two. Most of the children within this relatively deprived group turned out at least moderately well. But a substantial minority did not, and they were disproportionately those who had grown up in the most adverse conditions—including chronic poverty: "Two-thirds of the individuals with serious coping problems by age 31/32 had been high risk youth who had been exposed to poverty and family disorganization since early childhood and who subsequently developed records of school failure, repeated delinquencies, and/or mental health problems." In that especially high-risk group was also a group of about one-third who, despite being exposed to the same adverse conditions, generally prospered as children and adults—who were "vulnerable but invincible." One message of this study, accordingly, is that even the obstacle of being born into chronic poverty doesn't seal off the possibility of successful adulthood. But it does make growing up unscathed much harder.

The finding that even within a generally deprived population it is the *most* deprived children who face the greatest risks of delinquency and crime also stands out in another often-cited longitudinal study, this one done in South London, England, by Donald West and David Farrington of Cambridge University. The Cambridge Study of Delinquent Development followed over four hundred boys who were between eight and nine years old in the early 1960s—"a traditional white, urban, working class sample of British origin"—up to about age thirty-two. The study shows that a wide range of factors, including family problems like poor child-rearing techniques, poor supervision, erratic or harsh discipline, and parental conflict or criminality, influence the likelihood of later delinquency, violence, and adult crime. But it also found that "the major risk factors for delinquency include poverty, poor housing, and living in public housing in inner-city, socially disorganized communities." As in many other studies, delinquency was not strongly correlated with a general measure of the boys' "social class" based on their parents' occupation. But *poverty* was another matter. *Within* this basically working-class and decidedly unaffluent group, ninety-three of the boys, at age eight, lived in families defined as having "low income" compared with the sample as a whole. Of those ninety-three, about 42 percent became involved in violence as teenagers, versus 26 percent of the others. Even more significantly, 24 percent of the "low-income" boys—but less than 9 percent of the rest—were *convicted* of violent offenses as adults. "In the light of the clear link between poverty and antisocial behaviour," writes David Farrington, "it is surprising that more prevention experiments targeting this factor have not been conducted."

The same pattern appears in studies that examine the distribution of serious violent crime "cross-sectionally"—across different cities, or different neighborhoods within a city. In a 1996 study, Lauren Krivo and Ruth Peterson of Ohio State University divided census tracts in Columbus, Ohio, into those with low, high, and "extreme" levels of poverty ("extreme" meaning that 40 percent or more of the residents were poor). Not unexpectedly, rates of violent crime generally increased as the percentage of poor residents increased; violence was more likely in the areas of high poverty than in the low group. But there was an especially sharp upward jump in the level of violent crime once a neighborhood's poverty rate went above 40 percent: the difference between the extreme and the high poverty areas was much greater than that between the high and the low neighborhoods. When Krivo and Peterson put together a composite measure of "disadvantage," which included not only poverty rates but levels of male joblessness, the percentage of children living outside of two-parent families, and the presence of professional or managerial people in the neighborhood, the connection with violent crime—already astonishingly strong for extreme poverty alone—was even higher and explained a very large proportion of the variation in violence among Columbus's neighborhoods.

Krivo and Peterson's research also suggests that it is this strong link between extreme disadvantage and violence which underlies much of the association between *race* and violent crime in the United States. Columbus was a particularly fruitful place to study this issue, because it is one of the relatively few major American cities that have several neighborhoods with high concentrations of the *white* poor. And the same strong connection between extreme disadvantage and violence appeared in neighborhoods that were mostly or entirely white as in those that were mostly black. Rates of violence in the most deprived white neighborhoods were not quite as high as in the most deprived black ones—suggesting that there is something about the experience of black poverty in particular that exacerbates the common pressures of social disadvantage (an earlier study by these researchers, in fact, found a clear and consistent relationship between racial residential segregation and rates of violent crime). But they were close. The annual rate of reported violent crime per 1,000 population was 29 in extremely poor black neighborhoods; 23 in extremely poor white neighborhoods; and 18 in black neighborhoods with high but not extreme poverty. The poorest white neighborhoods, in other words, suffered more violence than somewhat less poor, but still deprived, black communities. And they suffered almost twice the violent crime rate of black neighborhoods characterized by "low" poverty.

* * *

The links between extreme deprivation, delinquency, and violence, then, are strong, consistent, and compelling. There is little question that growing up in extreme poverty exerts powerful pressures toward crime. The fact that those pressures are overcome by some individuals is testimony to human strength and resiliency, but does not diminish the importance of the link between social exclusion and violence. The effects are compounded by the absence of public supports to buffer economic insecurity and deprivation, and they are even more potent when racial subordination is added to the mix. And this—rather than "prosperity"—helps us begin to understand why the United States suffers more serious violent crime than other industrial democracies, and why violence has remained stubbornly high in the face of our unprecedented efforts at repressive control.

These conclusions fly in the face of the common conservative argument that government efforts to reduce poverty and disadvantage have no effect on crime—or, in a more extreme version, that the expansion of the "welfare state" is itself to blame for high crime rates. It's often said that though we've spent "trillions" of dollars on antipoverty programs since the 1960s, crime has risen anyway, and that, accordingly, public spending on the poor is not the solution and may indeed be the problem. But that argument is misleading, on two counts. To begin with, it both exaggerates the amount of "antipoverty" spending in America and, as importantly, reverses the direction of the recent trend. Welfare spending per child in poverty dropped by *a third* between 1979 and 1993, reflecting the fact that while the number of poor children rose substantially, welfare spending remained basically level. Most crucially, of course, the argument that the welfare state causes crime founders against the reality that those countries with the most developed welfare states have far less violence than the United States, the industrial nation with the *least* developed welfare state.

19. THE CIVIL RIGHTS ACT OF 1964
THE SOCIAL CLASS EXCLUSION
Janis E. Johnston

> That the poor are invisible is one of the most important things about them. They are not simply neglected and forgotten as in the old rhetoric of reform; what is much worse, they are not seen (Harrington, 1962, pp 6–7).

In 1962, Michael Harrington called the poor "invisible" and suggested that people who lived in poverty were so removed from mainstream society that for most people in the U.S. it was almost as though the poor didn't exist (for a complete discussion, see Harrington, 1997, pp. 1–18). While over 40 years have passed since Harrington first discussed the plight of the poor, their situation is still much the same as the one Harrington identified. One might even argue that the poor have become even further removed from the middle and upper class experience—even more invisible. Although the invisibility of the poor permeates all aspects of their lives, this discussion focuses on access to the courts and particularly, on the rights of the poor to challenge discriminatory behavior in the courts.

For most of U.S. history there were no legal protections for people who experienced discrimination. The Civil Rights Act of 1964 changed that for people who could prove that they had been discriminated against because of their race, color, religion, sex, or national origin, but it did not extend this protection to the poor and the near-poor. It is important to understand the history that led to the Civil Rights Act and to understand the implications of excluding people from the bottom of the social strata from protections through the courts. First, consider the history.

In the late 1800s, laws in much of the United States mandated segregation between whites and non-whites and in particular, prevented nonwhites from riding in rail cars designated for Whites. There were those, however, who sought to challenge those laws. In 1892 Homer Plessy, a man who was "seven-eighths Caucasian" but considered Black by cultural standards, was part of a planned action to challenge the separation of Blacks and Whites into separate rail cars (Zimmerman, 1997; Oyez, 2005). After purchasing a first class ticket, Plessy entered the "Whites only" car and took an empty seat. The train's conductor asked Plessy to find a seat in the car designated for "persons not of the white race" but he refused to move and was arrested. If convicted, Plessy faced a possible $25 fine or imprisonment in the parish prison for not more than twenty days (*The Multiracial Activist,* 1998).

According to Zimmerman (1997), Plessy's arrest had been planned to allow a group in Louisiana to challenge the "1890 Louisiana Separate Car Act" that mandated separate cars to keep the races apart. By choosing someone who was racially mixed, lawyers hoped to show that the law was arbitrary and unconstitutional and more specifically, that the Separate Car Act violated the Thirteenth and Fourteenth Amendments to the Constitution.

The Thirteenth Amendment abolished slavery and the Fourteenth Amendment was added to ensure "absolute equality" between the races. In other words, Amendment Fourteen required the law to be color blind (Introduction to the Court, 2005). In particular, Amendment Fourteen extended concepts such as "due process"; the requirement that the Government "respect all of a person's legal rights ... when the government deprives a person of life, liberty, or property" ("Due Process" *Wikipedia,* 2006), and "equal protection"; a mandate that required that all people be treated the same in the eyes of the law (see also U.S. Constitution, 2005).

The trial judge for the initial case, John H. Ferguson, ruled that Louisiana law was not unconstitutional and therefore Plessy was guilty of the charges against him. Ferguson's decision was appealed to the Louisiana State supreme court in 1893 where it was upheld, at which point lawyers petitioned the U.S. Supreme Court to hear the case. In its ruling, the Supreme Court upheld the lower court's decision and found that Louisiana was not violating the Constitution by providing separate facilities for Whites and Blacks. Writing for the majority, Justice Henry B. Brown argued that Louisiana's law did not conflict with the Thirteenth Amendment regarding slavery and as for the Fourteenth Amendment; the Railroad was not violating the law but instead was simply keeping with the traditions of the people at the time. Brown wrote, "We cannot say that a law which authorizes or even requires the separation of the two races in public conveyances is unreasonable, or more obnoxious to the Fourteenth Amendment than the acts of Congress requiring separate schools for colored children" (Introduction to the Court, 2005, para 14).

Justice John Harlan, the lone dissenter, argued that the "Constitution was colorblind" and further suggested that State sanctioned segregation would result in Black individuals feeling inferior, which did violate the presumed equality of the races under the Fourteenth Amendment. (For a complete discussion of Justice Harlan's dissent, see *Plessy v. Ferguson* at "Introduction to the Court," 2005 or Thompson, 1996.) In spite of Harlan's objection, the Court's decision ushered in an era that allowed the separation of the races in what became known as the "separate but equal" principle, or doctrine. Because of the separate but equal principle, virtually all aspects of life for White and Black Americans were maintained separately; transportation remained segregated, restaurants maintained separate seating, even drinking fountains were segregated.

In 1954, the Supreme Court heard a case that overturned *Plessy v. Ferguson*. That case was *Oliver L. Brown et al. v. Board of Education of Topeka, (KS) et al.* and came about to challenge the idea that separate schools for Whites and Blacks were indeed, equal. Linda Brown's name is the most recognized in the case, but twelve families were included in the Kansas lawsuit. The suit questioned why these African American children were not allowed to attend the schools in their neighborhoods but were bussed to Black schools in other neighborhoods. Moreover, the suit contended that the all-Black schools were inferior to the all-White schools. The suit was filed with aid from the National Association for the Advancement of Colored People (NAACP), and argued that the Black schools had substandard buildings, resources, personnel, and curricula, and therefore the separate but equal doctrine violated the Fourteenth Amendment (Brown Foundation, 2004).

The case that finally went to the Supreme Court was really a compilation of five cases, the Brown lawsuit and similar actions that had been filed in Delaware, South Carolina, Virginia, and Washington D.C. that all addressed the constitutionality of separate schools, although the combined lawsuit is still known by the name, *Brown v. Board of Education* (Brown Foundation, 2004). The 1954 Supreme Court decision was unanimous with the nine Justices ruling that segregated schools denied African American children equal protection and therefore violated the Fourteenth Amendment to the Constitution. *Brown v. Board of Education* thereby overturned the decision creating the separate but equal doctrine that had been in place since the *Plessy v. Ferguson* decision (see also, Brown v. Board Issue, n.d.; Brown v. Board, *Wikipedia*, 2006).

Although *Plessy v. Ferguson* was not the earliest case to challenge segregation and *Plessy v. Ferguson* and *Brown v. Board of Education* were just two among many cases that came to challenge the racial segregation, these two cases in particular represent the legal and cultural climate that people in the United States operated in in the 19th and 20th Centuries. These cases also lead us into a discussion of the Civil Rights Act of 1964.

The period leading up to 1964 was a tumultuous time in the United States, and particularly in the South. Southern Black students were pushing state governments to enforce the *Brown v. Board of Education* decision and demanding that they be allowed access to "White" schools, because although the law had passed, there was resistance to implementing the law. The result of their struggles was national attention to civil rights at even the highest level of government. The Civil Rights Act of 1964 was the culmination of work begun by early civil rights activists resulting in a bill promised by President John F. Kennedy in his "Civil Rights Address" of 1963. The reason for Kennedy's speech was two-fold. First, the speech was a call to action to engage people in pushing their State and local legislatures to act on civil rights questions. Second, Kennedy announced to the American public he was going to ask Congress to enact legislation to guarantee that "race [would have] no place in American life or law" (Kennedy, 1963, para 10).

Introduced into the House by Congressman Emanuel Celler (D-Brooklyn) and to the Senate by Majority Leader Michael J. Mansfield (D-Montana), the Civil

Rights Act was intended to ensure that the rights of Blacks were being upheld. The original legislation sought protection for individuals by preventing discrimination on the basis of race, color, religion, or national origin. In spite of the fact that the President supported the Bill, however, it was meeting with resistance in Washington. In November 1963, President Kennedy was assassinated and Lyndon B. Johnson became the thirty-seventh president of the United States. Johnson, who had never been a strong supporter of the Bill, took on the task of personally ensuring that Kennedy's vision regarding civil rights would be fulfilled upon being sworn into office (Whalen and Whalen, 1985).

The discussions that took place behind the scenes on Capitol Hill are evidence of the division among people in terms of how they felt about guaranteeing civil rights to people regardless of their race. Notice also that as originally introduced, the bill did not include protection based on an individual's sex. Providing legal protection against sex discrimination was added as an amendment to the original bill. Howard W. Smith (D-West Virginia) suggested the one-word amendment, adding the word "sex" to the list of protected statuses. The reason for Smith's amendment is clouded. There are strong arguments for the idea that Smith added protection for women in an attempt to keep the bill from passing. Smith was known for his opposition to the Civil Rights Act and there are those who argue that Smith believed that his amendment would prevent passage of the bill. Smith, however, stated he added sex to the list of protected statuses at the urging of a woman who had written him regarding the inclusion of women for equal protection (Whalen and Whalen, 1985 pp. 115–116). With the amendment in place, protection against discrimination changed from a focus on men, to protections for both men and women.

The Civil Rights Act began its journey through the House of Representatives June 20, 1963 when H.R. 7152 (House of Representatives 7152—the working name of the bill) was introduced into a Subcommittee of the Judiciary Committee. Seven months later, the bill came before the entire House and after a nine-day, continuous debate on just this one bill, members of the House sent the bill on to the Senate. In none of the discussion in the Subcommittee, nor in any of the discussions in the House, *did the issue of social class come up*. When the Civil Rights Act got to the Senate, it was subject to the longest filibuster in history, 13 weeks, and still the members of the lowest social classes remained invisible.

After 83 days in the Senate, H.R. 7152 passed and was signed into law July 2, 1964. In its final form, the Civil Rights Act gave protected status to groups of people based on race, color, religion, sex, or national origin. This meant that if people felt they had been discriminated against, they had "standing," or the right to initiate a lawsuit in the courts. So for example, if a group could prove it had been discriminated against because of race, members of the group could find remedy through the courts. The exclusion of class, however, meant that if people in the lowest classes were discriminated against they did not have standing in the courts.

A strong case can be made that the poor are discriminated against in a variety of situations, but consider education for a specific example. School districts receive about half of their revenue from local taxes, therefore poor neighborhoods tend to have substandard schools. Thus, much like the argument in *Brown v. Board of Education,* poor children go to inferior schools with substandard buildings, resources, personnel, and curricula. It would seem that since people who live in poor neighborhoods do not have the same access to education as their counterparts in more affluent neighborhoods that they should have the right to go to court and push for better schools. That is only true, however, if the neighborhood is primarily minority, predominantly women, is comprised of people who follow the same religion, or individuals who share the same nationality. If, however, the neighborhood is comprised of a heterogeneous group of men and women who are poor, there can be no lawsuit.

People in the lower classes are often negatively affected by decisions made by those with power, whether those decisions are regarding housing, employment, or public accommodations. When only a portion of the affected population is afforded a remedy for the discrimination through the courts, tensions between races and between males and females may evolve or intensify. Moreover, denying class as a protected status forces society's focus to stay on issues of race, gender, and religion, even if class is the underlying issue.

The Civil Rights Act provided a very important remedy for people who had been intolerably discriminated against. That discrimination still exists and therefore it is vital that the Civil Rights Act continues to be available as a tool to rectify structural and individual conditions that allow discrimination to continue. I would like to put forward a question, however, and that is, "What kind of world would we live in today if the Civil Rights Act had included social class among its categories for protected status"? Hurricane Katrina in 2005 profoundly affected many in the South, and especially impacted members of the lower class. There have been questions regarding the government's slow response to the disaster, with suggestions that the slow response was because the people who were the most affected were African American. Was the government slow to respond because of the race, ethnicity, national origin, or sex of the people who were in the devastating path of the hurricane? If so, these individuals have standing in the courts and may seek a legal remedy. Was the government slow to respond because of the social class of the people who were so profoundly affected? If so, no remedy exists. Until people in the lower social classes are afforded protection via the courts, a portion of our population will remain without recourse ... and without an option to redress their grievances.

According to The Dirksen Congressional Center, the Civil Rights Act "did not resolve all problems of discrimination. But it opened the door to further progress by lessening racial restrictions on the use of public facilities, providing more job opportunities, strengthening voting laws, and limiting federal funding of discriminatory aid programs" (Dirksen, n.d., para 7). Moreover, before signing the Civil Rights Act President Lyndon B. Johnson stated:

> We believe that all men [sic] are created equal—yet many are denied equal treatment. We believe that all men [sic] have certain inalienable rights. We believe

that all men [sic] are entitled to the blessings of liberty—yet millions are being deprived of those blessings, not because of their own failures, but because of the color of their skins.

The reasons are deeply embedded in history and tradition and the nature of man [sic]. We can understand without rancor or hatred how all this happens. But it cannot continue. Our Constitution, the foundation of our Republic, forbids it. The principles of our freedom forbid it. Morality forbids it. And the law I sign tonight forbids it.... (Dirksen, n.d., para 92, 93).

The time has come to extend Civil Rights Act protections to members of the lower and under classes. It is time for the poor to move into the consciousness of our society and to ensure that the impoverished become visible. Making the poor visible in the courts is a first step.

REFERENCES

Brown Foundation for Educational Equity, Excellence and Research. 2004. "In Pursuit of Freedom & Equality: Brown v. Board of Education of Topeka." [Online]. Available http://brownvboard.org/index.htm.

"Brown v. Board of Education." 2006. *Wikipedia—the free encyclopedia.* [Online]. Available http://en.wikipedia.org/wiki/Brown_v._Board_of_Education.

"Brown v. Board of Education Issue: Racial Segregation in Public Schools." No date. [Online]. Available http://www.pbs.org/jefferson/enlight/brown.htm.

"Civil Rights Act of 1964." [Online]. Available http://usinfo.state.gov/usa/infousa/laws/majorlaw/civilr19.htm.

"Civil Rights Act of 1964." *Wikipedia—the free encyclopedia.* [Online]. Available http://en.wikipedia.org/wiki/Civil_Rights_Act_of_1964.

The Dirksen Congressional Center. n.d. "Major Features of the Civil Rights Act of 1964." [Online]. Available http://www.congresslink.org/print_basics_histmats_civilrights64text.htm.

"Due Process." 2006. *Wikipedia—the free encyclopedia.* [Online]. Available http://en.wikipedia.org/wiki/Due_process.

Harrington, Michael. 1962. *The Other America: Poverty in the United States.* New York: Macmillan.

———. 1997. *The Other America: Poverty in the United States.* New York: Touchstone.

Introduction to the Court Opinion on the Plessy V. Ferguson Case. 2005. [Online]. Available http://usinfo.state.gov/usa/infousa/facts/democrac/33.htm.

Kennedy, John F. 1963. "Civil Rights Address." [Online]. Available http://www.americanrhetoric.com/speeches/johnfkennedycivilrights.htm.

The Multiracial Activist. 1998. "United States Supreme Court Case: Plessy v. Ferguson." [Online]. Available http://www.multiracial.com/government/plessy.html.

The Oyez Project, Oyez: Plessy v. Ferguson, 163 U.S. 537 (1896). 2005. [Online]. Available http://www.oyez.org/oyez/resource/case/307/.

"Plessy v. Ferguson." 2006. *Wikipedia—the free encyclopedia.* [Online]. Available at http://en.wikipedia.org/wiki/Plessy_v._Ferguson.

Supreme Court of the United States: Brown v. Board of Education, 347 U.S. 483 (1954) (USSC+). 1954. [Online]. Available http://www.nationalcenter.org/brown.html.

Thompson, Charles. 1996. "Harlan's Great Dissent." [Online]. Available http://library.louisville.edu/law/harlan/harlthom.html.

U.S. Constitution—Amendment 14. 2005. [Online]. Available http://www.usconstitution.net/xconst_Am14.html.

Whalen, Charles and Barbara Whalen. 1985. *The Longest Debate: A Legislative History of the Civil Rights Act.* Cabin John, MD: Seven Locks Press.

Zimmerman, Thomas. 1997. *Plessy v. Ferguson.* [Online]. Available http://www.bgsu.edu/departments/acs/1890s/plessy/plessy.html.

Chapter 9
Natural Disasters

Social class position can make a life or death difference in natural disasters. For example, when the transatlantic luxury liner *Titanic* rammed an iceberg in 1912, only 3 percent of the first-class female passengers died, compared to 16 percent of the second-class passengers and 45 percent of the third-class passengers (Lord, 1955: 107).

The poor and the near-poor are more likely than middle- or upper-class people to be profoundly affected by natural disasters, for a variety of reasons. They live where land is the cheapest and the most vulnerable (in the flood plain or below sea level). Their homes are more likely to be unsafe (as in the case of mobile homes). Or they may not even have homes, which makes them the most vulnerable of all.

When tornado warning sirens sound, people are told to go to a basement and to leave mobile homes entirely; but many members of the lower classes have no immediate access to safe locations in an acute disaster. When hurricane warnings are announced, people are told to evacuate, especially from low-lying areas and those near human-created structures such as dams and levees; but many members of the lower classes lack access to transportation out of the area and have nowhere to go even when they are able to vacate their homes and apartments.

In extreme heat or extreme cold, survival depends on access to air conditioning or heat, which many members of the lower classes do not have. In the face of rising energy costs, even those with furnaces or air conditioners often cannot afford the cost of operating them. Being without air conditioning in sustained heat can be as devastating as lacking heat in extreme cold. In July 2006, heat was blamed for the deaths of more than 140 California residents. Yet, as George Luber of the Center for Disease Control's Division of Environmental Hazards and Health Effects noted, many heat-related deaths are avoidable. Luber specifically stated that "using air conditioning" can prevent heat-related illness and death (Minerd, 2006) and further argued that as few as three hours of air conditioning per day could have saved lives (Luber, in Reinberg, 2006). Those at risk were the elderly, the infirm, and members of the lower classes.

The three readings in this section focus on two natural disasters. The first, an interview with Eric Klinenberg, deals with the Chicago heat wave of 1995. According to Klinenberg's data, the people most likely to die were those who had been socially isolated and without resources. The next two readings consider the intersection of social class and race in the New Orleans flood caused by Hurricane Katrina in 2005. Jason DeParle describes the situation just days after the hurricane, and Peter Wagner and Susan Edwards supply data comparing Louisiana, New Orleans, and the Lower Ninth Ward in New Orleans (the worst-hit ward in the city) along with comparable data for the U.S. population overall.

References

Lord, Walter. 1955. *A Night to Remember.* New York: Henry Holt.

Minerd, Jeff. 2006. "Heat-Related Deaths Strike Men More Often," MedPage Today (July 27). Available online at http://www.medpagetoday.com/PublicHealth-Policy/Environmental Health/tb/3820.

Reinberg, Steven. 2006. Heat-Related Deaths in U.S. on the Rise. *Healthfinder,* U.S. Department of Health and Human Services. Available online at http://www.healthfinder.gov/news/newsstory.asp?docID=534068.

20. Dying Alone
AN INTERVIEW WITH ERIC KLINENBERG
University of Chicago Press

Question: Take us back to July 1995 in the city of Chicago. How hot was it? What were the city and its residents going through?

Klinenberg: Chicago felt tropical, like Fiji or Guam but with an added layer of polluted city air trapping the heat. On the first day of the heat wave, Thursday, July 13, the temperature hit 106 degrees, and the heat index—a combination of heat and humidity that measures the temperature a typical person would feel—rose above 120. For a week, the heat persisted, running between the 90s and low 100s. The night temperatures, in the low to mid-80s, were unusually high and didn't provide much relief. Chicago's houses and apartment buildings baked like ovens. Air-conditioning helped, of course, if you were fortunate enough to have it. But many people only had fans and open windows, which just recirculated the hot air.

The city set new records for energy use, which then led to the failure of some power grids—at one point, 49,000 households had no electricity. Many Chicagoans swarmed the city's beaches, but others took to the fire hydrants. More than 3,000 hydrants around Chicago were opened, causing some neighborhoods to lose water pressure on top of losing electricity. When emergency crews came to seal the hydrants, some people threw bricks and rocks to keep them away.

The heat made the city's roads buckle. Train rails warped, causing long commuter and freight delays. City workers watered bridges to prevent them from locking when the plates expanded. Children riding in school buses became so dehydrated and nauseous that they had to be hosed down by the Fire Department. Hundreds of young people were hospitalized with heat-related illnesses. But the elderly, and especially the elderly who lived alone, were most vulnerable to the heat wave.

After about forty-eight hours of continuous exposure to heat, the body's defenses begin to fail. So by Friday, July 14, thousands of Chicagoans had developed severe heat-related illnesses. Paramedics couldn't keep up with emergency calls, and city hospitals were overwhelmed. Twenty-three hospitals—most on the South and Southwest Sides—went on bypass status, closing the doors of their emergency rooms to new patients. Some ambulance crews drove around the city for miles looking for an open bed.

Hundreds of victims never made it to a hospital. The most overcrowded place in the city was the Cook County Medical Examiners Office, where police transported hundreds of bodies for autopsies. The morgue typically receives about 17 bodies a day and has a total of 222 bays. By Saturday—just three days into the heat wave—its capacity was exceeded by hundreds, and the county had to bring in a fleet of refrigerated trucks to store the bodies. Police officers had to wait as long as three hours for a worker to receive the body. It was gruesome and incredible for this to be happening in the middle of a modern American city.

Question: How many people died as a result of the heat wave?

Klinenberg: In 1995 there were no uniform standards for determining a "heat related death," so officials had to develop them. Edmund Donoghue, Cook County's chief medical examiner, used state-of-the-art criteria to report 465 heat-related deaths for the heat wave week and 521 heat deaths for the month of July. But Mayor Richard M. Daley challenged these findings. "It's hot," the mayor told the media. "But let's not blow it out of proportion.... Every day people die of natural causes. You cannot claim that everybody who has died in the last eight or nine days dies of heat. Then everybody in the summer that dies will die of heat." Many local journalists shared Daley's skepticism, and before long the city was mired in a callous debate over whether the so-called heat deaths were—to use the term that recurred at the time—"really real."

Medical examiners around the country confirmed that Donoghue's heat-related death criteria were scientifically sound and endorsed his findings. But perhaps the best measure of heat deaths comes from another figure—the "excess death" rate—which counts the difference between the reported deaths and the typical deaths for a given time period. According to this measure, 739 Chicagoans *above the norm* died during the week of 14 to 20 July—which means that Donoghue had been conservative in his accounts.

Daley's skepticism had a big impact on the public debate, and it still does. Today if you ask Chicagoans about the heat wave they will likely tell you that not all the deaths were "really real." That's a direct legacy of the politics of the disaster.

Question: Who were these 739 people? Was there a "typical" victim?

Klinenberg: The US Centers for Disease Control and Prevention did a thorough study of individual-level risk factors for heat wave victims, and they came up with a list of conditions of vulnerability: living alone, not leaving home daily, lacking access to transportation, being sick or bedridden, not having social contacts nearby, and of course not having an air conditioner.

Given these factors, experts assumed that female victims would outnumber male victims in the heat wave deaths, because women are more prevalent among those who are old and who live alone. But in fact men were more than twice as likely to die as women. This is just one of the surprises that emerged during my study of the Chicago heat wave. To understand this we have to look at the social relationships that elderly women retain but that elderly men tend to lose.

The ethnic and racial differences in mortality are also significant for what they can teach us about urban life. The actual death tolls for African Americans and whites were almost identical, but those numbers are misleading. There are far more elderly whites than elderly African Americans in Chicago, and when the

Chicago Public Health Department considered the age differences, they found that the black/white mortality ratio was 1.5 to 1.

Another surprising fact that emerged is that Latinos, who represent about 25 percent of the city population and are disproportionately poor and sick, accounted for only 2 percent of the heat-related deaths. I wrote *Heat Wave* to make sense of these numbers—to show, for instance, why the Latino Little Village neighborhood had a much lower death rate than African American North Lawndale. Many Chicagoans attributed the disparate death patterns to the ethnic differences among blacks, Latinos, and whites—and local experts made much of the purported Latino "family values." But there's a social and spatial context that makes close family ties possible. Chicago's Latinos tend to live in neighborhoods with high population density, busy commercial life in the streets, and vibrant public spaces. Most of the African American neighborhoods with high heat wave death rates had been abandoned—by employers, stores, and residents—in recent decades. The social ecology of abandonment, dispersion, and decay makes systems of social support exceedingly difficult to sustain.

Question: So would you call the heat wave deaths primarily a social disaster, rather than a natural one?

Klinenberg: Of course forces of nature played a major role. But these deaths were not an act of God. The authors of an article in the *American Journal of Public Health* said that the most sophisticated climate models "failed to detect relationships between the weather and mortality that would explain what happened in July 1995 in Chicago." Hundreds of Chicago residents *died alone,* behind locked doors and sealed windows, out of contact with friends, family, and neighbors, unassisted by public agencies or community groups. There's nothing natural about that.

The death toll was the result of distinct dangers in Chicago's social environment: an increased population of isolated seniors who live and die alone; the culture of fear that makes city dwellers reluctant to trust their neighbors or, sometimes, even leave their houses; the abandonment of neighborhoods by businesses, service providers, and most residents, leaving only the most precarious behind; and the isolation and insecurity of single room occupancy dwellings and other last-ditch low-income housing. None of these common urban conditions show up as causes of death in the medical autopsies or political reports that establish the official record for the heat disaster.

Chicago had such a high mortality rate because it is, as Mayor Daley quipped during the heat wave, the classic American city of extremes. It is a city of great opulence and of boundless optimism, but—as William Julius Wilson says—Chicago also suffers from an everyday "emergency in slow motion" that its leaders refuse to acknowledge. The heat wave was a particle accelerator for the city: It sped up and made visible the hazardous social conditions that are always present but difficult to perceive. Yes, the weather was extreme. But the deep sources of the tragedy were the everyday disasters that the city tolerates, takes for granted, or has officially forgotten.

Question: What about the response from the city? Did the city government do enough to warn residents of the danger, provide cool shelter, or help people who were in trouble? What could Chicago do differently in future heat waves?

Klinenberg: It is not fair to blame any single organization or individual for an event in which hundreds of people die alone. The heat disaster was a collective failure, and the search for scapegoats—whether the mayor, the media, or the medical system—is just a distraction from the real issues.

Yet there is no question that the city government did not do everything it could to prevent the catastrophe. The city failed to implement its own heat emergency plan, waiting until Saturday, July 15, after hundreds of bodies had already been delivered to the county morgue, to declare an official emergency. The Fire Department refused its paramedics' requests to call in more staff and secure more ambulances, thereby assuring continued delays in its emergency health response. The Police Department did not use its senior units to attend to the elderly residents they were supposed to protect. And since there was no system to monitor the hospital bypass situation, at one point eighteen hospitals were simultaneously refusing new emergency patients.

The city also aggressively used its tremendous public relations apparatus to first deny there was a disaster and then to define the disaster as natural and unpreventable. The city's public statements about the heat deaths, including the executive summary of a special mayor's commission, defended the government's role while obscuring the social roots of the death toll.

But the city did learn from its mistakes. In 1999, when Chicago experienced another severe heat wave, the city issued strongly worded warnings and press releases to the media, opened cooling centers and provided free bus transportation to them, phoned elderly residents, and sent police officers and city workers door-to-door to check up on seniors who lived alone. That aggressive response drastically reduced the death toll of the 1999 heat wave: 110 residents died, a fraction of the 1995 level but still catastrophic. The policy lesson is that there are limits to what any emergency plan can accomplish.

We know that more heat waves are coming. Every major report on global warming—including the recent White House study—warns that an increase in severe heat waves is likely. The only way to prevent another heat disaster is to address the isolation, poverty, and fear that are prevalent in so many American cities today. Until we do, natural forces that are out of our control will continue to be uncontrollably dangerous.

Note

Eric Klinenberg is author of *Heat Wave: A Social Autopsy of Disaster in Chicago.* Available at http://www.press.uchicago.edu/Misc/Chicago/443213in.html.

21. The Nation: Cast Away
Broken Levees, Unbroken Barriers
Jason DeParle

The white people got out. Most of them, anyway. If television and newspaper images can be deemed a statistical sample, it was mostly black people who were left behind. Poor black people, growing more hungry, sick and frightened by the hour as faraway officials counseled patience and warned that rescues take time.

What a shocked world saw exposed in New Orleans last week wasn't just a broken levee. It was a cleavage of race and class, at once familiar and startlingly new, laid bare in a setting where they suddenly amounted to matters of life and death. Hydrology joined sociology throughout the story line, from the settling of the flood-prone city, where well-to-do white people lived on the high ground, to its frantic abandonment.

The pictures of the suffering vied with reports of marauding, of gunshots fired at rescue vehicles and armed bands taking over the streets. The city of quaint eccentricity—of King Cakes, Mardi Gras beads and nice neighbors named Tookie—had taken a Conradian turn.

In the middle of the delayed rescue, the New Orleans mayor, C. Ray Nagin, a local boy made good from a poor, black ward, burst into tears of frustration as he denounced slow moving federal officials and called for martial law.

Even people who had spent a lifetime studying race and class found themselves slack-jawed.

"This is a pretty graphic illustration of who gets left behind in this society—in a literal way," said Christopher Jencks, a sociologist glued to the televised images from his office at Harvard. Surprised to have found himself surprised, Mr. Jencks took to thinking out loud. "Maybe it's just an in-the-face version of something I already knew," he said. "All the people who don't get out, or don't have the resources, or don't believe the warning are African-American."

"It's not that it's at odds with the way I see American society," Mr. Jencks said. "But it's at odds with the way I want to see American society."

Last week it was how others saw American society, too, in images beamed across the globe. Were it not for the distinctive outlines of the Superdome, the pictures of hovering rescue helicopters might have carried a Somalian dateline. The Sri Lankan ambassador offered to help raise foreign aid.

Anyone who knew New Orleans knew that danger lurked behind the festive front. Let the good times roll, the tourists on Bourbon Street were told. Yet in every season, someone who rolled a few blocks in the wrong direction wound up in the city morgue.

Unusually poor (27.4 percent below the poverty line in 2000), disproportionately black (over two-thirds), the Big Easy is also disproportionately murderous—with a rate that was for years among the country's highest.

Once one of the most mixed societies, in recent decades, the city has become unusually segregated, and the white middle class is all but gone, moved north across Lake Pontchartrain or west to Jefferson Parish—home of David Duke, the one-time Klansman who ran for governor in 1991 and won more than half of the state's white vote.

Shortly after I arrived in town two decades ago as a fledgling reporter, I was dispatched to cover a cheerleading tryout, and I asked a grinning, half-drunk accountant where he was from, city or suburb. "White people don't live in New Orleans," he answered with a where-have-you-been disdain.

For those who loved it, its glories as well as its flaws, last week brought only heartbreak. So much of New Orleans, from its music and its food to its architecture, had shown a rainbow society at its best, even as everyone knew it was more complicated than that.

"New Orleans, first of all, is both in reality and in rhetoric an extraordinarily successful multicultural society," said Philip Carter, a developer and retired journalist whose roots in the city extend back more at least four generations. "But is also a multicultural society riven by race and class, and all this has been exposed by these stormy days. The people of our community are pitted against each other across the barricades of race and class that six months from now may be last remaining levees in New Orleans."

No one was immune, of course. With 80 percent of the city under water, tragedy swallowed the privilege and poor, and traveled spread across racial lines.

But the divides in the city were evident in things as simple as access to a car. The 35 percent of black households that didn't have one, compared with just 15 percent among whites.

"The evacuation plan was really based on people driving out," said Craig E. Colten, a geologist at Louisiana State University and an expert on the city's vulnerable topography. "They didn't have buses. They didn't have trains."

As if to punctuate the divide, the water especially devastated the Ninth Ward, among city's poorest and lowest lying.

"Out West, there is a saying that water flows to money," Mr. Colten said. "But in New Orleans, water flows away from money. Those with resources who control where the drainage goes have always chosen to live on the high ground. So the people in the low areas were hardest hit."

Outrage grew as the week wore on, among black politicians who saw the tragedy as a reflection of a broader neglect of American cities, and in the blogosphere.

"The real reason no one is helping is because of the color of these people!" wrote "myfan88" on the Flickr blog. "This is Hotel Rwanda all over again."

"Is this what the pioneers of the civil rights movement fought to achieve, a society where many black people are as trapped and isolated by their poverty as they were by legal segregation laws?" wrote Mark Naison, director of the urban studies program at Fordham, on another blog.

One question that could not be answered last week was whether, put to a similar test, other cities would fracture along the same lines.

At one level, everything about New Orleans appears sui generis, not least its location below sea level. Many New Orleanians don't just accept the jokes about living in a Banana Republic. They spread them.

But in a quieter catastrophe, the 1995 heat wave that killed hundreds of Chicagoans, blacks in comparable age groups as whites died at higher rates—in part because they tended to live in greater social isolation, in depopulated parts of town. As in New Orleans, space intertwined with race.

And the violence? Similarly shocking scenes had erupted in Los Angeles in 1992, after the acquittal of white police officers charged with beating a black man, Rodney King. Newark, Detroit, Washington—all burned in the race riots of the 1960's. It was for residents of any major city, watching the mayhem, to feel certain their community would be immune.

With months still to go just to pump out the water that covers the city, no one can be sure how the social fault lines will rearrange. But with white flight a defining element of New Orleans in the recent past, there was already the fear in the air this week that the breached levee would leave a separated society further apart.

"Maybe we can build the levees back," said Mr. Carter. "But that sense of extreme division by class and race is going to long survive the physical reconstruction of New Orleans."

22. New Orleans by the Numbers
Peter Wagner and Susan Edwards

Rank of New Orleans compared to other large cities with population over 100,000:

Percentage of population that is African-American: **5th**
Percentage of population in poverty: **8th**

Rank of Louisiana compared to other states:

Percent of population living in poverty areas: **1st**
Percent of population born in state of residence: **1st**
Lowest median household income: **3rd**
Portion of households headed by single women with children: **2nd**
Portion of workforce that is unemployed: **3rd**

The city of New Orleans and the state of Louisiana were in trouble long before Hurricane Katrina flooded the city and long before the Federal Emergency Management Agency decided that the director's dinner engagements were more important than the plight of hurricane victims running out of food in the Superdome.

The tables below compare the Lower Ninth Ward in New Orleans to the city as a whole, to the state of Louisiana, and to the United States. The Lower Ninth Ward, very poor and almost entirely Black, was one of the most heavily damaged areas of the city. Its residents, along with tens of thousands of other New Orleanians, have been dispersed around the country.

The glimpse that Census data offer of the city's demographics may offer at least a partial explanation for why the powers-that-be don't seem too upset about what is beginning to look like the permanent dispersal of Katrina's survivors.

RACE

Only four large cities (Gary, Ind.; Detroit, Mich.; Birmingham, Ala.; and Jackson, Miss.) have a larger portion of their population that is Black than New Orleans. The Lower Ninth Ward is 99% Black.

Table 9.1

	Race Black
United States	12%
Louisiana	32%
New Orleans	67%
Lower Ninth Ward	99%
Source: U.S. Census	SF1 P3

HOME OWNERSHIP

Black people are less likely than the general population to own their own homes, but home ownership in the Lower Ninth Ward was more prevalent than in either New Orleans as a whole or among Blacks generally. If the government refuses to help the uninsured residents of the Lower Ninth Ward rebuild, it will have destroyed what was actually a shining example of Bush's often touted "ownership society."

Table 9.2

	Own Their Home	
	Total Population	Blacks
United States	66%	49%
Louisiana	68%	53%
New Orleans	47%	43%
Lower Ninth Ward	59%	57%
Source: U.S. Census	SF1 H14	SF1 H11B

BIRTHPLACE AND PLACE OF RESIDENCE FIVE YEARS AGO

The United States is generally a mobile society; people move quite frequently. Louisiana, New Orleans and the Lower Ninth Ward are exceptions to that rule. Despite all the social ills in Louisiana and New Orleans, residents had deep roots and were invested in their communities.

Table 9.3

	Percent of Population Born in the State They Live in Now
United States	60%
Louisiana	79%
New Orleans	77%
Lower Ninth Ward	92%

Source: U.S. Census   SF3 P21

Table 9.4

	Place of Residence, 5 Years Ago		
	In same house	In same county/parish	In same state
United States	54%	79%	89%
Louisiana	59%	84%	93%
New Orleans	57%	85%	91%
Lower Ninth Ward	74%	97%	98%

Source: U.S. Census   SF3 P24   SF3 P24   SF3 P24

EDUCATION

Residents of New Orleans and of Louisiana are more likely to lack a high school education than residents of the United States as a whole. But New Orleans residents are more likely to have a college education than residents of either the state of Louisiana or the entire country.

However, New Orleans did not invest in all its communities equally. Forty percent of the adult residents of the Lower Ninth Ward lack a high school diploma or GED.

Table 9.5

	Education (Adults 25+)		
	Percent without High School Diploma or GED	Percent with High School/ GED only	Percent with at least bachelor's degree
United States	20%	29%	24%
Louisiana	25%	32%	19%
New Orleans	25%	23%	26%
Lower Ninth Ward	40%	29%	7%
Source: U.S. Census	SF3 P37	SF3 P37	SF3 P37

INCOME AND POVERTY

The people of New Orleans are poor, and in the Lower Ninth Ward even more so. Poverty is a confusing concept that requires some explanation. The federal government sets one national poverty line that is supposed to indicate, for families of various sizes and for individuals living alone, whether they are making enough money to meet basic needs. Based on a 1960s model in which food represented 1/3 of a family's budget, the poverty line was calculated as three times the cost of meeting minimum nutritional needs. People with incomes below that line are determined to be in poverty.

Table 9.6

	Poverty					
	Median Household Income	Percent of population in poverty	Percent of population living at less than 1/2 poverty line	Percent of population living at more than 2x poverty line	Percent of children in poverty	Percent of Adults 65+ in poverty
United States	$41,994	12%	6%	70%	17%	10%
Louisiana	$32,566	20%	9%	60%	27%	17%
New Orleans	$27,133	28%	15%	50%	41%	19%
Lower Ninth Ward	$19,918	36%	16%	34%	48%	31%
Source: U.S. Census	SF3 P53	SF3 P87	SF3 P88	SF3 P88	SF3 P87	SF3 P87

The poverty line is adjusted annually based on inflation, but the model itself has never been revised. The calculation does not take into account regional differences in the cost of living, the additional expenses that families now face (such as child care), or disproportionate cost increases for essentials like housing, heating, and transportation. (See "Ask Dr. Dollar", Dollars & Sense, January/February 2006).

Because the poverty line is set so low, those living at less than 50% of poverty are in extreme, perhaps life threatening, poverty. Even people earning twice the poverty line may barely be getting by. For that reason, many federal and state programs use a multiple of the poverty line (often 125%, 150%, or 185%) to determine eligibility for assistance, and at least one—Massachusetts' Low-Income Home Energy Assistance Program—uses 200% of poverty for eligibility. Unfortunately, the Census Bureau does not provide data for poverty ratios above 200%, which would begin to give us a more useful measure of affluence and discretionary income.

Finally, poverty correlates strongly with age. While the number of children remains frighteningly high, the expansion of assistance programs for the elderly over the last few decades has reduced the percentage of older adults in poverty.

PUBLIC ASSISTANCE

The expansion of the social safety net and cash public assistance programs are responsible for the tremendous decline in the number of elderly living in poverty. The shredding of the social safety net for poor children and adults under 65 has left almost 11 million households with incomes below the poverty line, but with no access to cash assistance.

Table 9.7

Public Assistance

	Percent of households receiving cash assist.	Percent of households in poverty that do not receive cash assist.
United States	3%	87%
New Orleans	3%	90%
Louisiana	5%	87%
Lower Ninth Ward	8%	85%
Source: U.S. Census	SF3 HCT25	SF3 HCT25

UNEMPLOYMENT

Census data aren't as timely as Bureau of Labor Statistics data, but they are the only available source for data at the neighborhood level, such as the Lower Ninth Ward.

Table 9.8

Unemployed (civilian labor force, 16+)

	Total	White	Black
United States	6%	5%	11%
Louisiana	7%	5%	14%
New Orleans	9%	4%	13%
Lower Ninth Ward	14%	0%	14%
Source: U.S. Census	SF3 P43	SF3 P150A	SF3 P150B

No Vehicle Available

City-dwellers often do not have cars because they can rely on public transportation, and poor people rarely have cars because they cannot afford them. In the days after Katrina, pundits blamed the residents of New Orleans for not evacuating; they should have looked at the facts to see whether evacuation was even possible.

Table 9.9

	No vehicle available		
	Total	White	Black
United States	10%	8%	24%
Louisiana	12%	6%	25%
New Orleans	9%	4%	13%
Lower Ninth Ward	32%	0%	33%
Source: U.S. Census	SF3 H44	SF3 HCT33A	SF3 HCT33B

Note

Peter Wagner is executive director of the Prison Policy Initiative. Susan Edwards is a government documents librarian at Amherst College. Together they are writing a book on how to use Census data for research and advocacy.

CHAPTER 10

UNEQUAL SACRIFICE IN WAR

In the 1960s the United States was embroiled in a bitter war in Vietnam. A lottery-style draft forced men to serve in the military, with exclusions provided for college students (e.g., the 2-S student deferment). Men who were between eighteen and twenty-five years of age during the Vietnam era could postpone or avoid military service by going to college. Thus, those who could afford college could avoid the war, while those who could not were drafted.

Researchers who studied the Korean War found that members of the lower classes suffered three times more casualties than members of the upper class (Mayer and Hoult, 1955). Later researchers who studied the Vietnam War found a similar pattern with regard to casualties and also noted that officers tended to be from the upper class while enlisted men were more likely to be drawn from the ranks of the lower classes (Badillo and Curry, 1976; Willis, 1975). Thomas Wilson (1995), using data from the General Social Survey to test whether the classes were equally represented in Vietnam, also argued that inequalities existed in Vietnam. Based on measures of social class such as father's education and profession, Wilson concluded that men whose fathers had high social status were less likely to serve in Vietnam than the sons of lower-social-status fathers—a finding that was especially true for members of the elite classes. Moreover, men whose fathers were professionals or managers were less likely to serve in the military than men whose fathers worked on a farm or had a service-sector job (for a complete discussion see Wilson, 1995).

The evidence clearly suggests that during the Korean and Vietnam wars, men from the lower social classes had a disproportionate burden in terms of both service and casualties. But the draft that forced military service ended in 1975, and since that time the United States has had an all-volunteer military. Therefore, using a college deferment to avoid the draft is no longer necessary. Does that mean that military service and serving in combat have become more equally distributed among the social classes?

The answer is no. Members of the upper classes still have many more options regarding life after high school, while members of the lower classes are faced with seeking options. The latter, both men and women, are less likely to have money for college education, and funds provided by government programs such as the Pell Grant that help the poor pay tuition have decreased. Consider, for example, that in the 1970s Pell Grants paid approximately 40 percent of the cost of attending a four-year private school. Today, that percentage is down to about 15 percent (*The USA Today,* 2004).

In addition, because the current conflicts in Afghanistan and Iraq are being fought with volunteers rather than with conscripts, the middle and upper classes are effectively exempted, leaving the fighting to the less fortunate. It is interesting to note that military service is marketed as a way up from the bottom for members of the lower classes—as an opportunity to grow and earn the respect of others while experiencing the world, and as a route to post-service educational prospects. And, indeed, the military still draws disproportionately from members of the lower class for its enlisted ranks. The following readings describe the unequal sacrifice of the lower classes in military service.

References

Badillo, Gilbert, and G. David Curry. 1976. "The Social Incidence of Vietnam Casualties," *Armed Forces & Society* 2: 397–406.

Mayer, Albert J., and Thomas Ford Hoult. 1955. "Social Stratification and Combat Survival," *Social Forces* 34: 155–159.

USA Today. 2004. "Low-Income College Students Are Increasingly Left Behind" (January 14). Available online at http://www.usatoday.com/news/education/2004-01-14-low-income-students_x.htm.

Willis, John. 1975. "Variations in State Casualty Rates in World War II and the Vietnam War," *Social Problems* 22: 558–568.

Wilson, Thomas C. 1995. "Vietnam-Era Military Service—A Test of the Class-Bias Thesis," *Armed Forces & Society* 21: 461–471.

23. Sacrifices of War Remain Unshared
Chuck Raasch

On the Fourth of July, a B-1 bomber from Ellsworth Air Force Base will thunder low over the tiny town of Frederick, S.D., population less than 300, where 26 local residents serve in the military.

The flyover will be part of a ceremony honoring those who served in the war in Iraq.

Frederick's high percentage of service members is typical of small-town America, where the military still is seen as a viable option for upward mobility and where patriotism is an unquestioned trait of community spirit.

But the small-town flyover also will symbolize something else: the unshared sacrifice of the terrorism wars.

If a similar percentage of New York City's population were in the military, for instance, you could field armies twice the size of those that fought in Iraq.

And therein lies a fundamental challenge of the long-term fight against terror.

The burden is not being shared equally.

Those fighting and dying come from a diminished pool of applicants: minorities, small-town kids, and others who—like wounded and captured Army Pfc. Jessica Lynch—see the military as their only gateway to a college degree.

In this respect, the volunteer military operates through a form of class warfare.

You don't see many K Street lobbyists or trial lawyers or CEOs doing their patriotic duty in the National Guard.

Yes, the volunteer military produces superior fighting attributes and beneficial social effects.

The armed services remain prime examples of minority success in a meritocracy (see former Joint Chiefs Chairman Colin Powell and Lt. Gen. Vincent Brooks, a top U.S. military spokesman in the war in Iraq).

Yet as an institution, it is a melting pot of the lower end of the economic strata.

Even in rural states like South Dakota, there is a huge divide between rural and urban economics.

A study released this month by the Center for Rural Affairs in Walthill, Neb., said that in Iowa, Kansas, Minnesota, Nebraska, North Dakota, and South Dakota, rural workers earned less than half—48 cents on the dollar—of what those employed in the region's big cities earned.

The study said the gap had widened considerably since 1990, when rural workers, on the whole, earned 58 cents for every dollar earned by residents of big cities in those six states.

So increasingly in places like Frederick, the U.S. military will be the biggest-opportunity employer.

And the sacrifice divide will continue.

The "Greatest Generation" of World War II vets, who now are dying at the rate of 1,000 a day, [was] the greatest example of shared sacrifice in war.

The draft of that generation virtually guaranteed that every family touched a veteran in some way or another. That's no longer the case.

So it's no surprise that the Pentagon is launching a new advertising campaign to reacquaint Americans with the military.

It took a poll last September and found that 52 percent cited television and the movies as their prime source of information about the armed services. Only 11 percent of adults mentioned the military as an option for children after high school.

The Pentagon will spend $1.7 million of your tax dollars buying ads in weekly news magazines this summer.

The ads, the Pentagon announced, are "designed to strengthen the personal bond between adult Americans and their military."

The Pentagon also will spend $10 million for other outreach efforts, including buying lists of potential recruits for mail appeals.

But as long as class dictates the ranks of the military, shared sacrifice will be an elusive condition.

24. Their Last Resort
Ann Scott Tyson

As sustained combat in Iraq makes it harder than ever to fill the ranks of the all-volunteer force, newly released Pentagon demographic data show that the military is leaning heavily for recruits on economically depressed, rural areas where youths' need for jobs may outweigh the risks of going to war.

More than 44 percent of U.S. military recruits come from rural areas, Pentagon figures show. In contrast, 14 percent come from major cities. Youths living in the most sparsely populated Zip codes are 22 percent more likely to join the Army, with an opposite trend in cities. Regionally, most enlistees come from the South (40 percent) and West (24 percent).

Many of today's recruits are financially strapped, with nearly half coming from lower-middle-class to poor households, according to new Pentagon data based on Zip codes and census estimates of mean household income. Nearly two-thirds of Army recruits in 2004 came from counties in which median household income is below the U.S. median.

Those patterns are pronounced in counties such as Martinsville, Va., that supply the greatest number of enlistees in proportion to their youth populations. All of the Army's top 20 counties for recruiting had lower-than-national median incomes, 12 had higher poverty rates, and 16 were nonmetropolitan, according to the National Priorities Project, a nonpartisan research group that analyzed 2004 recruiting data by Zip code.

"A lot of the high recruitment rates are in areas where there is not as much economic opportunity for young people," says Anita Dancs, research director for the NPP, based in Northampton, Mass.

Senior Pentagon officials say the war has had a clear impact on recruiting, with a shrinking pool of candidates forcing the military to accept less qualified enlistees—and presumably many for whom military service is a choice of last resort. In fiscal 2005, the Army took in its least qualified group of recruits in a decade, as measured by educational level and test results. The war is also attracting youths driven by patriotism, including a growing fringe of the upper class and wealthy, but military sociologists believe that greater numbers of young people who would have joined for economic reasons are being discouraged by the prolonged combat.

The Pentagon Zip code data, applied for the first time to 2004 recruiting results, underscores patterns already suggested by anecdotal evidence, such as analysis of the home towns of troops killed in Iraq. Although still an approximation, the data offer a more detailed portrait of the socioeconomic status of the Americans most likely to serve today.

Tucked into the Piedmont foothills of "southern Virginia, where jobs in the local economy are scarce as NASCAR fans are plentiful, Martinsville is typical of the lower-income rural communities across the nation that today constitute the U.S. military's richest recruiting grounds.

Albert Deal, 25, had struggled for years to hold onto a job in this rural Virginia community of rolling hills and shuttered textile mills. So when the lanky high school graduate got his latest pink slip, from a modular-homes plant, he took a hard look at life. Then he picked up the phone and dialed the steadiest employer he knew: the U.S. Army.

Two weeks later, on Oct. 27, Deal sat in his parents' living room and signed one enlistment document after another as his fiancée, Kimbery Easter, somberly looked on.

"This is the police check," said Sgt 1st Class Christopher A. Barber, a veteran Army recruiter, leading Deal through the stack of paperwork. "This is the sex-offender check...." Barber spoke in a monotone, like a tour guide who had memorized every word.

Left adrift, young people such as Deal "are being pushed out of their communities. They want to get away from intolerable situations, and the military offers them something different," says Morten G. Ender, a sociologist at the U.S. Military Academy at West Point.

To be sure, some young people who need jobs or college money also seek adventure and a chance to serve their country. Others come from towns with large bases or populations of veterans interwoven with a military culture that helps keep enlistments high. And a rising percentage of youth from wealthy areas is signing up, presumably for patriotic reasons.

But nationwide, data point above all to places such as Martinsville, where rural roads lined with pine and poplar trees snake through lonely, desolate towns, as the wellspring for the youth fighting America's wars.

"They are these untapped kids," Enders says "that nobody found."

Barber palms the steering wheel of his gray Dodge Stratus as he drives northwest into the steeply undulating backcountry surrounding Martinsville, where he commands a recruiting station.

Barber's territory spans 862 square miles in one of the country's most productive recruiting regions. Roaming in and out of cell-phone range through tiny towns, Barber and his partner post Army brochures at mom-and-pop groceries, work the crowd at NASCAR races at the local track, and log more than 100 miles a day meeting potential recruits.

In fiscal 2005, the Army's worst year for recruiting since 1999, they signed up 94 percent of their target, a relatively high number in one of the Army's top recruiting regions.

"We were pretty much dead-on," says Barber of Miami, attributing his success in part to the region's shrinking job market and the inability of families to afford college. Unemployment in Martinsville was 12.1 percent in 2004. Median income is $27,000, with a poverty rate of 17.5 percent, 2000 census data show.

"The job market is dwindling, and it's hard for a young man or woman to find something other than the fast-food business," Barber says on the way to the one-story home of Mike McNeely, Deal's stepfather.

Still, many young people such as Deal exhaust other options before considering the Army, making today's recruits older on average. "These kids have tested the labor market and gone on to college but didn't perform well," says Curtis Gilroy, director of accessions for the Pentagon. From 2000 to 2004, the number of teenagers joining the military dropped, while 20- to 25-year-olds rose from 31 to 36 percent.

As his fiancée stares impassively at a TV soap opera, Deal cradles Kadence, her fussy 6-month-old daughter, and explains how he turned to the Army after doors kept slamming in his face.

"I tried anything and everything to land a job, Deal says, ticking off glass and furniture companies and a local telemarketing firm. "No one ever called back." Divorced and the father of a 3-year-old son, Deal decided to call the recruiter because "it's a job to do," he says. "It's something to make a life of."

Sitting in a kitchen decorated with religious figurines, McNeely, 50, agrees. "You're not looking at a lot around here in terms of a future," says McNeely, who is disabled. He adds that the textile and furniture factories where he once worked have vanished or downsized.

But McNeely, Deal and Easter are uneasy over the prospect that the job will lead to Iraq. "That bothers me a lot," says McNeely, saying that his wife also likes to have Deal "in hollerin' distance."

Kadence spits up, and Deal rushes to get a rag to wipe off her mother's pants. Easter now supports Deal, after being angry at first over his plans to join the Army. Still, she hesitates to marry him before he leaves for boot camp. Deal, who wants a job as a tank driver, says he hopes he won't deploy.

"Believe me, I don't want to go over there." But, he says, "that's the risk I take."

It's just after lunch at Magna Vista High School south of Martinsville. Sgt. Michael Ricciardi strides through the door and is ushered inside by a smiling woman signing in visitors. He is soon joking with kids heading to class, including several future soldiers.

"This is pretty much my 'anchor' school," says Ricciardi, Barber's partner, who spends hours each week handing out Frisbees and footballs in the hallways. "They know me pretty well."

In contrast to some schools around the country that limit access to recruiters, Magna Vista, where half of students receive financial aid or free lunch, welcomes them. School officials give recruiters a list of seniors to contact, and encourage upperclassmen to take a vocational test required by the military.

"We expose them to the fact that the military is there," says guidance counselor Karen Cecil. "We're setting the stage for [students] to know it's an option" especially as a way to afford college, she says.

Indeed, like many heavy recruiting areas, Martinsville has more people seeking Army jobs than are qualified for them. Army recruiters here turn away scores of interested youths because they fail vocational tests, physicals or legal background checks. To fill its ranks nationwide, the Army in fiscal 2005 accepted its least qualified pool in a decade—falling below quota in high school graduates (87 percent) and taking, in more youths scoring in the lowest category of aptitude test (3.9 percent).

Support for military service among parents has dwindled nationwide, but many parents here view it as an opportunity, often phoning recruiters to urge them to enlist their children.

Senior Miyana Gravely, 17, had long talks with her mother before asking for approval to join the Army and go to boot camp last summer. "You can do it. I don't want you to grow up and say, 'Mama wouldn't let me,'" Gravely recalls her mother telling her.

Gravely sees soldiering as a ticket to an active life somewhere else. "I don't want to be one of the people still sitting around Martinsville," she says, adding she is contemplating airborne training and "wouldn't mind" going to Iraq.

Being black and female, Gravely contradicts a national decline over the past four years in the willingness of both blacks and women to consider military service—a shift polls attribute to the U.S. anti-terrorism effort and perceived discrimination. Blacks fell from 22.3 percent of Army recruits in fiscal 2001 to 14.5 percent this year; Hispanics rose from 10.5 percent to 13.2 percent, and whites, from 60.2 percent to 66.9 percent. Women dropped from 20 percent to 18 percent.

Gravely is active in the school's large Junior Reserve Officers' Training Corps (JROTC), which draws 300 of the 1,200 students each year and works closely with recruiters. JROTC programs are prolific in Virginia and across the rural South.

"The parents heavily support it. We've kept a lot of kids from getting kicked out of school," says JROTC instructor John Truini.

The program gives students military ranks and strips them away if they break discipline. "I don't want to say [we] control the kids, but we have influence over them," Truini says.

Davey Brooks, 17, grew up on a small farm; he says JROTC "changed everything about my life." He joined JROTC in hopes the military could fulfill his dream of learning to fly—"like 'Top Gun,'" he says.

Now, Brooks is "battalion commander" and leader of a nine-person Raider Team—modeled after Army Rangers—which competes in military skills such as evacuating casualties and orienteering. He plans a 20-year Army career.

I want to be in the Army and fly whatever I can get my hands on," Brooks says. He is eager to go to Iraq as a pilot, although he admits to one drawback: He's scared of heights. "But when I'm up there," he predicts, "I'll feel like I'm free and I'm in control of everything."

CHAPTER 11
ENVIRONMENTAL CLASSISM

Attention to the problem of environmental classism resulted from a groundbreaking book, *Dumping in Dixie: Race, Class, and Environmental Quality,* by Robert D. Bullard (1990). As first identified, the crux of the problem was that companies seeking sites for waste facilities were locating landfills, dumps, and hazardous waste sites in poor neighborhoods. The issue now encompasses a broad range of air, water, and land quality concerns, but it continues to focus on the question of how people in low-income areas are affected by noxious industries.

Waste facility siting is a complex matter. Companies identify land that is relatively cheap and seek the appropriate permits to construct a waste facility. Cheap land is usually associated with economically disadvantaged neighborhoods, but the problem goes beyond that fact. The people in poor neighborhoods have neither sufficient power by themselves nor sufficient influence with public officials to prevent the industry from moving into the neighborhood. And once the landfill or dump is in place, they typically have no way out of the neighborhood to escape the noise, odors, toxicity, and residual trash that accompany a waste dump. Ironically, some poor communities have courted these industries to bring jobs to the area.

Environmental factors and poverty combine in ways that are important to consider. As an example, think about poor families who live near a feedlot or garbage dump. During the summer months, noxious fumes emanating from waste sites mix with the heat of the sun and the breeze to permeate the neighborhood. But in this poor neighborhood, none of the families have air conditioning so their only escape from the stifling heat is to leave their windows open. The odors are not just unpleasant. Fumes from feedlots are associated with health problems such as headaches, nausea, and depression. And people in neighborhoods near feedlots are at risk for contracting diseases like swine flu or the bird flu if they come into contact with infected animals (CDC, 2005). Water near feedlots and garbage dumps may also be affected as waste by-products enter the water table.

Environmental classism manifests itself in many ways. It occurs when the soil in a poor neighborhood is contaminated by industries in the area, when a poor neighborhood is zoned for industrial development, when a major highway splits the neighborhood, and when members of the neighborhood are subjected to high levels of noise, pollution, and litter. The following readings consider the intersection of social class and human-created environmental issues.

REFERENCES

Bullard, Robert D. 1990. *Dumping in Dixie: Race, Class, and Environmental Quality.* Boulder, CO: Westview.

CDC (Center for Disease Control and Prevention). 2005. "Transmission of Influenza A Viruses Between Animals and People" (October 17). Available online at http://www.cdc.gov/flu/avian/gen-info/transmission.htm.

25. Bioethics, Social Class, and the Sociological Imagination
Leigh Turner

Last year I published a short article[1] urging bioethicists to carefully examine the question of what ought to constitute the canonical issues topics and questions driving research and teaching in bioethics. Why some subjects dominate the field whereas other topics are regarded as matters for scholars in other disciplines is a question that has intrigued me for nearly a decade. How are the boundaries of bioethics established? What factors influence research agendas and the creation of bioethics curricula? How do funding agencies, editors, and leading scholars shape the field of bioethics? These questions are increasingly receiving scrutiny from Charles Bosk, Raymond De Vries, and other researchers as they explore the sociology of bioethics and the "construction" of the "ethical enterprise."

One of the first papers I published[2] explored why particular topics are addressed or neglected by bioethicists. I wrote "Bioethics, Public Health, and Firearm-Related Violence: Missing Links between Bioethics and Public Health" during my time as a graduate student in the School of Religion and Social Ethics at the University of Southern California. When I wrote the article, I was living in one of the poorer, more socially disadvantaged neighborhoods of Los Angeles. My time in that social environment played a formative role in leading me to wonder why bioethicists pay relatively little attention to social inequalities, urban poverty, homelessness, firearm-related violence, and the disintegration of inner cities and the relationship of these topics to health, illness, and moral experience. At the time, anthropologists, sociologists, and cultural geographers were publishing detailed studies of homelessness, urban gangs and gang-related violence, and the collapse of inner city social infrastructures. Their work considered the relations among poverty, unemployment, ill health, and lack of access to basic healthcare and social services. In contrast, the literature of bioethics placed tremendous emphasis on ethical issues in end-of-life care, organ transplantation, and other topics associated with high-technology medical interventions. Bioethics, it seemed to me, was becoming fixated on an odd menagerie of dramatic, "cutting-edge" topics and neglecting the social, political, and economic contexts within which important ethical issues were unfolding. Living at the time in a low-income area, where community problems extended to the most basic social institutions, the literature of bioethics seemed dominated by middle-class preoccupations and fears. These issues were important—and remain significant today—but their dominant status pushed to the periphery of bioethics crucial aspects of health, illness, social life, and moral experience. When I was riding public transit and walking the streets of this low-income area, it took little effort to see how various interwoven social problems had profound ethical dimensions and were closely connected to medicine, illness, injury, and healthcare.

Unlike anthropologists and sociologists studying poverty, homelessness, structural inequalities, social suffering, and illness experiences, I cannot claim to have deliberately immersed myself in a social environment where I might explore these issues in depth. Rather, my sense that important issues were being placed too low on the agenda of bioethics emerged in a more accidental, circumstantial manner. I didn't find myself using the hopelessly inadequate public transit system or living near the intersection of 3rd and Vermont Avenue out of idealism, because I had some Marxist-inflected notion of siding with the proletariat, or because I had a cinema-mediated desire to experience Los Angeles in all its urban grittiness. To the contrary I was there because, as a graduate student, I simply couldn't afford to live in Westwood, Brentwood, or one of the other wealthier neighborhoods of Los Angeles. I had wanted to attend graduate school in the United States; prior to arriving in Los Angeles the evening before the start of my courses I gave little thought to where I might live.

The urban landscapes through which I traveled during my time in Los Angeles were quite unlike anything I encountered during my years living a relatively stable, safe, middle-class existence in rural Manitoba. To deter criminals, jagged pieces of glass were embedded into the top of walls. Coiled razor wire made already ugly buildings resemble bunkers. The public school nearest my apartment had a play area covered in asphalt, without even a small patch of grass, and signs on the mesh wire fences indicating handguns were not allowed on school grounds. Late at night, police helicopters buzzed through the darkness, their spotlights fingering the ground and tracking individuals on streets and rooftops. The popping sound of gunfire would occasionally accompany the constant background noise of car alarms, police car and ambulance sirens, and blaring stereos. To step onto the campus at the University of Southern California (USC), a wealthy, resource-rich, private university situated amid a low-income, high-crime neighborhood, was to enter a different and much safer world.

Visiting neighborhoods such as Compton, South Central, and Watts during trips to different hospitals affiliated with USC, I passed through neighborhoods that looked as though they must be in some desolate, poverty-stricken country rather than the United States. Shattered toilets and broken sofas were strewn along city curbs. Abandoned, burned-out cars sat beside walls covered with graffiti. In some city blocks, vacant lots were all that remained following what, depending on your political leanings and reaction to the outcome of the Rodney King trial, was either the "Los Angeles Riot" or the "Los Angeles Civil Disturbance" of 1992. Visiting various medical facilities, I found that staff at hospitals such as USC/Los Angeles County Medical Center and Martin Luther King/Drew Medical Center faced incredibly challenging patients and workplace environments. Guards patrolled the hallways. Metal detectors were located at entrances. Emergency rooms were constantly overcrowded.

When I visited these institutions, it was apparent that "medical" problems typically had significant social and economic dimensions. Patients with severe psychiatric illnesses lived homeless on the streets and reached the emergency room with multiple chronic illnesses and sometimes life-threatening diseases. Lacking options, individuals without health insurance waited hours to see ER doctors for their primary care. NICU staff faced the challenge of providing care to infants whose mothers had used crack during pregnancy. Residents specializing in emergency care or trauma medicine learned their craft on patients arriving with gunshot wounds and stab injuries. Overwhelmed social workers juggled unmanageable caseloads.

For many individuals living in the most impoverished, devastated parts of Los Angeles and other urban centers in America, poverty, poor health, frequent encounters with both criminals and paramilitary-style police forces, lack of economic opportunities, and limited access to healthcare and basic social services are not temporary challenges. Rather, poverty, unemployment, chronic illnesses, the risk of violence, and blocked educational opportunities are pervasive features of social life and everyday experience. In many respects, to live in Bel Air or South Central is to inhabit different worlds. Concrete freeways, and not any sense of social solidarity or a common fate, constitute the main links between these worlds.

While I am writing this essay in Princeton, one of the wealthiest, most economically privileged towns in the United States, the poorest neighborhoods of Los Angeles now seem very distant. Here, the problems individuals encounter are very different. When I encounter local undergraduates discussing their future prospects, I hear them dwelling on challenging questions such as whether to go to law school or medical school or attend graduate school at Brown or Penn. Such questions are never trivial for the individuals making such decisions. Furthermore, I readily acknowledge that I am much like these students in many of my preoccupations. When considering the choices and opportunities found in middle-class or upper-middle-class America, it is easy to forget that individuals in other places inhabit much different social worlds. When you are living in Princeton, the intersection at 3rd and Vermont in Los Angeles begins to seem rather distant.

I wrote that early article on missing links between bioethics and public health because I felt that firearm-related violence and all its ethical, medical, social, and economic dimensions ought to concern individuals working in bioethics. Firearm-related violence is a major topic of research in trauma medicine and public health. Firearm-related violence, medical specialists readily recognize, is not just a matter of particular individuals suffering gunshot wounds caused by weapons fired by specific assailants. Rather, firearm-related violence typically needs to be situated within a context of urban poverty, the breakdown of communities, ease of access to firearms, cultures of violence, gang-related activities, and lack of social, cultural, and economic opportunities. Firearm-related violence occurs in particular social and economic contexts; ignore the context and you have little understanding of what might be done to reduce the number of individuals suffering firearm-related wounds. Of course, in addressing this topic, I was not just attempting to draw attention to ethical and legal aspects of gun control and firearm-related violence. Rather, I was trying to encourage bioethicists to give greater consideration to many different social issues often neglected by bioethicists, yet explored by researchers in public health, medical anthropology, social medicine, and the sociology of health and illness.

What struck me when I first began to consider bioethics, public health, and firearm-related violence, as well as other social and economic issues addressed by public health specialists, was the relative lack of consideration bioethicists gave to questions concerning the breakdown of urban neighborhoods, radical social inequalities, poverty, and the "epidemic" of firearm-related injuries. If a patient received treatment in the ER, was transferred to the ICU, and then deteriorated, issues began to emerge that seemed to intrigue bioethicists. Should treatment be continued, withdrawn, or withheld? Was there an identifiable surrogate decision maker? Did the patient have an advance directive? How should death be defined? These topics are readily recognizable as issues bioethicists address. However, the various factors that led to the patient arriving in the ER with a gunshot wound were not matters that concerned most bioethicists. Rather, structural inequalities, urban poverty, and violence were apparently regarded as problems best left to medical sociologists, public health specialists, economists, and activist physicians.

To assert that bioethics is nothing more than ethics at the bedside or ethics within the clinical setting would ignore the contributions of all those individuals who have written about the need for universal health insurance, the importance of addressing social inequalities, and the value of connecting bioethics to public health. Clearly, bioethics has long included a tradition of addressing basic issues related to social inequalities and social justice. Still, in terms of relative emphasis, I think it fair to suggest that issues at the bedside—such topics as informed consent, capacity assessment, and end-of-life care, for example—receive considerably more attention than broader explorations of ethical issues related to what are often called the "social determinants" of health and illness. Moral analysis in bioethics is now typically placed in a "social context," but all too often that context is one occupied by the relatively wealthy and the comparatively privileged.

In the 1980s and 1990s, many bioethicists directed their attention toward ethical issues related to end-of-life care. Now, much more attention is focused on ethical, legal, and social issues related to genetics. This shift in emphasis is not simply a product of individual thinkers growing tired of one set of topics and cultivating new research agendas. Rather, major funding initiatives in such countries as Canada, the United Kingdom, and the United States offer powerful professional incentives to explore ethical, legal, and social issues related to genetics and biotechnology. In my more charitable moments, I recognize the importance of these topics and appreciate that funding is available to address ethical issues related to developments in the life sciences. Such topics as embryonic stem cell research, therapeutic cloning, germ line gene therapy, genetic enhancement, and xenotransplantation all raise ethical issues worth careful exploration. However, in my less charitable moments—and I have many of them—I worry that the funding available for the study of ethical issues related to genetics and biotechnology will lead to the neglect of other important topics that ought to concern bioethicists.

Acknowledging that major changes are occurring in the life sciences, recognizing the value of careful analysis before particular technologies emerge, appreciating that the provision of funding to study ethical issues related to genetics and biotechnology is not just a calculated strategy of co-opting possible critics, I find it nonetheless plausible to suggest that many of the gravest ethical and social issues we face have rather little to do with cloning, stem cells, neutraceuticals, biotechnology, nanotechnology, and gene therapy. It is for precisely this reason that I grow concerned when I consider the issues the President's Council on Bioethics chooses to address. I would feel much more favorably disposed toward their study of enhancement technologies and efforts to make humans "better than normal" if I knew that this group was also engaged in addressing ways to respond to the problems facing the 42 million Americans currently lacking health insurance. In the absence of such reflection, the President's Council on Bioethics, as with many other agenda-setting groups in bioethics, is neglecting some of the most important ethical issues related to health and illness.

To criticize the tremendous contemporary emphasis on ethical issues related to biotechnology and the life sciences is not to suggest that individual bioethicists addressing these issues are doing trivial work. Rather, I wish to make a more general point that is directed at bioethics as a field rather than toward individual scholars. Bioethics, if it is to remain significant, if it is to withstand the criticisms of anthropologists, sociologists, and social activists who see it as obsessed with the concerns of middle-class, relatively wealthy, sometimes rather narcissistic individuals, needs to remain attentive to broader social issues connected to poverty, social inequalities, lack of access to healthcare, the collapse of communities and social infrastructures, and public health.

When emergency room physicians in Los Angeles addressed the "social determinants" of firearm-related violence in the 1990s, they did not take a narrow view of gunshot wounds as seen only through the lens of emergency medicine and trauma surgery. Rather, drawing upon the disciplines of public health and social medicine, they exercised what C. Wright Mills called the "sociological imagination." They rightly addressed firearm-related violence in its social and economic settings. At the time, bioethicists simply did not see such issues—and other topics related to urban poverty, violence, and the deterioration of social institutions within inner cities—as significant matters for bioethics. With the current focus on ethical issues related to genetics and biotechnology, bioethics once again risks narrowing its scope of analysis and missing important ethical, legal, and social issues that deserve careful, critical reflection. If this attitude is a consequence of recognizing the immense complexity of such issues as urban poverty, health inequalities, and homelessness, then I quite understand the sense of resignation. Understandably, many bioethicists simply feel ill equipped to address such multifaceted, complex matters. Few of us are trained in epidemiology or public health. Most of us do not have a sophisticated understanding of the economic policies and social structures that generate or mitigate social inequalities. However, if these issues are seen as matters concerning economists, public health specialists, and sociologists and are of no personal, practical, or disciplinary importance to bioethicists, then I worry that the significance and promise of bioethics has been greatly exaggerated, and we will fail to grapple with the most important ethical and social issues facing our cities, communities, and citizens.

NOTES

1. Turner, L. Bioethics needs to rethink its agenda. *British Medical Journal* 2004; 328:175.
2. Turner, L. Bioethics, public health, and firearm-related violence: missing links between bioethics and public health. *Journal of Law, Medicine & Ethics* 1997;25:42–48.

26. Poverty and Pollution in the United States
Robert D. Bullard

Toxic Foods

The United States has one of the safest food supplies in the world. Still, food borne diseases cause approximately 76 million illnesses, 325,000 hospitalizations, and 5,000 deaths in the U.S. each year.[1] Known food borne pathogens account for 14 million of the illnesses, 60,000 hospitalizations and 1,800 deaths.[2] Unknown agents account for approximately 81 percent of food borne illnesses and hospitalizations and 64 percent of deaths.[3]

Number One Environmental Threat to Children

In many African cities, childhood lead poisoning can be as high as 90 percent. Even in the United States, lead poisoning continues to be the number one environmental health threat to children, especially poor children, children of color, and children living in inner cities.[4] Lead poisoning affects an estimated 890,000 American preschoolers or 4.4 percent of the under 5 age group.[5] African American children are five times more likely to be poisoned than white children. Some 22 percent of African American children living in pre-1946 housing are lead poisoned, compared with 5.6 percent of white children and 13 percent of Mexican American children living in older homes.

Geography of Air Pollution

The number of automobiles is increasing three times faster than the rate of population growth. According to National Argonne Laboratory researchers, 57 percent of whites, 65 percent of African Americans, and 80 percent of Hispanics live in 437 counties with substandard air quality.[6] In the heavily populated Los Angeles air basin, the South Coast Air Quality Management District estimates that 71 percent of African Americans and 50 percent of Latinos live in areas with the most polluted air, compared to 34 percent of whites. Air pollution costs Americans $10 to $200 billion a year.[7]

Asthma Epidemic

The number of asthma sufferers doubled from 6.7 million in 1980 to 17.3 million in 1998.[8] Over 4.8 million asthma sufferers are children.[9] Asthma hits poor, inner-city dwellers, and people of color hardest. African Americans and Latinos are almost three times more likely than whites to die from asthma.[10] In 1995, more than 5,000 Americans died from asthma.[11] The hospitalization rate for African Americans and Latinos is 3 to 4 times the rate for whites.[12] The Centers for Disease Control and Prevention reports that asthma accounts for more than 10 million lost school days, 1.2 million emergency room visits, 15 million outpatient visits, and over 500,000 hospitalizations each year. Asthma cost Americans over $14.5 billion in 2000.[13]

Toxic Wastes and Race

Nationally, three out of five African Americans and Latino Americans live in communities with abandoned toxic waste sites.[14] Discrimination influences land use, housing patterns, and infrastructure development. Zoning ordinances, deed restrictions, and other land-use mechanisms have been widely used as a "NIMBY"[15] (not in my back yard) tool, operating through exclusionary practices.[16] The U.S. General Accounting Office estimates that there are between 130,000 and 450,000 brownfields[17] (abandoned waste sites) scattered across the urban landscape from New York to California. Most of these brownfields are located in or near low-income, working-class, and people-of-color communities.[18]

Toxic Housing

A 2000 study by *The Morning News* and the University of Texas–Dallas found that some 870,000 of the 1.9 million (46 percent) housing units for the poor, mostly minorities, sit within about a mile of factories that reported toxic emissions to the Environmental Protection Agency.[19] Homeowners have been the most effective groups to use "NIMBY" (Not in My Back Yard) tactics and practices in keeping locally unwanted land uses (LULUs) out of their back yards and communities. However, racial discrimination prevents millions of people of color from enjoying the advantages of home ownership. A little over 46 percent of African Americans and Latinos own their homes compared with 73 percent of whites in 1999. If blacks and Hispanics owned homes at the same rate as whites of similar age and income, their homeownership rates would have been 61 percent in 1998 versus

72 percent for whites.[20] African American and Latino American households, on average, must pay discrimination "tax" of roughly $3,700.[21]

Toxic Schools

More than 600,000 students in Massachusetts, New York, New Jersey, Michigan and California were attending nearly 1,200 public schools that are located within a half mile of federal Superfund or state-identified contaminated sites.[22] No state except California has a law requiring school officials to investigate potentially contaminated property and no federal or state agency keeps records of public or private schools that operate on or near toxic waste or industrial sites.[23]

Toxic Jobs

Farm work is the second most dangerous occupation in the United States. Farm workers suffer from the highest rate of chemical injuries of any workers in the United States. EPA estimates that pesticide exposure causes farmworkers and their families to suffer between 10,000 to 20,000 immediate illnesses annually, and additional thousands of illnesses later in life.[24] Of the 25 most heavily used agricultural pesticides, 5 are toxic to the nervous system; 18 are skin, eye, or lung irritants, 11 have been classified by the U.S. Environmental Protection Agency (EPA) as cancer-causing; 17 cause genetic damage; and 10 cause reproductive problems (in test of laboratory animals).[25] Annual use of the pesticides causing each of these types of health problems totals between one and four hundred million pounds.[26]

Farms employing less than 10 workers are exempt from the Occupational Safety and Health Administration (OSHA). Over 85 percent of migrant farm workers work on farms with fewer than 10 employees. Over 80 percent of migrant farm workers in the U.S. are Latinos. An estimated 250,000 children of farm workers in the U.S. migrate each year, and 90,000 of them migrate across an international border; half of all migrant children have worked in fields still wet with pesticide and more than one third have been sprayed directly; over 72.8 percent of migrant children are completely without health insurance.

An estimated 137 American workers die from job-related diseases every day.[27] This is more than eight times the number of workers who die from job-related accidents. Fear of unemployment acts as a potent incentive for many workers to stay in and accept jobs that are health threatening. This practice amounts to "economic blackmail." Workers are often forced to choose between unemployment and a job that may result in risks to their health, their family's health, and the health of their community.

The U.S. Department of Labor estimates that more than half of the country's 22,000 sewing shops violate minimum wage and overtime laws.[28] Many of these workers labor in dangerous conditions including blocked fire exits, unsanitary bathrooms, and poor ventilation. Government surveys also reveal that 75 percent of U.S. garment shops violate safety and health laws.[29]

MILITARY TOXICS

The U.S. Department of Defense (DoD) has left its nightmarish nuclear weapons garbage on Native lands and the Pacific Islands. In fact, "over the last 45 years, there have been 1,000 atomic explosions on Western Shoshone land in Nevada, making the Western Shoshone the most bombed nation on earth."[30] Over 648 U.S. military installations, both active and abandoned, in Alaska are polluting the land, groundwater, wetlands, streams and air with extensive fuel spill, pesticides, solvents, PCBs, dioxins, munitions, and radioactive materials. Many of these military installations are in close proximity to Alaska Native villages and traditional hunting and fishing areas. Military toxics threaten the way of life of Alaska Natives.

The U.S. Navy has used the tiny island of Vieques, Puerto Rico as a bombing range since 1941.[31] Fifty years of military exercises including the use of bombs, artillery shells, depleted uranium ordnance, and napalm have left local communities with serious health problems and destroyed ecosystems. Nearly three-fourths of the island's 9,000 residents live in poverty. Soils are degraded and contaminated, and both Navy and independent testing of bombing areas have found at least 10 toxic constituents including metals, benzene, and chloroform.

RADIOACTIVE COLONIALISM

There is a direct correlation between exploitation of land and exploitation of people. It should not be a surprise to anyone to discover that Native Americans have to contend with some of the worst pollution in the United States. Native American nations have become prime targets for waste trading.[32] The vast majority of these waste proposals have been defeated by grassroots groups on the reservations. However, "radioactive colonialism" is alive and well. Winona LaDuke sums up this "toxic invasion" of Native lands as follows:

> While Native peoples have been massacred and fought, cheated, and robbed of their historical lands, today their lands are subject to some of most invasive industrial interventions imaginable. According to the Worldwatch Institute, 317 reservations in the United States are threatened by environmental hazards, ranging from toxic wastes to clearcuts.
>
> Reservations have been targeted as sites for 16 proposed nuclear waste dumps. Over 100 proposals have been floated in recent years to dump toxic waste in Indian communities. Seventy-seven sacred sites have been disturbed or desecrated through resource extraction and development activities. The federal government is proposing to use Yucca Mountain, sacred to the Shoshone, a dumpsite for the nation's high-level nuclear waste.[33]

Radioactive colonialism operates in energy production (mining of uranium) and disposal of wastes on Indian lands. The legacy of institutional racism has left many sovereign Indian nations without an economic infrastructure to address poverty, unemployment, inadequate education and health care, and a host of other social problems.

Eastern Navajo reservation residents have been struggling to prevent the Nuclear Regulatory Commission from permitting a uranium mine in Church Rock and Crown Point, New Mexico. The Mohave tribe in California, Skull Valley Goshutes in Idaho, and Western Shoshone in Yucca Mountain, Nevada are currently fighting proposals to build radioactive waste dumps on their tribal lands. Native and indigenous people all across the globe are threatened with extinction due to the greed of mining and oil companies and "development genocide." A growing grassroots multiracial transnational movement has emerged to counter this form of environmental racism.[34]

CLIMATE JUSTICE

Climate justice looms as a major environmental justice issue of the 21st century.[35] The United States emits one quarter of the world's gases that cause global warming. People of color are concentrated in cities that failed EPA's ambient air quality standards. Global warming is expected to double the number of cities that currently exceed air quality standards. A study of the fifteen largest American cities found that climate change would increase heat-related deaths by at least 90 percent. People of color are twice as likely to die in a heat wave. Global warming will increase the number of flood, drought and fire occurrences worldwide. Also, low-income people typically lack insurance to replace possessions lost in storms and floods. Only 25 percent of renters have renters insurance. Climate change will reduce discretionary spending because prices will rise across the board. Poor families will have to spend even more on food and electricity, which already represent a large proportion of their budgets. Indigenous people are losing traditional medicinal plants to a warming climate, and subsistence households are suffering from the loss of species that are unable to adapt.

CONCLUSION

The environmental justice movement emerged in response to environmental inequities, threats to public health, unequal protection, differential enforcement, and disparate treatment received by the poor and people of color. Poverty and environmental degradation are intricately linked and take a heavy toll on billions of people in developing and industrialized countries alike. Thus, any search for sustainable development must address the root causes of both poverty and pollution and seek solutions to this double threat.

Redefinition of Environmental Protection. The environmental justice movement redefined environmental protection as a basic right. It also emphasized pollution prevention, waste minimization, and cleaner production techniques as strategies to achieve environmental justice for all without regard to race, color, national origin, or income. Many countries have environmental and human laws to protect the health and welfare of its citizens—including racial and ethnic groups and indigenous peoples. However, all communities have not received the same benefits from their application, implementation, and enforcement.

Design a Holistic Approach to Environmental Protection. The environmental justice movement has set out clear goals of eliminating unequal enforcement of environmental, civil rights, and public health laws, differential exposure of some populations to harmful chemicals, pesticides, and other toxins in the home, school, neighborhood, and workplace, faulty assumptions in calculating, assessing, and managing risks, discriminatory zoning and land-use practices, and exclusionary policies and practices that limit some individuals and groups from participation in decision making. Many of these problems could be eliminated if existing environmental, health, housing, and civil rights laws were vigorously enforced in a nondiscriminatory way.

Clean and Affordable Energy. Governments should initiate an action program to make available finances and infrastructure to bring clean and affordable and sustainable energy sources to the 2 billion people who lack these energy services by 2012. Governments should adopt a target increasing the global share of new renewable energy sources to 15 percent by 2010.

Decrease Pesticide Use. Institute protocols and plan to decrease pesticide use, including prohibiting the export of banned or never registered pesticides, implement integrated pest management (IPM), evaluate the hazards posed by pesticide exports, and improve the quality and quantity of information about pesticide production, trade and use and publish information in the public record.

Reduce Children's Exposure to Neurotoxicants. Abate lead in older housing; completely phase-out leaded gasoline; target high-risk children, screening, early detection, treatment; increase allocation of medications that help reduce or remove lead; use new, safe lead removal techniques; and dietary improvements.

Strengthen Legislation and Regulations. A legislative approach may be needed where environmental, health, and worker safety laws and regulations are weak or nonexistent. However, laws and regulations are only as good as their enforcement. Unequal political power arrangements also have allowed poisons of the rich to be offered as short term economic remedies for poverty.

Design Strategies to Combat Economic Blackmail. There is little or no correlation between proximity of industrial plants and employment opportunities of nearby residents. Having industrial facilities in one's community does not automatically translate into jobs for nearby residents. Many industrial plants are located at the fence line with the communities. Some are so close that local residents could walk to work. More often than not, the poor are stuck with the pollution and poverty, while other people commute in for the industrial jobs.

Close Corporate Welfare Loopholes. Tax breaks and corporate welfare programs have produced few new jobs by polluting firms. However, state-sponsored pollution and lax enforcement have allowed many communities of color and poor communities to become the dumping grounds. Industries and governments (including the military) have often exploited the economic vulnerability of poor communities, poor states, poor nations, and poor regions for their unsound, "risky", and nonsustainable operations. Environmental justice leaders are demanding that no community or nation, rich or poor, urban or suburban, black or white, should be allowed to become a "sacrifice zone" or dumping grounds. They are also pressing governments to live up to their mandate of protecting public health and the environment.

Forge International Cooperative Agreements. Governments will need to take responsibility and develop policies that address global environmental racism. The poisoning of African Americans in Louisiana's "Cancer Alley," Native Americans on reservations, and Mexicans in the border towns all have their roots in the same economic system, a system characterized by economic exploitation, racial oppression, and devaluation of human life and the natural environment.

Environmental Reparations. The call for environmental and economic justice does not stop at the U.S. borders but extends to communities and nations that have been the "victims" of economic exploitation via the export of hazardous wastes, toxic products, "dirty" industries, indigenous resource extraction, and nonsustainable development practices. Much of the world does not get to share in the benefits of the United States' high standard of living. From energy consumption to the production and export of tobacco, pesticides, and other chemicals, more and more of the world's peoples are sharing the health and environmental burden of the United States' wasteful throw-away culture. Hazardous wastes and "dirty" industries have followed the "path of least resistance." Poor people and poor nations are given a false choice of "no jobs and no development" versus "risky low-paying jobs and pollution."

Building A Global Environmental Justice Movement. The environmental justice movement has begun to build a global network of grassroots groups, community based organizations, university-based resource centers, researchers, scientists, educators, and youth groups. Better communication and funding is needed in every area. Resources are especially scarce for environmental justice and antiracist groups in developing countries. The Internet has proven to be a powerful tool for those groups who have access to the worldwide web. Erasing the "digital divide" becomes a major strategy to combat environmental racism.

NOTES

Robert D. Bullard is the Ware Professor of Sociology and Director of the Environmental Justice Resource Center, Clark Atlanta University, 223 James P. Brawley Drive, Atlanta, GA 30314. Phone: (404) 880–6911; Fax: (404) 880–6909; E-mail: ejrc@cau.edu.

1. P.S. Mead, L. Slutsker, V. Dietz, L.F. McCaig, J.S. Bresee, C. Shapiro, P.M. Griffin, and R.V. Tauxe, "Food-Related Illness and Death in the United States," *Emerging Infectious Diseases Journal* 5 (September-October 1999).
2. Ibid.
3. Ibid.
4. National Institute of Environmental Health Sciences. Environmental Diseases from A to Z. NIH Publication No. 96–4145 (1996); NIEHS, "Lead—The #1 Environmental Hazard to many Children," *NIEHS Fact Sheet* #8, LEAD (March, 1997). http://www/niehs.nih.gov/oc/factsheets/fslead.htm.
5. U.S. Department of Health and Human Services, "HHS Helps in Effort to Eliminate Childhood Lead Poisoning," *HHS Fact Sheet* (March 4, 2002).
6. D. R. Wernett, D. R. & L. A. Nieves. Breathing polluted air: Minorities are disproportionately exposed. *EPA Journal*, 18: (1992): 16–17.
7. Robert D. Bullard. "Climate Justice and People of Color." http://www.ejrc.cau.edu/climatechgpoc.htm.
8. "Asthma's At-A-Glance 1999." http://www.cdc.gov/nceh/asthma_old/ataglance/default.htm.
9. Ibid.
10. Centers for Disease Control, "Asthma: United States, 1980–1990," Morbidity and Mortality Weekly Report, 39 (1992), pp. 733–735. See also Robert D. Bullard, Glenn S. Johnson, and Angel O. Torres. *Sprawl City: Race, Politics, and Planning in Atlanta*, Washington, DC: Island Press, 2000.
11. "Asthma's At-A-Glance 1999." http://www.cdc.gov/nceh/asthma_old/ataglance/default.htm.
12. H.P. Mak, H. Abbey, and R.C. Talamo, "Prevalence of Asthma and Health Service Utilization of Asthmatic Children in an Inner City," *Journal of Allergy and Clinical Immunology* 70 (1982), pp. 367–372; I.F. Goldstein and A.L. Weinstein, "Air Pollution and Asthma: Effects of Exposure to Short-Term Sulfur Dioxide Peaks," *Environmental Research* 40 (1986), pp. 332–345; J. Schwartz, D. Gold, D.W. Dockey, S.T. Weiss, and F.E. Speizer, "Predictors of Asthma and Persistent Wheeze in a National Sample of Children in the United States," *American Review of Respiratory Disease* 142 (1990), pp. 555–562; F. Crain, K. Weiss, J. Bijur, et al., "An estimate of the Prevalence of Asthma and Wheezing among Inner-City Children," *Pediatrics* 94 (1994), pp. 356–362. See also Robert D. Bullard, Glenn S. Johnson, and Angel O. Torres. *Race, Equity, and Smart Growth: Why People of Color Must Speak for Themselves*. Atlanta, GA: Environmental Justice Resource Center, 2000.
13. "Asthma's At-A-Glance 1999." http://www.cdc.gov/nceh/asthma_old/ataglance/default.htm.
14. Commission for Racial Justice. *Toxic wastes and race in the United States*. New York: United Church of Christ, 1987.
15. Robert D. Bullard and Beverly H. Wright. "The Quest for Environmental Equity: Mobilizing the African-American Community for Social Change." *Society and Natural Resources*, Vol. 3, 1990: 301–311.
16. Robert D. Bullard. "The Legacy of American Apartheid and Environmental Racism." *St. John's Journal of Legal Commentary*, Vol. 9, Issue 2, (Spring 1994): 445–474; See also Robert D. Bullard, *Dumping in Dixie: Race, Class, and Environmental Quality* (3rd ed.). Boulder, CO: Westview Press, 2000.
17. R. Twombly. (1997). "Urban uprising." *Environmental Health Perspective* 105 (July): 696–701.
18. See Robert D. Bullard, Glenn S. Johnson, and Angel O. Torres. *Race, Equity, and Smart Growth: Why People of Color Must Speak for Themselves*. Atlanta, GA: Environmental Justice Resource Center, 2000.
19. "Study: Public Housing Is Too Often Located Near Toxic Sites." *Dallas Morning News*, October 3, 2000. See http://www.cnn.com/2000/NATURE/10/03/toxicneighbors.ap.
20. Robert D. Bullard, Glenn S. Johnson, and Angel O. Torres. *Race, Equity, and Smart Growth: Why People of Color Must Speak for Themselves*. Atlanta, GA: Environmental Justice Resource Center, 2000.

21. Robert D. Bullard, Glenn S. Johnson, and Angel O. Torres. *Race, Equity, and Smart Growth: Why People of Color Must Speak for Themselves*. Atlanta, GA: Environmental Justice Resource Center, 2000.

22. Child Proofing Our Communities Campaign. March 2001. *Poisoned Schools: Invisible Threats, Visible Actions*. Falls Church, VA: Center for Health, Environment and Justice; See also http://www.childproofing.org/mapindex.html.

23. Cat Lazaroff. "Pesticide Exposure Threatens Children at School." *Environmental News Service,* January 5, 2000.

24. Caroline Cox. "Working With Poisons on the Farm." *Journal of Pesticide Reform,* Vol. 14, No. 3, (Fall 1994): 2–5; U.S. General Accounting Office. *Pesticides on Farms: Limited Capability Exists to Monitor Occupational Illnesses and Injuries*. Report to the Chairman, Committee on Agriculture, Nutrition, and Forestry, U.S. Senate. Washington, D.C. (December 1993).

25. Caroline Cox. "Working With Poisons on the Farm." *Journal of Pesticide Reform,* Vol. 14, No. 3, (Fall 1994): 2–5; A. L. Aspelin. "Pesticide Industry Sales and Usage: 1992 and 1993 Market Estimates. U.S. EPA. Office of Prevention, Pesticides and Toxic Substances." Office of Pesticide Programs. Biological and Economic Analysis Division. Washington, D.C., (June 1994); D.P. Morgan. "Recognition and Management of Pesticide Poisonings." Washington, D.C.: U.S. EPA. Office of Pesticide Programs. Health Effects Division, 1989; U.S. EPA Office of Prevention, Pesticides and Toxic Substances. List of chemicals evaluated for carcinogenic potential. Memo from Reto Engler, senior science advisor, Health Effects Division to Health Division Branch Chiefs, et. al. Washington, D.C. (August 31, 1993); U.S. Department of Health and Human Services. Public Health Service. Centers for Disease Control. National Institute for Occupational Safety and Health. Registry of Toxic Effects of Chemical Substances. Microfiche Edition. Sweet, D.V. (ed.). Cincinnati, OH (January 1993).

26. Caroline Cox. "Working With Poisons on the Farm." *Journal of Pesticide Reform,* Vol. 14, No. 3, (Fall 1994): 2–5.

27. National Institute of Environmental Health Sciences. *Environmental Diseases from A to Z*. NIH Publication No. 96–4145. http://www.nieehs.nih.gov.

28. See Sweatshop Watch: Frequently Asked Questions. http://www.sweatshopwatch.org/swatch/questions.html.

29. "Sweatshops and Women of Color." http://www.incite-national.org/involve/sweatshops.html.

30. LaDuke, All Our Relations, p. 3.

31. Jessica Reaves and Mark Thompson, "Vieques under Fire: Standoff in Puerto Rico," TIME.com. Time website at http://www.time.com/time/printout/0,8816,107846,00.html.

32. Al Gedicks. The New Resource Wars: Native and Environmental Struggles Against Multinational Corporations. Boston: South Ends Press, 1993.

33. Winona LaDuke. All Our Relations: Native Struggles for Land Rights and Life. Boston: South End Press, 1999, pp. 2–3.

34. Al Gedicks, Resource Rebels: Native Challenges to Mining and Oil Corporations. Boston: South End Press, 2001.

35. Robert D. Bullard. "Climate Justice and People of Color." http://www.ejrc.cau.edu/climatechgpoc.html.

Part III
Reducing Inequality

CHAPTER 12

PROGRESSIVE SOLUTIONS FOR REDUCING INEQUALITY

Social stratification is inevitable; indeed, there will always be leaders and followers, successful and not-so-successful entrepreneurs, differences in talents and skills, and differences in society's rewards. Whether the inequality is great (as in the United States) or relatively small (as in the Scandinavian countries), policymakers are the ones responsible for crafting policies that determine the contours of the society's stratification system (Eitzen and Baca Zinn, 2006: 572–573). Addressing the issue of inequality, Claude Fischer and his colleagues make this related point:

> The answer to the question of why societies vary in their structure of rewards is ... political.... By loosening markets or regulating them, by providing services to all citizens or rationing them according to income, by subsidizing some groups more than others, societies, through their politics, build their ladders [the height and breadth of the rungs of the stratification system]. To be sure, historical and external constraints deny full freedom of action, but a substantial freedom of action remains.... In a democracy, this means that the inequality that Americans have is, in significant measure, the historical result of policy choices Americans—or, at least, Americans' representatives—have made. In the United States, the result is a society that is distinctly unequal. Our ladder is, by the standards of affluent democracies and even by the standards of recent American history, unusually extended and narrow—and becoming more so. (Fischer et al., 1996: 8)

In short, the level of inequality in the United States, which is greater than that found in other Western democracies, is by design (Fischer et al., 1996: 125).

Social policies determine society's design. Since the 1970s, decision-makers in the United States have deliberately shrunk the safety net established during the New Deal of the 1930s. Welfare programs have been eliminated or curtailed. Subsidies to low-income families for child care, food, housing, medical care, and job training have been cut. At the same time, taxes for the affluent have been reduced significantly. Such policies have dramatically increased the inequality gap.

Political conservatives believe that the unequal distribution of economic rewards is none of the government's business (Eitzen and Sage, 2007: 217). Seemingly regardless of the human cost, they value individualism, freedom, and the market economy. From their perspective, inequality is not evil but good because it motivates people to compete and weeds out the weak. Progressives, on the other hand, argue that this laissez-faire approach guarantees an exaggerated inequality and leads to what economists Robert Frank and Philip Cook (1995) have called a "winner-take-all" society.

The three readings in this concluding section describe the pernicious social problems that flow from the inequality gap in the United States and explore progressive means of reducing this gap.

REFERENCES

Eitzen, D. Stanley, and Maxine Baca Zinn. 2006. *Social Problems,* 10th ed. Boston: Allyn & Bacon.

Eitzen, D. Stanley, and George H. Sage. 2007. "The Role of Government in Achieving the Good Society." Pp. 217–226 in *Solutions to Social Problems from the Top Down: The Role of Government,* edited by D. Stanley Eitzen and George H. Sage. Boston: Allyn & Bacon.

Fischer, Claude S., Michael Hout, Martin Sanchez Jankowski, Samuel R. Lucas, Ann Swidler, and Kim Voss. 1996. *Inequality by Design: Cracking the Bell Curve Myth.* Princeton, NJ: Princeton University Press.

Frank, Robert H., and Philip J. Cook. 1995. *The Winner-Take-All Society.* New York: Free Press.

27. Narrowing the Income Gap Between Rich and Poor
Michael Hout and Samuel R. Lucas

The growing income gap between rich and poor Americans has become a key issue in this political season. The gap is larger now than at any point in the last 75 years. But a heated political and academic debate is under way about what the numbers mean. Some politicians and commentators try to dismiss income inequality with a variety of false assertions. They claim that inequality is inevitable because every society has its rich and poor; that it is a reflection of Americans' unequal talents; that it is necessary for economic growth; or that it may be unfortunate but must be tolerated because of the prohibitive expense of initiating government programs to redistribute wealth.

The results of a year-long research project that we and four colleagues in the sociology department at the University of California at Berkeley conducted contradict all of these propositions, as we document in *Inequality by Design: Cracking the Bell Curve Myth,* to be published by Princeton University Press next month. Social inequality is not a force beyond our control.

Recent American history and the experience of several European nations show that economic inequality depends on the choices we make—how we regulate corporations and unions, how we distribute the tax burden, how we finance or do not finance education, and how we set wages. Nor is "taxing and spending" our only option.

Perhaps the most telling argument against the inevitability of our current situation is that not only is the inequality in income between the richest and the poorest in the United States greater now than in the past, but it is also greater than that of any other populous, industrialized country. Workers in such countries also have had to deal with the globalization of trade and the disruptions caused by new technology; yet only workers in the United States have lost so much ground. For example, in 1974 the chief executive officers of American corporations made about $35 for every worker's dollar; in 1995, they made $224 for every worker's dollar. By contrast, the chief executive officers of German corporations make about 21 deutsche marks (about $14) for every one earned by workers. Clearly, different economic choices produce different outcomes.

While every society has its rich and poor, inequality is mainly a matter of degree. In 1974, when the gap between the incomes of the richest and poorest Americans was at a historic low, the top 10 percent of U.S. households had incomes 31 times those of the poorest 10 percent and four times those of median-income households. By 1994, those numbers were 55 times the poorest and six times the median. Not only is inequality growing; its growth is accelerating. Inequality surged between 1991 and 1993 as the most recent recession lowered incomes for all but the richest Americans. Executives killed jobs in ways that would be illegal in Germany and France—for example, shutting down plants in some regions and relocating them in jurisdictions with right-to-work laws. Wall Street rewarded the executives with a mid-recession rally that boosted the value of their stock options.

Viewing inequality as inevitable absolves us of responsibility for reducing it. The current differences among nations mean that Americans need to be activist, not fatalistic, in the face of growing inequality. They also suggest that inequality is not produced by the genetic or other immutable personal characteristics that doom many workers to low wages. In their controversial book *The Bell Curve: The Reshaping of American Life by Differences in Intelligence* (Free Press, 1994), the political scientist Charles Murray and the late psychologist Richard J. Herrnstein tried to explain the rising inequality of incomes in the United States by claiming that the economy now rewards intelligence more than in the past.

Our reanalysis of their data shows conclusively that the test scores that they relied on to gauge intelligence reflect home environments—particularly parents' socioeconomic levels—as well as the quality of the schools people attended. For example, if I.Q. tests measure innate ability, people's scores on them ought to correlate equally well with their educational achievements both before and after the test. But the data used by Mr. Murray and Mr. Herrnstein show that people's scores correlate much more closely with their educational achievements at the time of the test than they do with their subsequent educational achievements. Schools create intelligence; they do not merely certify it. Thus the "intelligence" measured by tests is affected by a person's environment and is not solely the result of inborn characteristics.

Certainly, cognitive skills—though not innate—are important to one's earnings. However, errors and omissions in *The Bell Curve* also exaggerate the role of I.Q. in American inequality. Our reanalysis of the book's data shows that refining and enriching people's social environment makes I.Q. just one variable among many affecting inequality. Would that talent alone decided where a person ended up in society. Being born rich is still at least as much of an advantage as performing well on tests.

Nor are growing disparities in income an unavoidable negative effect of economic growth. Our review of the latest economic research concludes that such disparities may actually hinder growth. Since 1945, societies that have had greater inequality in incomes between the richest and poorest families have tended to have lower, not higher, subsequent economic growth.

The German and Italian economies grew faster between 1975 and 1989 than did that of the United States, but the gap between the incomes of the richest and the poorest citizens in those countries did not increase. In the United States, the period from 1955 through 1974 was the era of the greatest economic growth in this century, and also the era of the greatest equality of incomes in this century.

The richest 5 percent of U.S. households saw their incomes go up rapidly during that period, but their share of total household income fell from 22 percent to 16 percent as the incomes of poor and middle-income households rose even faster.

Greater equality of income between the richest and poorest does not harm productivity, either. In a comparative analysis of Western nations spanning the 1970s and 1980s, the Northwestern University economist Rebecca Blank found that factors including job-security laws (such as tenure laws for workers in some European countries), homeowner subsidies (such as tax deductions for mortgage interest in the United States), health insurance, and public child care did not inhibit the flexibility of businesses to shift resources, for example from one set of priorities or products to another.

Growing inequality of incomes may actually be hurting our economic performance. In a study of more than 100 U.S. businesses, Douglass Cowherd of the Brookings Institution and our Berkeley colleague David Levine found that the smaller the wage gap between managers and workers, the higher the quality of the business's products. Considering how the gap between management compensation and workers' wages has grown in recent years, this analysis suggests that the quality of some companies' products may be suffering.

Do we have to raise taxes and spend on welfare programs to have less inequality of income? Research shows that many social programs can reduce inequality, but it also shows that many countries have low inequality without high spending on social programs. Rates of poverty among children are sensitive indicators of overall inequality. At 22 percent, the proportion of poor children in the United States is higher than that in any other populous, industrial country. Australia and Canada are next, with 14 percent of their children living in poverty—a rate more than 30 percent below that of the United States. The rate of childhood poverty is 10 percent in Britain and Italy, and in the single digits in Germany (7 percent), France (6 percent), and the Netherlands (6 percent).

Some countries achieve their lower rates with expensive social programs, but others don't. Childhood poverty would be substantially higher in France (25 percent) and in Britain (30 percent) if there were no taxes and no welfare programs to redistribute income in those two countries. Their welfare states bring their rates of childhood poverty below that of the United States. But the percentage of children living in poverty already is low before the government transfers any money to poor people in Germany (where the rate is 9 percent before counting the taxes and welfare spending that lower it to 7 percent) and in Italy (12 percent as opposed to the 10 percent after social spending). The rate of childhood poverty is moderate in the Netherlands (14 percent before social programs lower it to 6 percent). Those nations do not need extensive welfare spending to keep children out of poverty, because the economy itself does not generate as much inequality as we see in France, Britain, or the United States.

Germany, Italy, and the Netherlands have less poverty because they have no working poor. They boost the bottom of the income distribution with a minimum wage guaranteeing that full-time workers' children will not be poor. With the current minimum wage of $4.25 per hour, however, an American parent of two can work full time and still fall below the poverty line. Even though Congress has approved a bill raising the minimum wage to $5.25 in September 1997, that will still be true. Indeed, it would be true even if we raised the minimum wage to $6.50 per hour. The continuing debates about the minimum wage in this country have not contradicted this essential point: Young workers and their children are not as poor in countries with higher minimum wages.

Many European countries also use national wage agreements to control inequality. The details differ, but these countries all use some form of collective bargaining that makes management accountable to workers. In Austria and Norway, national associations of employers in different industries bargain with representatives of national unions to determine wages for workers in each sector of the economy. In Germany and Italy, bargaining goes on between unions and employers' associations in each industry or region. The government then routinely extends the terms of these agreements to nonunion workers and companies.

In the United States, workers' wages are negotiated with a specific employer, either by individual employees or by a local union. In many jobs, the employer simply offers the job at a preset wage with little or no negotiation. This extremely decentralized system weakens the bargaining power of workers. Research by the Harvard University economist Richard Freeman, reported in *Working under Different Rules* (Russell Sage Foundation, 1994), shows that the distribution of wages for workers of the same age, education, gender, and occupation is much wider in the United States than in countries with more centralized methods of setting wages.

Unions are the key to more uniform policies for setting wages. They help lower the inequality of income because they typically make management more accountable to workers, particularly when managers try to raise their own pay. The decline of unions in the United States in recent decades has meant that workers have lost the power to claim their share of economic growth. Between 1970 and 1990, the proportion of workers in the private sector belonging to unions dropped from 30 percent to just 11 percent, the lowest rate of union membership in the industrialized world except, possibly, for Japan.

Even as unions were declining, American workers set records in productivity (output per working hour). Between 1949 and 1974, increases in productivity were rewarded by increases in wages. Since 1974, productivity increased 68 percent in manufacturing and 50 percent in the service sector of the economy, but real wages grew less than 10 percent. The gains in productivity fueled both executive compensation—up 600 percent since 1974, according to research by the economic writer Graeff Crystal—and the stock market, where the Dow Jones Industrial Average has risen from 1,500 to more than 5,500 since 1974. Workers have set the table for an American economic feast for over two decades, but they have not received their slice of the growing pie.

The reports about economic inequality keep appearing. Political leaders, with the exception of the Republican Presidential candidate Patrick Buchanan, have been surprisingly passive. The action gap is almost as big as the income gap.

Our review of recent American history and of the actions of our competitors makes it clear that the country need not accept ever more extreme income disparities. Nor is the unpopular combination of high taxes and social spending our only remedy. In the past, investments in our schools and colleges helped to equalize opportunity for many citizens. Institutions such as labor unions empowered workers who wanted to claim a share of their own productivity. Today, the economies of countries that have national income policies that include a voice for workers are growing faster than is the economy of the United States, and they are doing a better job of sharing the wealth.

That suggests that the solutions to America's problems of inequality of income are in the classrooms, boardrooms, and workplaces around the country. Washington's role should be to foster opportunity through education and to find ways to bring employers and workers together on an equal footing, so they can solve economic problems directly. For example, we need changes in the policies of the National Labor Relations Board to make it easier to form unions and easier for unions to force employers to engage in binding arbitration over contracts and other disputes.

We can certainly do without the corrupt practices engaged in by some powerful unions in the past, but we do need a labor policy that will give today's workers more power to negotiate with employers. When workers have a voice in how wealth is distributed, they do not end up as working poor. Their paychecks keep them—and their children—above the poverty line. The problem right now is that American workers have a case to make, but their employers do not have to listen to it.

Note

Michael Hout is a professor of sociology and director of the Survey Research Center at the University of California at Berkeley. Samuel R. Lucas is an assistant professor of sociology at Berkeley. They are coauthors of the forthcoming *Inequality by Design* (Princeton University Press), along with Claude S. Fischer, Martin Sanchez Jankowski, Ann Swidler, and Kim Voss.

28. Millennium Development Goals for Children in the United States to Be Achieved by 2015

Childrens Defense Fund

"We are guilty of many errors and many faults but our worst crime is abandoning the children, neglecting the fountain of life. Many of the things we need can wait. The child cannot. Right now is the time his bones are being formed, his blood is being made, and his senses are being developed. To him we cannot answer 'Tomorrow.' His name is 'Today.'"
—Gabriela Mistral, Chilean poet, educator, Nobel Laureate

It is our responsibility and within our power to make our nation see all our children as the sacred gifts they are of our Creator and not just as fodder for war or as a consumer market. Adults must regain their moral bearing and teach our children that the most important things in life are not material things but love, justice, respect, service and integrity. We must challenge the glorification of violence in our culture. And we also must challenge families, religious, cultural, media and government leaders, and citizens to make our children's health, safety, education, family and community life our overarching national purpose.

Through the United Nations, the nations of the world have set Millennium Development Goals (MDGs) to, among other things, reduce child and maternal mortality and end extreme global poverty by 2015. We hope the United States will lead the world in assuring their achievement. We also hope we will challenge ourselves to set and honor similar goals in our nation for our own poor, uninsured and poorly educated children. Beginning now, we must demand that our leaders commit in 2006 and 2008, as a condition of our vote, to an America that:

- Ensures every child and their parents health insurance.
- Lifts every child from poverty.
- Gets every child ready for school through full funding of quality child care and Head Start and new investments in universal preschool education.
- Ends child hunger through adequate child and family nutrition investments.
- Makes sure every child can read by fourth grade and can graduate from school able to succeed at work and in life.
- Provides every child safe, quality after-school and summer programs so they can learn, serve, work and stay out of trouble.
- Ensures every child a place called home and every family decent affordable housing.
- Protects all children from neglect, abuse, and other violence and ensures them the care they need when families break down.
- Ensures families leaving welfare the supports needed to be successful in the workplace, including health care, child care, education and training.
- Creates jobs with a living wage.

29. Taxing Concentrated Wealth to Broaden the American Dream
Good Policy, Good Politics, Good for America
Dedrick Muhammad and Chuck Collins

Imagine listening to a presidential or senatorial campaign speech and hearing this proposal:

My fellow Americans, our country is facing a dangerous polarization of wealth and power. The growing disparity in assets and opportunity is becoming frighteningly un-American. America has a long and noble history of investing in its citizens and its citizens reinvesting in America. I have a proposal that would further this long and proud legacy. A half a century ago, our country made a substantial investment in broadening wealth. We invested in subsidized mortgages so that millions of Americans could purchase a home. Many more got debt-free college educations that vaulted them into the middle class.

Unfortunately, not all of our fellow American citizens had an equal opportunity to participate in these wealth-broadening programs, particularly Americans of color. This has left America to this day divided by race and wealth. We can and will no longer tolerate this. In Post 9/11 America we as a country cried out "United We Stand." Today I put forth a proposal that will help make this idea a reality.

I propose that we make a serious investment in the rising generation, to broaden their stake in America with wealth and opportunity, just as we did for our soldiers in the war against fascism so shall we do today as all of America stands up against terror. My "Wealth Opportunity Fund" will provide debt-free college educations and low interest mortgages to first time homebuyers, to all Americans. It will provide matching funds for universal savings accounts and invest in other forms of community wealth that increase our security and prosperity. This program will help to end the terror that plagues all families that live in poverty and will show to the world the democratic and humanistic core of our American society. The fund will be capitalized by an inheritance tax on accumulated fortunes over $10 million. This has the duel benefit of paying for and addressing the dangers that such dynastic accumulations of wealth pose to our democracy and commitment to equality of opportunity.

Such a speech might seem positively utopian in today's political climate. After all, much of the thrust of the Bush fiscal agenda seems to be reducing taxation on wealth and dismantling the ladder of economic opportunity. And Democrats are running scared of proposing anything that might require increased taxes.

But a bold proposal to link wealth taxation to a specific wealth-broadening agenda has the potential to shift public perceptions and politics if it addresses the deep desires and the unmet needs of the average American alienated from her/his own democratic government. Such an initiative could galvanize immobilized constituencies and dramatize the limitations of Bush's "want another tax cut?" social policy.

The progressive tax system is under attack at all levels of government. Neoconservatives are pushing their twenty year old con of "shrink, shift and shaft." This extremist fiscal agenda is aimed at shrinking the regulatory and welfare state (while enlarging the warfare/watchtower state); and shifting the tax burden off wealth and federal taxing bodies and onto income and consumption taxes and state and local taxes. The "shaft" is the deteriorating quality of life and opportunities faced by the overwhelming majority of the population that depends on vibrant public sector spending.

A key constituency to be mobilized to defend progressive taxation and promote a wealth-broadening program are those who aspire to own a home, start a business, and have greater economic security. This constituency is classic middle America, those who believe and are working toward fulfilling the American dream. There is a nascent "wealth broadening movement" made up of community development organizations promoting stable housing and homeownership, credit unions and individual development accounts helping members to save, and savings and investment clubs in religious congregations. These efforts aspire to broaden their impact through state and federal legislation to expand the number of people who benefit. But there will be no meaningful investment in asset solutions in the current austere fiscal environment with multitrillion dollar budget deficits projected over the coming decade. As Dr. Martin Luther King stated forty years ago the American promissory note has been returned to too many Americans and it has been marked insufficient funds.

Progressives need a policy initiative that recaptures the possibility and potential of affirmative activist government. A bold wealth-broadening proposal could greatly strengthen equality of opportunity and reduce wealth disparities, particularly the racial wealth gap. Such an initiative could move progressive constituencies and candidates off of defense ("We want half of Bush's tax cut") and in favor of a comprehensive solution rooted in American values of opportunity.

A campaign to broaden wealth, at this time of historic inequalities, could have the quality of a moral crusade for equality of opportunity. A campaign such as this could take us to fulfill the next phase of the American Civil Rights Movement. A young Civil Rights activist Stokely Carmichael articulated two problems of the African Americans: "We are black and we are poor." The Civil Rights movement was able to push forth legislation that outlawed gross white supremacist practices but were never that successful in adequately addressing the economic legacies of white supremacy. Efforts such as Dr. King's Poor People's Campaign or Lyndon Johnson's War on Poverty were never successfully institutionalized into the American agenda. The Wealth Broadening Campaign can play a significant role in healing one of the most serious scars on American Society, the racial wealth gap. It has been shown that wealth is the great equalizing factor in America. Cutting across racial lines families with equitable wealth have equitable educational results, economic practices, and more equitable health conditions.

A wealth-broadening program could reconnect the American people with the potential for positive government spending like the G.I. Bill for education and the post–World War II homeownership expansion. Such a program would deepen and mobilize constituencies that have a stake in preserving a progressive tax system. By linking revenue more directly to the practical aspirations for opportunity, security and prosperity of the average American, this program could help breathe new life into a democratic process that most Americans see as too corrupt and removed to be of any benefit.

At the same time, this emerging movement must defend existing safety nets and investments in opportunity as a foundation for moving forward. Individual wealth-broadening alone has its limitations and is not a substitute for a robust social safety net and adequately funded Social Security program.

LAST CENTURY'S WEALTH BROADENING PROGRAM

In the two decades after World War II, the U.S. embarked on a substantial effort to broaden wealth ownership and opportunity, putting millions of families onto the private wealth building train. Between 1945 and 1968, the percentage of American families living in owner-occupied dwellings rose from 44 percent to 63 percent. This was due in large part to a massive public commitment to subsidized and insured mortgages from the Federal Housing Authority (FHA), the Veteran's Administration (VA) and Farmers Home Administration (FmHA).

Prior to the FHA, mortgages averaged 58 percent of the property value, excluding all but those with substantial savings. FHA and other mortgage subsidies enabled lenders to lengthen the term of the mortgage and dramatically lower the down payment to less than 10 percent. Government guarantees alone enabled interest rates to fall 2 or 3 points.

Between World War II and 1972, 11 million families bought homes, another 22 million improved their properties, according to Kenneth Jackson in his history of the FHA, *Grabgrass Frontier*. The FHA also insured 1.8 million dwellings in multifamily projects. The biggest beneficiary was white suburbia where half of all housing could claim FHA or VA financing in the 1950s and 1960s. All these housing subsidy programs provided a wealth stake for 35 million families between 1933 and 1978. This does not include the other substantial benefits of the Home Mortgage Interest Deduction and the indirect subsidy of interstate highway construction opening up inexpensive land for suburban commuters.

Unfortunately, for a host of reasons—including racial discrimination in mortgage lending practices, housing settlement patterns, income inequality, and unequal educational opportunity—many nonwhite and Hispanic families were left standing at the wealth-building train station. Homeownership rates for blacks and Latinos are currently stalled at the level where whites were at the end of World War II. While now, over 70 percent of non-Hispanic whites own their own home, homeownership rates for blacks and Hispanics average 48 percent.

This post–World War II investment in middle-class wealth expansion was paid for by a system of progressive taxation. The top income tax rate coming out of the War was 91 percent and the estate tax included a provision that taxed fortunes over $50 million at a 70 percent rate (no such top rate exists today). In turn, many of the widely shared benefits of postwar spending meant that the progressivity of the tax system enjoyed widespread political support.

GOOD POLICY, GOOD POLITICS, GOOD FOR AMERICA

The current debates about health care, education and inequality are impoverished by the lack of bold solutions to people's deeply felt needs. Instead, we've instituted three years of federal tax cuts that have disproportionately benefited the very wealthy. In five decades, we've gone from a system of progressive taxation that funded America's biggest middle class expansion to an increasingly regressive federal tax system that has inadequate resources to invest in something as basic as a full prescription drug benefit for elders.

The conservative agenda of shrinking government spending (except on the military) has succeeded in dampening what is politically possible. Is there anyone who might dare propose a wealth-broadening program that would touch 35 million more families, particularly those barred by discrimination from the last generation's housing wealth boom?

A farsighted initiative, however, to broaden wealth by taxing concentrated wealth could be both good policy and good politics. Consider how such a program would work from a policy and constituency mobilization perspective. A universal wealth-broadening "trust fund" could be capitalized by a dedicated estate tax paid primarily by fortunes over $10 million. Two ideas that alone are politically problematic gain some power when fused together.

The estate tax could initially generate $20 to $25 billion a year for a wealth opportunity fund. But in the coming decades, an enormous intergenerational transfer of wealth will occur and estate tax revenue will grow to between $157 billion to $750 billion a year, depending on one's estimated annual growth rate. In addition, if the estate tax was made more progressive, with a top rate returning to 70 percent on fortunes over $100 million, it would generate even more revenue for a wealth broadening commitment on scale with the G.I. Bill.

A wealth-broadening program would be a constructive solution to the polarization of wealth and assets and break down the racial boundaries that have fractured this nation. A wealth-broadening program can help march this country toward greater equality, to "a more perfect union." British commentator Will Hutton observes that current "US society is polarizing and its social arteries hardening. The sumptuousness and bleakness of the respective lifestyles of rich and poor represent a scale of difference in opportunity and wealth that is almost medieval."

Between 1983 and 1998, the share of wealth held by the richest one percent of households grew from 34 to 39 percent. And the disparities within this top one percent are also enormous, with a huge percentage of wealth gains accruing to people with household net worth over $50 million. As Edward N. Wolff has observed, "The 1990s also saw an explosion in the number of millionaires and multimillionaires. The number of households worth $1,000,000 or more grew by almost 60 percent; the number worth $10,000,000 or more almost quadrupled."

Meanwhile, the number of households without assets, who have zero or negative net worth, is increasing. The national savings rate has plummeted and, according to recent Survey of Consumer Finance information, racial wealth disparities have widened again. Between 1998 and 2001, median net worth for whites rose 16.9 percent to $120,900. But for all nonwhite/Hispanic people, net worth fell 4.5 percent, to $17,100. A wealth-broadening program would address this current abomination.

A political benefit to a wealth-tax funded program is that it could mobilize constituencies to defend progressive taxation, such as the federal estate tax. The federal estate tax is our country's most progressive tax, falling only on the estates of multimillionaires. Under the 2001 tax cut, the estate tax will be phased out and then abolished in 2010, but only for one year. Hence there is a rigorous debate over whether to make the tax cut permanent versus reforming the tax and retaining it on larger fortunes.

From the outset in the estate tax debate, there has been a political mismatch of constituencies. The wealthy individuals and business interests that pay the tax are highly motivated to abolish it. On the other side, the constituencies that have a stake in retaining the estate tax are immobilized, for they do not see a government that is active in creating better opportunities for them and are thus unable to discern the direct threat of its abolition.

The benefits of the tax are seemingly remote to the broader public because they flow into the general treasury. Last year, the estate tax added $28 billion to the Treasury and stimulated an estimated $10 billion a year in charitable giving. But their benefits are one step removed, compared to local property taxes and K–12 education.

Linking estate tax revenue to a wealth-broadening "trust fund" would galvanize a more direct constituency for its preservation. While there are downsides to earmarking taxes for specific spending items, here we can potentially save the most progressive tax and make the case that there is a relationship between the source of the money and its benefits. The estate tax, falling on those who have benefited disproportionately from our nation's fertile ground for wealth creation, recaptures and recycles that public investment that will build this system for the next generation.

MAKING THE AMERICAN DREAM AN AMERICAN REALITY

There are very good proposals and pilot projects that are focused on broadening assets and reducing wealth disparities. These include promotion of "asset-based solutions" such as savings incentives and homeownership. Taken together, these ideas form the modest beginning of a policy agenda for greater wealth equality. And they could be fully funded by a modest tax on wealth.

One example is a new wealth-broadening initiative that was just instituted in England, sponsored by Tony Blair's Labor Party. In 2003, British Parliament established what has become known as "baby bonds," a small child trust fund for each newborn in the country. Modest amounts of funds will be deposited and invested for each newborn infant and available for withdrawal at the age of 18.

In 1998, former U.S. Senator Robert Kerrey introduced similar legislation to create what he called "KidSave" accounts. "Under our proposal," said Kerrey, "every baby in America would enter life owning a piece of their country."

The KidSave initiative would guarantee every child $1000 at birth, plus $500 a year for children ages one to five, to be invested until retirement. Through compound returns over time, the account would grow substantially, provide a significant supplement to Social Security and other retirement funds, and enable many more Americans to leave inheritances to their children. This would strengthen economic opportunities and wealth-building across the generations. The KidSave accounts would be administered like a social security program.

There is a national demonstration project involving Individual Development Accounts (IDAs), where low-income people receive matching funds for their savings. While the number of households that benefit from IDAs has been small to date, the idea is to ramp up this concept, through expanded public funding, to assist many more households. At the same time, many community-based organizations are working to expand homeownership opportunities using a patchwork of development subsidies, low-interest mortgages, and down-payment assistance programs.

But the challenge for all of these wealth-broadening programs, including the British Baby Bond, is that they don't have an adequate or dedicated source of revenue to bring the effort to meaningful scale. Here is where some interesting theoretical proposals are emerging as to how to pay for asset programs.

Yale professors Bruce Ackerman and Anne Alstott put forward a radical "equality of opportunity" proposal in their 2001 book, *The Stakeholder Society*. They advocate using a wealth tax and "privilege tax" to fund an $80,000 stake given to every American when they turn 21, conditioned on graduating from high school. They argue that as young people come of age, the brunt of America's inequality of opportunity hits them. Those without parental help for education, homeownership, and business startups have vastly different opportunities than their upper income cohorts.

This notion of "stakeholding," providing a wealth stake as people come of age, has a long history. In 1797, Tom Paine argued that all new democratic republics, including France and the United States, should guarantee every 21-year-old citizen a wealth stake. And in the U.S., land grants and subsidized housing loans have been among the ways in which government has helped individuals to build substantial wealth.

Another interesting source of revenue for wealth building is the "sky trust" concept which addresses both the problem of asset building and environmental degradation. Recognizing that the environmental "commons" is being destroyed, Peter Barnes, in his book *Who Owns the Sky*, proposes creating a sky trust, capitalized by pollution credits as a revenue stream for asset building. Polluting companies would purchase carbon and sulfur permits (rather than being given them free) and funds would be paid into the "sky trust." Barnes cites the example of the Alaska Permanent Fund, which pays annual dividends to Alaska residents from the state's oil wealth.

The cumulative impact of a program to broaden wealth by taxing wealth would be to dramatically reduce, over a generation, the disparities of wealth in America. The implementation of such policies now when America is committed to including all of its citizens will strengthen the American community for generations to come. There are obvious questions about how such a program should be designed. Should wealth-broadening go beyond our notions of individual wealth ownership to include community wealth? For instance, public or community-owned housing that charges low monthly fees may not represent private wealth for an individual, but is a tremendous source of economic stability and security. Should the wealth creation vehicles have strings attached, with funds restricted to education, homeownership and retirement? How should we recognize, in some financial way, the legacy of racial discrimination in wealth-building? And what are the politically winnable forms of taxing wealth?

The good news is that the constituency for this program already exists. Local wealth building efforts need a source of substantial money. State and federal organizations working to defend the progressivity of the tax system, and the estate tax in particular, need a broader affirmative program. Wealth taxation and asset development, in sum, need each other. Taxing concentrated wealth and linking those revenues to wealth-spreading in the next generation is the political heart of a winning strategy to broaden equality of opportunity, ownership of wealth, and reaffirming that America is a nation for the people and by the people.

NOTE

Dedrick Muhammad coordinates the Racial Wealth Divide program at United for Fair Economy. Chuck Collins is co-founder and associate director at United for Fair Economy and co-author, with Bill Gates Sr. of *Wealth and Our Commonwealth: Why America Should Tax Accumulated Fortunes* (Beacon 2003).

WEBSITES

Inequality.org is a website that includes teaching tools, articles, and videos on the issue of social class. The site also includes an interesting series of "inequality quotes," and information about conferences on the issue of class.
    Inequality.org
    http://www.demos.org/inequality/

The public broadcasting site offers a variety of topics on social class. Do a basic search in the "Explore by topic" option to find them. The site also includes sponsored links from questia.com and healthline.com that provide access to additional information on class.
    Public Broadcasting
    http://www.pbs.org

The Economic Policy Institute provides a wide range of sources on social class. Issues include living wages, social security, welfare, unemployment, and trade and globalization. Books, articles, and news briefs are included as sections within this wide-ranging site on social class.
    Economic Policy Institute
    http://www.epinet.org/

The U.S. Census Bureau site links to census data for the 2000 census as well as information on topics such as poverty, health insurance, income, maps, and news releases on relevant topics.
    U. S. Census
    http://www.census.gov/

The Center on Budget and Policy Priorities collects information on a variety of policy issues affecting low-income individuals. Links to information on low-income housing, poverty/income, social security, state budget and tax, unemployment insurance, welfare reform and TANF (temporary assistance for needy families), and health policies are included in the site.
    Center on Budget and Policy Priorities
    http://www.cbpp.org

The Federal Reserve System site focuses on monetary and financial systems. This site allows people to learn "About the Fed" and about monetary policy. There are links to data sets, economic research and data, consumer information, and community development.
>Board of Governors of the Federal Reserve System
>*http://www.federalreserve.gov*

The Population Reference Bureau is a wide-ranging site that provides information on a number of topics that are pertinent to studies in the United States and in other countries. Here, researchers can access information about the environment and population trends and investigate topics such as aging, education, health, poverty, and race and ethnicity.
>Population Reference Bureau
>*http://www.prb.org/*

The Institute for Research on Poverty is an interdisciplinary organization that focuses on issues of poverty and social inequality in the United States. The site has a wealth of information on poverty and also provides access to other excellent websites, including the University of Kentucky Poverty Research Center, the West Coast Poverty Research Center, the Public Policy Institute of California, and the National Poverty Center.
>Institute for Research on Poverty
>*http://www.ssc.wisc.edu/irp*

The Joint Center for Poverty Research provides links to policy working papers, policy briefs, and poverty research. The focus of the Center is to explore "what it means to be poor in America."
>Joint Center for Poverty Research
>*http://www.jcpr.org*

The National Bureau of Economic Research allows researchers to access information on policies. Researchers can find information on individuals, industries, hospitals, and demographic and vital statistics, as well as economic indicators and economic releases.
>National Bureau of Economic Research
>*http://www.nber.org*

The Institute for Women's Policy Research provides information on women and is concerned with issues such as employment, education, poverty, welfare, work and family, and health and safety.
>Institute for Women's Policy Research
>*http://www.iwpr.org*

The Children's Defense Fund considers issues affecting children. This broad site offers information on programs and policies and a wide variety of data on issues affecting children.
    Children's Defense Fund
    http://www.childrensdefense.org

The U.S. Census Bureau Fact Finder provides an easy search for census information on populations by zip code or by state. A variety of demographic data combined with maps that provide a graphic representation of the data are available.
    U.S. Census Bureau Fact Finder
    http://factfinder.census.gov

The Panel Study of Income Dynamics follows a longitudinal study that began in 1968. Data on a large, random sample provides a description of economic, demographic, sociological, and psychological measures for the original respondents and their families in this ongoing project.
    Panel Study of Income Dynamics
    http://psidonline.isr.umich.edu

The National Center for Children in Poverty provides a variety of information regarding childhood poverty. Information on issues such as economic security, family stability, early childhood, and demographics is available at this website. In addition, the site contains a "data wizard" that allows the researcher to make state by state comparisons for a large number of variables.
    National Center for Children in Poverty
    http://www.nccp.org

The Cornell University Center for the Study of Inequality is focused on social and economic inequalities and the processes that contribute to inequality. Along with a listing of publications, the site has an interactive quiz that measures peoples' "inequality quotient."
    Cornell University Center for the Study of Inequality
    http://www.inequality.cornell.edu/

The Center on Urban Poverty and Social Change is specifically concerned with urban poverty and seeks to address questions on how inequality affects low-income communities. Specifically, the site has links to research topics such as welfare, children and families, neighborhood change, and community safety.
    Center on Urban Poverty and Social Change
    http://povertycenter.cwru.edu

A site produced by the U.S. Department of Human Services, the Administration for Children and Families provides access to information on a variety of children's

issues including TANF (Temporary Assistance for Needy Families), Head Start, Energy Assistance, and child support.
Administration for Children and Families
http://www.acf.hhs.gov/

Formerly known as the Welfare Information Network, the Economic Success Clearinghouse has information on policies, programs, and strategies for low-income and poor families. Links include welfare, income supplements, workforce development, asset development and work supports.
Economic Success Clearinghouse
http://www.welfareinfo.org

CREDITS

Chapter 1: Janny Scott and David Leonhardt, "Shadowy Lines That Still Divide," http://www.nytimes.com/2005/05/15/national/class/OVERVIEWFINAL.html?ex=1144468800&ei=5070, pp. 1–8. Copyright © 2005 by *The New York Times* Co. Reprinted with permission. • Michael D. Yates, "A Statistical Portrait of the U.S. Working Class," *Monthly Review* 56 (April 2005): 12–31. http://www.monthlyreview.org/0405yates.htm. Used with permission. • Jonathan Alter, "The Other America: An Enduring Shame," *Newsweek* (September 19, 2005): 40–48. Used with permission.

Chapter 2: "Tilting the Tax System in Favor of the Rich," *The New York Times* (October 4, 2005): Editorial/Op-Ed, pp 1–4. Copyright © 2005 by *The New York Times* Co. Reprinted with permission. • Woodrow Ginsberg, "Income and Inequality: Millions Left Behind," fifth ed., Americans for Democratic Action , (January 2006): 5–12. Used with permission. • Clara Jeffery, "The Perks of Privilege," *Mother Jones* 31 (May/June 2006): 24–25. Used with permission.

Chapter 3: Louise Auerhahn, "Our Society's Middle Is Shrinking from View," *The Mercury News* (July 26, 2005). Used with permission. • Griff Witte, "The Vanishing Middle Class," *The Washington Post National Weekly Edition* (September 27–October 3):6–9. Used with permission.

Chapter 4: Paul Krugman, "The Death of Horatio Alger: Our Political Leaders Are Doing Everything They Can to Fortify Class Inequality," *The Nation* (January 5, 2004). Used with permission. • Reprinted by permission of the publisher from Bernard Wasow, "Rags to Riches? The American Dream Is Less Common in the United States Than Elsewhere," The Century Foundation, Copyright 2004, The Century Foundation, Inc.

Chapter 5: Joel Wendland, "Still Not Getting By in Bush's America," *.Znet* (August 21, 2004): 1. http://www.zmag.org/content/showarticle.cfm?ItemID=6076. Used with permission. • Beth Shulman, "America's Low-Wage Workers: The Demography of a Caste," in *The Betrayal of Work,* New York: The New Press, 2003, 69–79. Used with permission.

Chapter 6: Lila Guterman, "As the Rich Get Richer, Do People Get Sicker? Researchers Debate Whether Income Inequality Impairs Public Health," *The Chronicle of Higher Education* (November 28, 2003): A22–A23. Used with permission. • Robert Sapolsky, "Sick of Poverty," *Scientific American* 293, no. 6 (December 2005). Reprinted with permission © 2005 by Scientific American, Inc. All rights reserved.

Chapter 7: Richard Rothstein, "A Wider Lens on the Black-White Achievement Gap," *Phi Delta Kappan* 86 (October 2004): 105–110. Used with permission • Ross Douthat, "Does Meritocracy Work?" *The Atlantic Monthly* 296 (November 2005), 120–26. Used with permission.

Chapter 8: From Jeffrey Reiman, *The Rich Get Richer and the Poor Get Prison: Ideology, Class and Criminal Justice,* 7/e, 145–46. Published by Allyn and Bacon, Boston, MA. Copyright © 2004 by Pearson Education. Reprinted by permission of the publisher. • Elliott Currie, "Poverty and Violent Crime," first published as "The depths of social exclusion" from *Crime and Punishment in America* by Elliott Currie © 1998 by Elliott Currie. Reprinted with permission of Henry Holt and Company, LLC. • Janis E. Johnston, "The Civil Rights Act of 1964: The Social Class Exclusion." Used with permission of the author.

Chapter 9: "Dying Alone: An Interview with Eric Klinenberg," University of Chicago Press (2002), 1–5, http://www.press.uchicago.edu/Misc/Chicago/443213in.html. Copyright © 2002 by the University of Chicago Press. Used with permission of the publisher and Eric Klinenberg. • Jason DeParle, "The Nation: Cast Away; Broken Levees, Unbroken Barriers," *The New York Times* (September 4, 2005): 1–3. Copyright © 2005 by The New York Times Co. Reprinted with permission. • Peter Wagner and Susan Edwards, "New Orleans by the Numbers," *Dollars & Sense* (March/April 2006): 54–55. Reprinted with permission of *Dollars & Sense,* a progressive economics magazine <www.dollarsandsense.org>.

Chapter 10: Chuck Raasch, "Sacrifices of War Remain Unshared," *Fort Collins Coloradan* (June 28, 2003), A11. Used with permission. • Ann Scott Tyson, "Their Last Resort: Youths in Rural U.S. Are Drawn to the Military" (November 4, 2005). Copyright © 2005, *The Washington Post,* reprinted with permission.

Chapter 11: Leigh Turner, "Bioethics, Social Class, and the Sociological Imagination," *Cambridge Quarterly of Healthcare Ethics* 14 (2005), 374–378. Copyright © 2005 Cambridge University Press 096=1801/05. Reprinted with the permission of Cambridge University Press. • Robert D. Bullard, "Poverty and Pollution in the United States," Atlanta: Environmental Justice Resource Center, Clark Atlanta University, 2002. Used with permission.

Chapter 12: Michael Hout and Samuel R. Lucas, "Narrowing the Income Gap Between Rich and Poor," *The Chronicle of Higher Education* (August 16, 1996): Section 2, B1–B2. Used with permission. • Marian Wright Edelman, "Millennium Development Goals for Children in the United States to Be Achieved by 2015," *Stand Up for Children Now! State of America's Children® Action Guide,* Children's Defense Fund, 2006. Retrieved from www.childrensdefense.org. • Dedrick Muhammad and Chuck Collins, "Taxing Concentrated Wealth to Broaden the American Dream: Good Policy, Good Politics, Good for America," United for a Fair Economy (February 2004): 1–6. Used by permission.

INDEX

Abbott, David H., 114
Academic achievement, 40, 129, 137; black-white gap and, 120, 122; differences in, 121; income and, 127; influence of, 120; lead exposure and, 123; by lower-class children, 121, 122, 123, 128; by middle-class children, 121, 122, 123, 124; school reform and, 127; social class and, 122, 123; social/economic inequalities and, 127; student mobility and, 121; wealth and, 122
Access, 2; to education, 130, 134, 135, 136; to health care, 103, 104, 108, 111, 112, 183; improvements in, 134; social class and, 9; to transportation, 157, 160, 162
"AccessUVa" program, 134
Achievement gap, 127; after-school/summer programs and, 128; black-white, 120, 122; closing, 124, 126, 128; existing-persistent, 120; minorities and, 126; race, 123, 124–125; school reform and, 124, 126; size of, 124–125; social-class, 123, 124–125; socioeconomic reforms and, 124
Ackerman, Bruce, 210
Action gap, income gap and, 202
Adjudication process, conviction and, 143
Adler, Nancy E., 113, 114, 115
Admissions process, 129, 131
Advantages, transmitting, 12, 16
Affirmative action, 13, 40, 133, 135
Afghanistan War, 96, 172
After-school programs, 126, 128, 204
Agostino, Fred, 74
Air conditioning, 157, 159, 160

Air pollution, geography of, 186–187
Air quality standards, 190
Alaska Natives, military toxics and, 189
Alaska Permanent Fund, 210
Alger, Horatio, 19, 85, 86
Alstott, Anne, 210
Alternative minimum tax (AMT), 48–49
American Dream, 79; as American reality, 209–211; belief in, 86; as privilege, 70; social mobility and, 81, 82; subscribing to, 13, 71, 93; upward mobility and, 85–86
American Dream (DeParle), 36
American Enterprise Institute, 15, 49, 135
American Idol (television show), 17
American Journal of Public Health, on weather/mortality, 161
"Anatomy of Racial Inequality, The" (Loury), 40
Annenberg Political Fact Check group, 67
Annunzio, Frank, 143, 144
Anthony, Kenneth, 39
Antidiscrimination laws, 86
Antipoverty programs, 15, 37, 149
Antisocial behavior: lower classes/higher classes compared, 125; poverty and, 148
Apprentice, The (television show), 17
Arrests: discrimination in, 141, 142; social class and, 139
Assets: broadening, 209; disparity in, 204; environmental degradation and, 210; polarization of, 208; prices of, 28; taxing, 13
AT&T Corp., 75
Atlantic, The, 131

Baby Bond, 209
Bank accounts, establishing, 38
Bankruptcy, 10, 72
Barber, Christopher A., 175, 176, 177
Barnes, Peter: sky trust and, 210
Beast: saving, 51–52; starving, 51, 52
Becker, Gary S.: on mobility, 14
Bell Curve: The Reshaping of American Life by Difference in Intelligence, The (Murray and Herrnstein), 132, 133, 200
Bernstein, analysis by, 20, 31
Bethlehem Steel, pension obligation of, 62
Bezruchka, Stephen: on income/life expectancy, 114
Biden, Joseph, Jr.: on white collar crime, 144
Big Test, The (Lemann), 136
Bioethics, 182, 184; boundaries of, 181; public health and, 183; research/teaching in, 181; significance of, 185
"Bioethics, Public Health, and Firearm-Related Violence: Missing Links between Bioethics and Public Health" (Turner), 181
Biotechnology, 184, 185
Blacks: academic achievement by, 40, 120, 122; asthma and, 187; heat-related deaths and, 161; homeownership and, 166, 207; inequality and, 147; low-wage workforce and, 97; military service and, 177; wage rates for, 22
Blair, Tony, 209
Blank, Rebecca: analysis by, 201
BLS. *See* Bureau of Labor Statistics
Bosk, Charles: bioethics and, 181
Bowen, William, 130, 133, 134, 135
Bowles, Samuel, 88
Boyer, Robert, 76
Brin, Sergey, 2
British Medical Journal, 106, 107
Bronfenbrenner, Kate: on outsourcing, 31
Brooks, Davey, 178
Brooks, David: bat mitzvah party by, 62
Brooks, Vincent, 173
Brown, Henry B.: *Plessy* and, 151
Brown, Linda: separate schools and, 152
Brown, Wanda: on middle class, 14
Brownfields, number of, 187
Brown v. Board of Education (1954), 38; desegregation and, 120, 152; poor children and, 154

Buchanan, Patrick: economic inequality and, 202
Bullard, Robert D., 179
Bureau of Labor Statistics (BLS), 31, 96, 169; job growth and, 30; on mobility decline, 15
Bush, George H. W., 53–54, 84
Bush, George W., 84; antipoverty idea of, 37; capital gains tax and, 48; criticism of, 39, 74; economy and, 96, 205; Hurricane Katrina and, 40; job performance and, 24; legacy of, 40; NCLB and, 37; ownership society and, 166; poor and, 37; recession and, 95; social policy and, 205; standard of living and, 58; starving the beast and, 52; tax cut by, 51, 61; tax policies and, 96; unemployment and, 95
Business Week, 83, 84, 93

Cambridge Study of Delinquent Development, 148
Cancer Alley, 192
Capital gains, 83, 95
Capital gains tax: decline in, 50; Hurricane Katrina and, 48; investment/economic growth and, 48; rate for, 48, 49; rich and, 47; war on, 45, 47–49
Capitalist class, described, 2
Capital One Financial Corp, 73
Capital spending, increase in, 32
Carmichael, Stokely, 206
Carnevale, Anthony, 130, 133, 134
Carter, Philip, 164, 165
Cashin, Sheryll, 38
Caste society, 84
CBP. *See* Center on Budget and Policy Priorities
Cecil, Karen, 177
Celler, Emanuel, 152–153
Census Bureau, 58, 169; rich-poor gap and, 95; shrinking middle class and, 67
Center for American Progress, 60
Center for Rural Affairs, 173
Center on Budget and Policy Priorities (CBP), 37; report by, 43–44; social mobility and, 81
CEOs. *See* Chief executive officers
Chaves, Mark A., 17
Cherlin, Andrew: on poor, 36

Chicago Federal Reserve, 15
Chicago Fire Department, heat-related deaths and, 159, 162
Chicago Police Department, heat-related deaths and, 162
Chicago Public Health Department, 161
Chief executive officers (CEOs): compensation for, 1, 24, 30, 37–38, 44, 60 (table), 61, 62, 64 (fig.), 93, 201; perks for, 62; and workers' wages compared, 201
Child care, 98, 99, 100, 168, 201, 204; funding, 198, 204; reducing, 70
Child hunger, ending, 204
Child poverty programs, 96
Child-rearing patterns, 121
Children: investing in, 18, 203; poverty rates for, 25
Children's Defense Fund (CDF), 203–204
Circuit City, 73, 76–78
Civil Rights Act (1964), 150–155; discrimination and, 154; protections by, 154–155
"Civil Rights Address" (Kennedy), 152
Civil rights laws, enforcement of, 191
Civil rights movement, 164, 206
Clark, Kathy, 74, 75–76
Clark, Scott, 77, 79; layoff for, 74; politicians and, 74; Viasystems and, 75; work of, 71, 72, 75
Class, 9, 103; attributes of, 13–14; diversity and, 17; eliminating, 13; encountering, 12; gauging, 14; language, 14; military ranks and, 174; multicultural society and, 164; power of, 11; race and, 17, 40, 163; social complexity and, 13–14; structure, 2–5, 19; understanding, 11
Class struggle, 28, 83; volunteer military and, 173; workers and, 34
Climate change, 190
Climate justice, 190
Clinton, Bill, 14, 36, 39
Cognitive skills, 125, 200
College admissions, 119, 129, 130
College education, 18, 98; economic advantages of, 131, 136; economic/social achievement and, 129; high achievers and, 136; long-term unemployment and, 78; low-income students and, 135; money for, 172, 204; upper-middle-class students and, 136; years spent earning, 118
College Pipeline, 137
Colten, Craig E., 164
Communication skills, 101
Community, 38, 40
Congressional Budget Office (CBO), 83, 96; income inequality and, 7; income/tax statistics from, 58
Consumer spending, 32, 33, 38
Consumption, 17, 33; debt and, 34
Consumption taxes, 205
Convictions: adjudication process and, 143; discrimination in, 141
Cook, Philip, 198
Cook County Medical Examiners Office, 159
Corporate regulation, 83, 199
Corporate taxes, 83; avoiding, 49; cutting, 50, 85
Corporate Tax Shelters in a Global Economy (Shaviro), 49
Corporate welfare, closing loopholes to, 192
Cowherd, Douglas, 201
Crime, 37; corporate, 145; drop in, 36; economic class bias among, 144; poor and, 145; poverty and, 148, 149; race and, 149; risk of, 148; street, 142, 145; violent, 145, 146, 147, 148, 149; wealthy and, 145; welfare state and, 150; white-collar, 139, 143, 144, 145
Crime and Drugs Subcommittee (Senate Judiciary Committee), 144
Crime bills, 33
Criminal justice system: bias of, 144, 145; lower-class and, 144; social class and, 4; wealthy and, 142
Crystal, Graeff, 202
Culture, meritocracy and, 133

Daley, Richard M.: heat-related deaths and, 160, 161
Dancs, Anita, 175
Deal, Albert, 175, 176, 177
Deal, Kadence, 176, 177
Death by a Thousand Cuts: The Fight over Taxing Inherited Wealth (Graetz and Shapiro), 46

Death penalty, homicides and, 146
Death tax, 45, 46, 47
Debt, 28, 45–46; consumption and, 34; credit card, 32, 68
Deficit, 51, 96
Deindustrialization, income gap and, 43
Delinquency: risk factors for, 148; social class and, 148; violence and, 149
Delphi, Miller and, 62
Democracy, 53, 206
Democratic Party, diversity and, 134
Denver Post, on C-470, 10
DeParle, Jason, 36, 158
Deprivation, 145, 147, 149
Development genocide, 190
De Vries, Raymond: bioethics and, 181
DiCicco, Albert, 78
Digital divide, 192
Dilulio, John, 37
Dirksen Congressional Center, Civil Rights Act and, 154
Disadvantage, 122; composite measure of, 148–149; social, 147; violence and, 149
Discrimination, 98, 187; arrests/sentencing and, 141; challenging, 150; Civil Rights Act and, 154; hiring, 100; informal contact, 38; mortgage lending, 207; poor and, 153–154; protection against, 153; racial, 37, 142, 207, 211; taxes, 188
Diversity, ix, 129; class and, 17; elite and, 17, 18; social, 11; socioeconomic, 130, 132, 133, 134
Division of Environmental Hazards and Health (Centers for Disease Control and Prevention), 157
DoD. *See* U.S. Department of Defense
Donoghue, Edmund: heat-related deaths and, 160
"Dot-commer" industry, 10
Double tax, 45, 46, 47
Dow Jones Industrial Average, 202
Duke, David, 164
Dumping in Dixie: Race, Class, and Environmental Quality (Bullard), 179

Early-admissions programs, 131
Earned income tax credit (EITC), 33, 36
Easter, Kimberly, 175, 176, 177

Econometric studies, 125
Economic advantage, 15, 129
Economic blackmail, 188, 191
Economic exploitation, victims of, 192
Economic goals, theory for, 106
Economic growth, 16, 36, 52, 70, 199; capital gains tax/investment and, 48; distribution of, 54; income inequality and, 200–201; median family income and, 54; sharing, 202; tax system and, 48
Economic hardship, measures of, 26
Economic inequality, 199, 202; academic achievement and, 127; health and, 105; homicide rates and, 146; school reform and, 127; suffering, 53; violence and, 146
Economic mobility, 86, 87 (fig.), 88–89, 88 (fig.); in other countries, 90 (fig.)
Economic Policy Institute, 19
Economic resources: classification and, 2; disparities in, 1; distribution of, 2
Economist, The: on social class, 81
Education, 2, 12, 72, 93, 96, 107, 117, 210; access to, 130, 134, 135, 136; class and, 14; costs of, 33, 95, 199; debate about, 207; early childhood, 15, 126, 204; gaps in, 19; getting ahead and, 12; immigrants and, 101; importance of, 17; inadequate, 190; inequality in, 4, 130; income and, 88, 98; jobs and, 102; low-wage workforce and, 97–98; meritocracy and, 129; poor and, 87; quality of, 4; rich and, 87; social class and, 117; social mobility and, 117; social stratification and, 133; upward mobility and, 85; wealth and, 206; women and, 100. *See also* College education; Higher education
Educational opportunity, 2; inequality of, 4; race and, 207
Education Trust, claims by, 123
Edwards, John: two Americas and, 38
Edwards, Susan, 158
EITC. *See* Earned income tax credit
Elite: diversity of, 17, 18; isolation of, 18; net worth of, 28. *See also* Rich
Ellis, Delores, 38
Ellison, Larry, 61
Ellsworth Air Force Base, 173
Employment: growth of, 24, 32, 34;

poverty-level, 23, 24 (table); primary, 58; recovery and, 24. *See also* Jobs
Ender, Morton G., 175, 176
Enron, 62, 145
Entitlements, increase in, 135
Environmental classism, 179–180; social class and, 5
Environmental degradation, 192; asset building and, 210; poverty and, 190
Environmental issues, 5, 189, 192; social class and, 180; poverty and, 179; standardized examinations and, 117
Environmental justice movement, 190, 191, 192
Environmental laws, 191
Environmental protection, 96, 107, 192; holistic approach to, 191; redefining, 191
Environmental racism, 5, 190, 192
EPA. *See* U.S. Environmental Protection Agency
Equality, 151, 154
Equity and Excellence in American Higher Education (Bowen), 130
Estate tax, 48, 61, 209; as progressive tax, 47; cost of, 45–46; debate over, 208; decline in, 45, 50; opposition to, 40, 45, 46–47, 85; revenue from, 208; wealth opportunity and, 208
Ethical issues, 181, 184, 185
Evacuation, problems with, 157, 164, 170
Evangelical Christians, 17
Evans, Robert G., 111, 116
ExxonMobil, 62, 93

"Failures of Integration, The" (Cashin), 38
Faith-based initiatives, 37
Fallows, James, 131
Family and Medical Leave Act (1993), 99
Family leave, 99, 101
Family structure, class lines and, 18
Family-supportive policies, 99
Farmers Home Administration (FmHA), 207
Farm work, toxicity of, 188
Farrington, David, 148
Federal Bureau of Investigation (FBI): Index crime, 143; white-collar crime and, 139
Federal Emergency Management Agency (FEMA), 165

Federal Housing Authority (FHA), 207
Federal Reserve Bank of Boston, 15
Federal Reserve Bank of New York, 72
Federal Reserve System, 28
Feldstein, Martin, 29
Ferguson, John H., 151
Financial aid, 132; availability of, 130, 131; low-income students and, 134
Firearm-related violence, 181, 184; dimensions of, 183, 185
Fischer, Claude: on inequality, 197
Food: budget for, 25; subsidies for, 198; toxic, 186
Food stamps, 36, 61; cut in, 40, 51
Forbes 400, 12, 61
Foreign policy, 35
For-profit schools: governments/public universities and, 135–136; Web-based, 136
Fourteenth Amendment, Louisiana Separate Car Act and, 151
Frank, Robert H., 73, 198
Franklin, Benjamin, 14, 19
Frazier, Ernie, 13
Frederick, S.D.: Iraq War and, 173–174
Freeman, Richard, 202
Free trade, 30–31
Friedman, Benjamin M., 52

Gartner, Rosemary, 146
Gates, Bill, 14, 111
Gatreaux model, 39
General Motors, 16
General Social Survey, 171
Genetics, issues related to, 184, 185
Georgia Pacific, 77
G.I. Bill, 206, 208
Gilded Age America, 83, 84
Gilroy, Curtis, 176
Gini coefficient, 3
Gintis, Herbert, 88
Globalization, 17, 43
Global warming, 162, 190
Goldin, Claudia: Great Compression and, 83
Goldman Sachs, 18
Google, 2
Gora, Ewa, 103

Government: drowning, 52; privatization of, 85
Government spending, 51, 52, 208
Grabgrass Frontier, 207
Graetz, Michael J., 46
Grand Central Terminal, 19
Gravely, Miyana, 177
Great Compression, 83
Great Depression, 27, 70
Greater Richmond Technology Council, 76
Greenspan, Alan, 28, 78

Halliburton, 93
Harlan, John, 151
Harrington, Michael, 150
Harris, Joycelyn, 38–39
Hartmann, Heidi, 99
Harvard Law Review, 142
Harvard School of Public Health, 106
Have-nots: haves and, 3, 11, 56, 84, 115; tax cuts and, 46
Hazardous wastes, 179, 192
Head Start, 117, 204
Health: economic disparities and, 105; gaps in, 19; income inequality and, 107, 108, 109, 114, 115; lower-class children and, 127; poor and, 115; problems, social/economic dimensions of, 182–183; SES and, 110–111, 112, 113, 114, 115, 116; social capital and, 116; social class and, 2, 121; social determinants of, 184; wealth and, 105–107, 108, 112
Health care, 2, 5, 71, 85, 93, 96, 113, 185, 192, 204; access to, 103, 104, 108, 111, 112, 183; costs of, 95, 116; debate about, 207; distribution of, 4; inadequate, 36, 190; poverty and, 110; publicly financed, 107; social class and, 9, 104; social status and, 103–104; subsidies for, 198; universal, 115
Health insurance, 14, 71, 183, 184, 201; children and, 204; immigrants and, 101; lack of, 38; number without, 1
Health laws, 189, 191
Health of Nations: Why Inequality Is Harmful to Your Health, The (Kawachi and Kennedy), 106
Health spending, 70, 146
Heat-related deaths, 165; as social disaster, 161, 162; blame for, 162; ethnic/racial differences in, 160
Heat Wave (Klinenberg), 161
Heat waves: emergency plans for, 162; global warming and, 162; interview about, 159–162
Heavy-metal contamination, 117
Heffernan, William, 102
Henderson, David R., 73
Henrico County Economic Development Authority, 74
Henwood, Doug, 95, 96
Heritage Foundation, 84, 123
Herrnstein, Richard J., 132, 200
Hertzman, Clyde, 107, 108
Higher education, 167; access to, 134; class-defined, 133; costs of, 131, 135; funding for, 134–135; gap in, 130; meritocracy and, 130; minorities and, 129; politics of, 136; socioeconomic diversity in, 132; state involvement in, 135; stratification of, 118–119. *See also* College education; Education
High school diplomas, life chances and, 118
Hilton, Paris, 63
Hispanics: air pollution and, 186–187; asthma and, 187; heat-related deaths and, 161; homeownership and, 207; low-wage workforce and, 97; military service and, 177; toxic housing and, 187; wage rates for, 22
Holzer, Harry J., 100
Home Depot, 76
Homelessness, 1, 181, 182, 185
Home Mortgage Interest Deduction, 207
Homeostatic balance, 112
Homeownership, 209, 210; blacks and, 166, 207; expansion of, 207; Hispanics and, 207; subsidies for, 201
Homicides, 146
Hoover, Herbert, 24
HOPE scholarship, 132
Hourglass economy, 69, 70
House of Representatives, Civil Rights Act and, 153
House Subcommittee on Financial Institutions Supervision, Regulation, and Insurance, 143

Housing, 110, 168; affordable, 204; costs of, 95; delinquency and, 148; low-income, 121; stable, 121; subsidies for, 32, 198, 207; toxic, 187–188; vouchers, 39
Hout, Michael, 14
Hubbard, Glenn, 84
Human exploitation, land exploitation and, 189
Hurricane Katrina, 38–39; capital gains tax and, 48; debt before, 45–46; estate tax and, 45; evacuation and, 170; federal response to, 39; government programs and, 51; impact of, 35–36; lower class and, 154; Lower Ninth Ward and, 166; New Orleans and, 35–36, 158, 165; politics and, 39, 40; racism and, 39; relief provision for, 62; social class and, 5; tax code and, 46; tax cuts and, 46, 52
Hutton, Will, 208

Illness, 110, 188; food borne, 186; inequality and, 114; social determinants of, 184
Immigrants: communication skills and, 101; educational barriers for, 101; illegal, 97; increase in, 101; jobs for, 34, 98, 101; low-wage workforce and, 100–101, 102; prosperity for, 86; rights of, 34–35
Immigration, 46, 100–101
Income: academic achievement and, 127; aggregate, percentage distribution by, 43 (table); average, 1, 44, 57 (table), 59; blacks and, 54; causal channels/intergenerational transmission of, 89 (fig.); class and, 14; compression of, 68; distribution of, 19, 26, 59; economic growth and, 54; education and, 88, 98; family, 122; family shares, 55–56, 58, 58 (table); fathers'/sons' compared, 87, 88–89, 88 (fig.), 89n1, 90 (fig.); growth in, 26 (table), 54; Hispanics and, 54; inequality and, 52–56, 58–60; intelligence and, 200; life expectancy and, 114; maldistribution of, 1; mean household, 174; median household, 54, 59, 61, 69, 73, 165, 174; median real family, 55 (table); middle-class, 56, 58 (table); poverty and, 168; race and, 88; real family, 54 (fig.), 55 (fig.); regressive shift in, 53; share of disposable, wealthiest/poorest 30 percent, 60 (table); share of total, 56 (table); wealth and, 25; whites and, 54; women's, 100
Income distribution, 52, 53–54, 69, 70, 84, 86, 201; change in, 67; facts on, 83; minorities and, 20
Income gap: action gap and, 202; growth in, 43, 44, 72; narrowing, 83
Income inequality, 16, 26–27, 29, 54, 56, 58, 84, 109, 126, 203; debate about, 199; economic growth and, 200–201; growth in, 14–15, 72, 201; health and, 107, 108, 114, 115; jump in, 17–18; measuring, 106 (fig.); mortality and, 107, 108, 109; neomaterialist interpretation of, 115; pollution and, 107; postwar, 53; psychosocial stress and, 115; public expenditures and, 115; race and, 207; social support and, 115; unemployment and, 107; in United States, 59
"Income Mobility and the Fallacy of Class-Warfare Arguments" (Heritage Foundation), 84
Income share, top 1 percent, 27 (fig.)
Income taxes, 50, 205, 207
Individual Development Accounts (IDAs), 210
Inequality: addressing, 5, 93, 197; blacks and, 147; class, 83; debate about, 207; degree of, 199–200; growth in, 3, 26, 29, 52, 53, 200; health and, 108, 109; illness and, 114; income and, 52–56, 58–60; inevitability of, 200; life expectancy and, 114; poverty and, 146, 147; social effects of, 12; technologically driven, 30; United States/other industrial nations compared, 59–60; violent crime and, 146; wealth broadening and, 207
Inequality by Design: Cracking the Bell Curve Myth (Hout and Lucas), 199
Inequality gap, 3, 44, 198
Inequality Matters (Moyers), 4
Inequities, 1, 53
Inflation, 61, 73
Inheritance tax, 83, 205
Institute for Policy Studies, 1

Institute for Women's Policy Research, 99
Integrated pest management (IPM), 191
Intelligence: income and, 200; measuring, 132, 200; stratification by, 132
Interest rates, 34, 96
Internal Revenue Service (IRS), 62; estate tax and, 40; overseas profits and, 49
Investment, 33; capital gains tax/economic growth and, 48; virtuous cycle of, 32; untaxing of, 45, 47–49
I.Q.: class division by, 133; lead exposure and, 122–123; racial differences in, 132; tests, 200
Iraq War, 34; Frederick, S.D. and, 173–174; patriotism and, 175; resources for, 96; volunteers for, 172
Isolation, poverty and, 38

Jackson, Kenneth, 207
Jencks, Christopher S., 17, 163
Jobs, 93; education and, 102; female-dominated, 98–99; hazardous/unhealthy, 101; high-paying, 99; for immigrants, 34, 98, 101; lost, 72, 74, 95; low-paying, 22–23, 72; male-dominated, 98; manufacturing, 31, 38, 72; middle-class, 69; minimum-wage, 38; minorities and, 100; recovery and, 96; tech, 72, 76, 78; temporary, 100; toxic, 188–189; for undocumented workers, 102. *See also* Employment
Job-security laws, 201
John, Elton, 63
Johnson, Lyndon B., 37; civil rights and, 153; Civil Rights Act and, 154–155; War on Poverty and, 206
Joint Committee on Taxation, 45
Junior Reserve Officers' Training Corps (JROTC), 178
Justice system, social class and, 139, 140

Kane, Thomas, 135
Kaplan, George A., 107, 109
Kawachi, Ichiro, 106, 109, 110; on inequality/health, 108; on Milyo, 108; social capital and, 115, 116
Kennedy, Bruce P., 106
Kennedy, John F.: civil rights and, 152, 153

Kerrey, Robert: "KidSave" accounts and, 209
Kerry, John, 67
"KidSave" accounts, 209–210
King, Martin Luther, Jr., 206
King, Rodney, 165, 182
Kingston, Paul: on class/social complexity, 13–14
Kletzer, Lori G.: on tech jobs, 72
Klinenberg, Eric: interview with, 158, 159–162
Kmart, 16
Korean War, lower classes and, 171
Kotz, David, 32
Krivo, Lauren: study by, 148, 149
Krugman, Paul, 67–68

Labor, 25; attack on, 27; immigrant, 34
Labor market institutions, strong, 32
Labor Party, wealth-broadening initiative by, 209
Lackey, Diana: on downsizing, 13
LaDuke, Winona: radioactive colonialism and, 189
Landscape, blurring of, 16–19
Latinos. *See* Hispanics
Lead exposure, 122–123
Lead poisoning, threat of, 186
Learning, social class and, 118, 121–123
Left Business Observer, 95
Legal Services Corporation (LSC), 140
Lemann, Nicholas, 136
Levine, David I., 16, 18, 201
Levy, Frank, 72, 73, 78
Lewis, John, 39
"Life at the Top in America Isn't Just Better, It's Longer" (Scott), 103
Life chances, ix, 2; high school diplomas and, 118
Life expectancy, 116; income and, 114; inequality and, 114; wealth and, 106, 109
Lifestyle, 103, 104
Literacy, 117, 121
Little Village, death rate in, 161
Locally unwanted land uses (LULUs), 187
Los Angeles Civil Disturbance/Los Angeles Riot, 182
Louisiana Separate Car Act (1890), 151
Louisiana State Supreme Court, *Plessy* and, 151

Index 227

Loury, Glenn C., 38, 40
Lovell, Vicky, 99
Low-income families, subsidies for, 198
Lower class, 3; air conditioning and, 157; characteristics of, 122; criminal justice system and, 144; escape from, 16; Hurricane Katrina and, 154
Lower-class children: academic achievement by, 121, 122, 123, 128; college costs and, 131; health and, 127; noncognitive skills and, 126; standardized tests and, 124
Lower middle class, 3, 76; EITC and, 36
Lower Ninth Ward, 158; blacks in, 166; demographics of, 166; devastation in, 164; education in, 167–168, 168 (table); homeownership in, 166 (table); Hurricane Katrina and, 166; place of residence in, 167 (table); poverty in, 168, 168 (table), 169; public assistance in, 169 (table); racial makeup of, 166 (table); rebuilding, 166; roots in, 167, 167 (table); transportation in, 170 (table); unemployment in, 169 (table)
Lowe's, 78
Low-Income Home Energy Assistance Program, 169
Low-income students: college degrees for, 135; financial aid for, 134
Low-wage workforce, 22–23, 93; education and, 97–98; gender and, 98; immigrants and, 100–101, 102; makeup of, 97; minorities and, 98, 102; race and, 98; struggles of, 29; women and, 98, 99, 102
Luber, George, 157
Luce, Stephanie: on outsourcing, 31
Lucent Technologies Inc., 75
Lumina Foundation, 131
Luxembourg Income Study, 59
Lynch, Jessica, 173
Lynch, John W., 107, 109, 115

Ma Bell, 73–75
Mansfield, Michael J., 152–153
Manufacturing jobs, loss of, 31, 38, 72
Margo, Robert, 83
Marmot, Michael G., 111
Martin Luther King/Drew Medical Center, 182

Marx, Karl: on class, 13
Math, gaps in, 125
McNeely, Mike, 176
Medicaid, 38, 51, 127, 145
Medical care. *See* Health care
Medicare, 36, 50, 51
Mellor, Jennifer M., 107, 108
Meritocracy, 18, 137; education and, 129, 130; high-achieving kids and, 133; inherited privilege and, 12; wealth/culture and, 133
Messner, Steven, 146
Miami University, tuition at, 135
Middle class, 72, 79; choices for, 183; disappearing, 67–68, 69, 70, 73; Great Depression and, 70; growth of, 71, 73, 74; income share of, 56, 58 (table); natural disasters and, 157; police treatment of, 142; tax cuts and, 46; transformation of, 71; understanding, 11, 73
Middle-class children: academic achievement by, 121, 122, 123, 124; college costs and, 131; noncognitive skills and, 126
Miele, Jean, 103
Military service: blacks and, 177; Hispanics and, 177; lower classes and, 172; postponing/avoiding, 171; support for, 177; upper classes and, 171–172; women and, 177
Military toxics, 189
Millennium Development Goals, 203–204
Miller, Robert, 62
Millionaires, increase in, 61, 208
Milyo, Jeffrey, 108
Minimum wage, 38; increase in, 29, 32, 37, 53, 202; inflation and, 61; poverty and, 19; purchasing power of, 23–24; real, 29. *See also* Wages
Minimum-wage laws, violation of, 188
Minorities, 97; achievement gap and, 126; better paying jobs and, 100; higher education and, 129; income distribution and, 20; low-wage workforce and, 98, 102; poverty rates for, 25; temporary jobs and, 100; unemployment and, 21; wages/incomes of, 20

Miranda v. Arizona (1966), 139, 140
Mobility, 17, 167; decline in, 10, 15, 86; faith in, 19; income, 84, 86, 87; optimal range of, 15; research on, 11; social, 3, 14, 81, 82, 83, 102, 117; student, 121; surprise about, 16; upward, 3, 10, 12, 15, 81, 85–86, 93. *See also* Economic mobility
Mohave tribe, 189
Moore, Chuck, 77, 78
Moore, Terry, 77
Moral Consequences of Economic Growth, The (Friedman), 52
Morning News, The: on toxic housing, 187
Mortality, 105, 114, 161; income inequality and, 107, 108, 109; Robin Hood index and, 107
Mortgage lending, discrimination in, 207
Moyers, Bill: on social class, 4
Multicultural society, race/class and, 164
Multimillionaires, increase in, 208
Multiracial transnational movement, 190
Murnane, Richard J., 72, 78
Murphy, Kevin, 84
Murray, Charles, 132, 200

NAFTA. *See* North American Free Trade Agreement
Nagin, C. Ray, 163
Naison, Mark, 164
Nanotechnology, 185
National Argonne Laboratory, 186
National Association for the Advancement of Colored People (NAACP), *Brown* and, 152
National Guard, 173
National Labor Relations Board, 203
National Priorities Project (NPP), 175
Native peoples, radioactive colonialism and, 189
Natural disasters, 158; middle class and, 157; social class and, 5, 9, 157; upper class and, 157
NCLB. *See* No Child Left Behind
Neoconservatives, con by, 205
Neurotoxicants, 191
Neutraceuticals, 185
New Deal: income gaps and, 83; repeal of, 70; safety net and, 197

New Division of Labor, The (Murnane and Levy), 78
New Orleans: blacks in, 165; class in, 163, 165; education in, 167–168, 168 (table); foreign aid for, 163; homeownership in, 166 (table); homicide in, 163; Hurricane Katrina and, 35–36, 158, 165; multicultural society in, 164; place of residence in, 167 (table); poverty in, 165, 168, 168 (table), 169; public assistance in, 169 (table); race in, 163, 165, 166 (table); roots in, 167, 167 (table); segregation in, 164; transportation in, 170 (table); unemployment in, 165, 169 (table)
Newsweek, 38, 39
New York Times, 4, 11, 12, 103
Nicks, Stevie, 62
NIMBY tool, 187
No Child Left Behind (NCLB), 37, 117
Noncognitive skills, 125–126; lower-class children and, 126; middle-class children and, 126; social-class gaps in, 125
Nonsupervisory workers, wage rates for, 23 (table)
Norquist, Grover, 40, 52
North American Free Trade Agreement (NAFTA), 20, 31, 33
North Lawndale, death rate in, 161
Nuclear Regulatory Commission, 190

Obama, Barak, 35–36, 39, 40
Occupational Safety and Health Administration (OSHA), 188
OECD. *See* Organization for Economic Cooperation and Development
Offshoring, 73
Opportunity, 19; boundless, 16; broadening, 205, 206–207, 210; difference in, 205, 208; educational, 2, 4, 207; equal, 11, 53, 120, 203, 205, 211; inequality of, 210; social class and, 87; social networks and, 87; strengthening, 209; values of, 206; wealth, 207–209
Organization for Economic Cooperation and Development (OECD), 59, 99, 106
Outsourcing, 31, 34, 70, 71, 73, 74, 95
Overtime laws, 188
Ownership society, 166

Page, Larry, 2
Paine, Thomas, 210
Part-time workforce, women and, 99
Patriotism, 175, 176
Payroll taxes, 85; increase in, 50–51; social security and, 50
Pell Grants, 131, 132, 136, 172
Pensions, 18, 71, 101
Perlo, Art, 95
Pesticides, 188, 191
Peterson, Ruth: study by, 148, 149
Philip Morris USA, 73
Pickens, Boone, 62
Pikerty, Thomas, 83, 85
Plessy, Homer, 150–151
Plessy v. Ferguson (1896), 151, 152
Police forces, 142, 183
Political Affairs, 95
Politics, 136; class alignments in, 17; Hurricane Katrina and, 39, 40; social class and, 2
Pollin, Robert, 32, 33
Pollution: air, 186–187; income disparity and, 107; land, 189; poverty and, 191; state-sponsored, 192; sustainable development and, 190
Poor, 37, 86; being, 114; crime and, 142, 145; discrimination against, 141–142, 153–154; economic vulnerability of, 28, 192; education and, 87; energy costs and, 62; feeling, 113–114, 114–115; health and, 110, 115; income of, 95; inequality and, 147; invisible, 150; number considered, 41 (fig.); power of, 179; privacy and, 142; social support for, 113; tax burden and, 51; tax cuts and, 46; working, 36, 201
Poor People's Campaign, 206
Poverty, 14, 15, 23, 44, 106, 164, 182, 183, 184; addressing, 190; antisocial behavior, 148; attention for, 181; black, 149; childhood, 25, 148, 201, 204; chronic, 147, 148; crime and, 146, 148, 149; culture of, 37; decline of, 16, 20, 36, 40, 149; delinquency and, 148; economic remedies for, 191; elderly in, 169; endurance of, 35, 86, 115; environmental factors and, 179, 190; fighting, 36, 37; health care and, 110; incidence of, 26; income and, 168; increase in, 36, 37, 52; inequality and, 146, 147; isolation and, 38; low, 149; minimum wage and, 19; minorities and, 25; number living in, 41 (fig.); pollution and, 191; racism and, 39; rates of, 20, 25, 175, 201; social issues and, 185; stressors and, 113; sustainable development and, 190; threshold, 25, 26; urban, 184, 185
Poverty line, 3, 36, 93, 134, 163, 168, 169; dropping below, 1, 202, 203; Wal-Mart employees and, 61
Powell, Colin, 173
Power, 2, 11, 179; polarization of, 205; purchasing, 20, 23–24
Pratt, Michael: on middle class, 74
Preschool, 117, 204
President's Council on Bioethics, 185
President's Crime Commission, survey by, 141
Private production workers, wage rates for, 23 (table)
Privatization, 85
Productivity, 26, 34, 202; income equality and, 201; increase in, 20–21; wages and, 20, 24
Progressives, 198, 206
Progressive taxes, 45, 47, 68, 209; support for, 206, 207
Property taxes, 208
Prothrow-Stith, Deborah, 106
Provo, Lawrence: job for, 76
Psychosocial stress, 112–113, 115
Public health, 184, 185, 191; bioethics and, 183; gaps in, 105; inequality and, 108; protecting, 192
Public housing, 39, 211; delinquency and, 148
Purchasing power, 20; minimum wage, 23–24

Race, 154; class and, 17, 40, 163; crime and, 149; educational opportunity and, 207; income and, 88, 207; low-wage workforce and, 98; multicultural society and, 164; space and, 165; toxic wastes and, 187; violent crime and, 149; wealth and, 28, 206

Race riots, 165, 182
Racial mixing, 151
Racism, 40, 142, 208, 211; class-based, 37; environmental, 5, 190, 192; Hurricane Katrina and, 39; institutional, 190; poverty and, 39
Radar magazine, on Wilson, 63
Radioactive colonialism, 189–190
Reading: early childhood, 117, 121, 204; gaps in, 125
Reagan, Ronald, 53–54
Recession, 22, 25, 33
Recovery: employment growth and, 24; jobless, 20, 22, 23; jobs and, 96; workers and, 27
Recruiting, 174, 175, 176–177
Regressive taxes, 132, 208
Regulatory state, shrinking, 205
Religious affiliation, as class marker, 17
Republican Party, diversity and, 134
Reservations, nuclear waste dumps on, 189
Retirement, 18, 93, 211; baby boomer, 78; supplementing, 209–210
Ricciardi, Michael, 177
Rich: advantages for, 87; capital gains tax and, 47; education and, 87; financial assets of, 28. *See also* Elite
Richmond, economy of, 72–73, 76, 77
Richmond Works, 74, 75
Rich-poor gap, 16, 44, 46, 59, 95, 104, 199
Right-to-work laws, 200
Rise of Meritocracy, The (Young), 132
Robin Hood hypothesis, 108, 109, 110
Robin Hood index, 106, 106 (fig.); mortality and, 107
Roman Catholics, rise of, 17
Rose, Stephen, 130, 133, 134
Ross, Wilbur, 62
Ruling class, 2
Rural economy, urban economy and, 173
Russell Sage Foundation, 12

Sacrifice zones, 192
Saez, Emmanuel, 83, 85
Safety laws, violation of, 189
Safety net, 32, 169; defending, 206; shrinking, 70, 116, 146, 197
Santa Clara County: economy in, 70; income inequality in, 69

SAT, 129, 131, 132, 134, 136
Savings, 32, 209
Savings and loans criminals, prosecuting, 144
Scholarships, merit-based, 132
School reform, 128; academic achievement and, 127; achievement gap and, 126; in-school, 124, 126; insufficiency of, 123–124; social/economic inequalities and, 127
Schools: poor neighborhood, 117–118; subsidized, 32; Superfund sites and, 188; toxic, 188
Schuber, Margaret, 40, 42
Schumer, Charles: on income inequality, 56
Scott, Janny, 103
Segregation, 150–151, 164; educational, 132; housing, 38; social, 38; transportation, 151
Semi-skilled workers, 74
Senate Judiciary Committee, 144
Sentencing, 141, 143–145
Separate but equal, 150–151, 152
Service sector, 70, 95
SES. *See* Socioeconomic status
Shapiro, Ian, 46
Shaviro, Daniel N., 49
Silicon Valley, economy of, 69, 70
Skilled workers, 78; unemployment of, 31; unskilled workers and, 30
Sklar, Holly: on middle class, 3
Skull Valley Goshutes, 190
Sky trust, 210
Smith, Howard W., 153
Social capital, 115–116
Social class: academic achievement and, 122, 123; changing, 81; conceptualizing, 43, 120; delinquency and, 148; differences in, 2, 3, 120, 123, 125, 126; discipline and, 121; education and, 117, 118, 121–123; environmental issues and, 180; exclusion, 150–155; graduation and, 118; health and, 104, 121; importance of, 4, 10, 123; lines between, 9; justice system and, 4, 139; natural disasters and, 157; opportunity and, 87; short-term change and, 126–127; social/economic manifestations by, 121

Social complexity, class and, 13–14
Social exclusion, 145, 149
Social inequalities, 184, 185, 199; academic achievement and, 127; attention for, 181; complexities of, ix; school reform and, 127
Social isolation, 37, 165
Social issues, 17, 185
Social mobility, 3, 14, 102; American Dream and, 81, 82; decline of, 82, 83; education and, 117
Social networks, 2, 87, 103
Social policy, 205; society's design and, 197–198
Social problems: ethical dimensions of, 182; inequality gap and, 198
Social reforms, 124, 125, 127
Social Security, 32, 36; benefits from, 51; cuts in, 51; funding, 51, 206; payroll taxes and, 50; as portion of GNP, 146; privatization of, 70; supplementing, 209–210; trust fund for, 51
Social services, 37, 53, 181, 183; cuts in, 96
Social stratification, 197; education and, 133
Socioeconomic diversity, 130, 132, 133, 134
Socioeconomic status (SES), 122, 147; examining, 110; health and, 110–111, 112, 113, 114, 115, 116; objective/subjective, 113; psychosocial consequences of, 112; stressors and, 113
Solon, Gary: on inequality, 15
South Coast Air Quality Management District, 186
Stakeholding, 210
Standardized examinations, 117, 124, 129, 131, 132, 134, 136
Standard of living, 13, 52; deterioration of, 58; improvement in, 12, 53
State of Working America (SWA), 19, 22, 23, 28, 31, 32, 33, 34; income/wage inequality and, 29; labor market data in, 20
Stewart, Martha, 16
Stock-market bubble, 34, 83
Stolle, Robert J.: on Richmond economy, 76
Stratification, 2, 118–119, 132, 140; social, 133, 197
Stress hormone, 114

Stressors: control over, 113; physical, 112, 113; poverty and, 113; psychological, 115; psychosocial, 113; social, 115
Structural inequalities, 182, 184
Subcommittee of the Judiciary Committee, Civil Rights Act and, 153
Sullivan, Martin, 49
Summer programs, 126, 128, 204
Sundance Film Festival, 62
Superdome, disaster at, 163, 165
Superfund sites, 188
Superiority-inferiority scale, ix
"Supersize This: How CEO Pay Took Off While America's Middle Class Struggled" (Center for American Progress), 60
Sustainable development, poverty/pollution and, 190
SWA. See *State of Working America*
Swagel, Phillip: on upward mobility, 15

Tax avoidance, 49–50
Tax burden: nonrich and, 51; sharing, 45, 199; shifting, 205
Tax code, 5, 45, 46
Tax cuts, 45, 61, 205; crisis by, 51; have-nots and, 46; high-end, 51; Hurricane Katrina and, 46, 52; middle class and, 46; poor and, 46; windfall from, 96; zeal for, 46–47
Taxes, 33, 85, 93, 96, 203; earmarking, 209; economic growth and, 48; importance of, 52
Tax holiday, 50
Tax shelters, 49–50, 85
Technology: advances in, 72; safety, 9; wage inequality and, 30; worker conditions and, 30–31
Temporary workers, 71, 72, 99, 100
Tenure laws, 201
Testing: limitations of, 124–125; standardized, 117, 124, 129, 131, 132, 134, 136
Thirteenth Amendment, Louisiana Separate Car Act and, 151
Thurow, Lester: on economic failure, 52
Titanic (ship), passenger deaths aboard, 5, 157
Toll roads, social class and, 10

Toskes, Raffael, Sr., 76
Toxic invasion, 186, 187, 189
Trade: free, 30–31; globalization of, 199; imbalance, 34; jobs in, 78
Transportation, 93; access to, 157, 160, 162; public, 115, 170; segregation in, 151
Trickle down theory, 48
Truini, John, 178
Trump, Donald, 61
Trust funds, 208, 209
Tuition, 118, 135, 136

Underclass, 3
Underemployment, 96
Undocumented workers, jobs for, 102
Unemployment, 34, 52, 96, 169, 183; attention for, 181, 190; college degrees and, 78; compensation, 32; fear of, 188; hidden, 22; income inequality and, 107; increase in, 20; long-term, 25, 72, 78; minority, 21; recruiting and, 176; skilled worker, 31; wages and, 22, 37; women and, 21–22
Unemployment rates, 21, 21 (table), 22, 25, 31; decrease in, 20, 24; increase in, 95
Unions, 72, 74, 83; bargaining with, 202; decline of, 29, 33, 37, 85, 202; empowerment of, 203; impact of, 116; regulation of, 199; strong, 32, 68; teachers, 37; wage setting and, 202
United: executive bonuses at, 62; pension/salary cuts by, 62
United for a Fair Economy, 1
University of Virginia, access program at, 134
Unskilled workers, skilled workers and, 30
Upper class, 2, 9, 14; natural disasters and, 157; shrinking/stagnant, 70; understanding, 11
Upper middle class, 3; choices for, 183; college degrees and, 136; self-described, 14
Upward mobility, 3, 12, 81; American Dream and, 85–86; barriers to, 15; education and, 85; reality of, 10; work ethic and, 93
Urban economy, rural economy and, 173
USA Today, on college enrollment, 118

USC/Los Angeles County Medical Center, 182
U.S. Centers for Disease Control and Prevention, 150, 157, 187
U.S.-China Economic and Security Review Commission, 31
U.S. Department of Agriculture, 25
U.S. Department of Defense (DoD): advertising campaign by, 174; demographic data from, 174; military toxics and, 189; recruiting by, 175
U.S. Department of Education, data from, 118, 137
U.S. Department of Labor, 102; law violations and, 188; wage trend and, 78
U.S. Environmental Protection Agency (EPA): air quality standards and, 190; pesticide exposure and, 188; toxic housing and, 187
U.S. General Accounting Office, brownfield estimate by, 187
U.S. News & World Report, rankings by, 134
U.S. Supreme Court, *Plessy* and, 151

VA. *See* Veteran's Administration
Values, social class and, 2
Vanity Fair, Ellison and, 61
Vedder, Richard: tuition vouchers and, 135
Veteran's Administration (VA), 207
Viasystems Inc., 74, 75, 76
Vieques island, 189
Vietnam War, studying, 171
Violence: delinquency and, 149; deprivation and, 149; disadvantage and, 149; economic inequality and, 146; firearm-related, 181, 183, 184, 185; social disadvantage and, 147; social exclusion and, 149; urban, 184, 185; welfare state and, 150
Violent crime: deprivation and, 147; higher levels of, 145; international differences in, 145; poverty and, 146, 148, 149; race and, 149
Virchow, Rudolph: on poor/physicians, 110
Virtuous cycle, 32, 33, 34

Wage gap, 29, 201
Wage inequality, 22; aspects of, 23–24; growth in, 20, 29, 31; technology and, 30

Wages, 34; decrease in, 50, 78; distribution of, 202; gender disparity in, 22, 98; increase in, 22, 32; national averages in, 95; productivity gains and, 20, 24; racial disparity in, 22; real, 20, 22, 23 (table), 33, 78; setting, 199, 202; taxing, 50; unemployment and, 22, 37; unions and, 29, 202; workers', 201, 202. *See also* Minimum wage
Wagner, Peter, 158
"Waking Up From the American Dream" (*Business Week*), 83
Waldfogel, Jane: on family gap, 100
Wal-Mart, 46, 76, 84; employees, poverty line and, 61; heirs of, 1
Wanner, Eric: on barriers, 12
War on Poverty, 206
War on terror: unshared sacrifice of, 173; white-collar crime and, 139
Washington Post, The, 72
Wealth: academic achievement and, 122; advantages of, 106; broadening, 205, 206, 207, 208, 209, 210–211; class and, 14; concentration of, 58; creation of, 209, 210; difference in, 208; distribution of, 1, 19, 26, 28, 55, 59, 106, 107, 199, 208; dynastic accumulations of, 205; education and, 206; health and, 105–107, 112; income and, 25; inherited/self-made, 12; life expectancy and, 106, 109; meritocracy and, 133; ownership of, 210–211; polarization of, 205, 208; racial division of, 28; share of total earned/income group, 65 (fig.); taxation of, 205
Wealth gap, 109–110; health and, 108; race and, 206
Wealth inequality, 58–59, 83
Wealth opportunity, estate tax and, 208
Wealth Opportunity Fund, 205
Wealth taxes, 210, 211
Wealthy: criminal justice system and, 141–142, 145; secession of, 115
Weber, Max: on class, 13
Welfare, 38; corporate, 192; denial of, 33
Welfare programs, elimination of, 197
Welfare reform, challenges of, 36

Welfare state: crime and, 150; expansion of, 149; shrinking, 205; violence and, 150
Werner, Emmy, 147
West, Donald, 148
West, Kanye, 39
Western Electric, 74
Western Shoshone, 189, 190
White-collar crime, 145; extent/seriousness of, 143; prosecuting, 143, 144; war on terror and, 139
Wilkinson, Richard G., 107; economic goals and, 106; psychosocial stress and, 115; public health and, 105; Robin Hood hypothesis and, 109; SES/health gradient and, 114
Williams, Joan, 99
Wilson, Owen, 63
Wilson, Thomas, 171
Wilson, William Julius, 161
Wisconsin National Primate Research Center, 114
Wolff, Edward N., 58, 208
Women: education and, 100; family-supportive policies and, 99; low-wage workforce and, 97, 98, 99, 102; military service and, 177; part-time workforce and, 99; unemployment for, 21–22
Woods, Tiger, 62
Worker safety laws, 191
Workers: class struggle and, 34; future of, 34; recovery and, 27
Work ethic, upward mobility and, 93
Workforce, 97; restructuring of, 71, 72, 73
Working class, 3; economic appeal to, 17; federal spending and, 96; prosperity for, 86; state of, 20; understanding, 11
Working mothers: barriers for, 100; increase in, 99
Working under Different Rules (Freeman), 202
Worldwatch Institute, 189

Yahoo News, 39
Young, Michael, 132, 133
Youth Opportunity Grant, 39
Yucca Mountain, dumpsite at, 189, 190

ABOUT THE EDITORS

D. Stanley Eitzen is professor emeritus of sociology at Colorado State University, where he taught for twenty-one years, the last as John N. Stern Distinguished Professor. Prior to that he taught at the University of Kansas where he earned his Ph. D degree. His most recent book is *Solutions to Social Problems from the Top Down: The Role of Government* (Allyn & Bacon 2006), coauthored with George H. Sage. Eitzen is editor of *Sport in Contemporary Society: An Anthology* (Paradigm 2005). He was editor of *The Social Science Journal* from 1978 to 1984. His specialty areas in sociology are social inequality, power, family, criminology, and sport.

Janis E. Johnston received her Ph.D. from Colorado State University, where she is currently working as an adjunct instructor. She has published several articles in the area of permutation statistics. Her specialty areas are social inequality, environmental sociology, quantitative analysis, and research methods.